IMAGES
of America

KUYAHOORA TOWNS

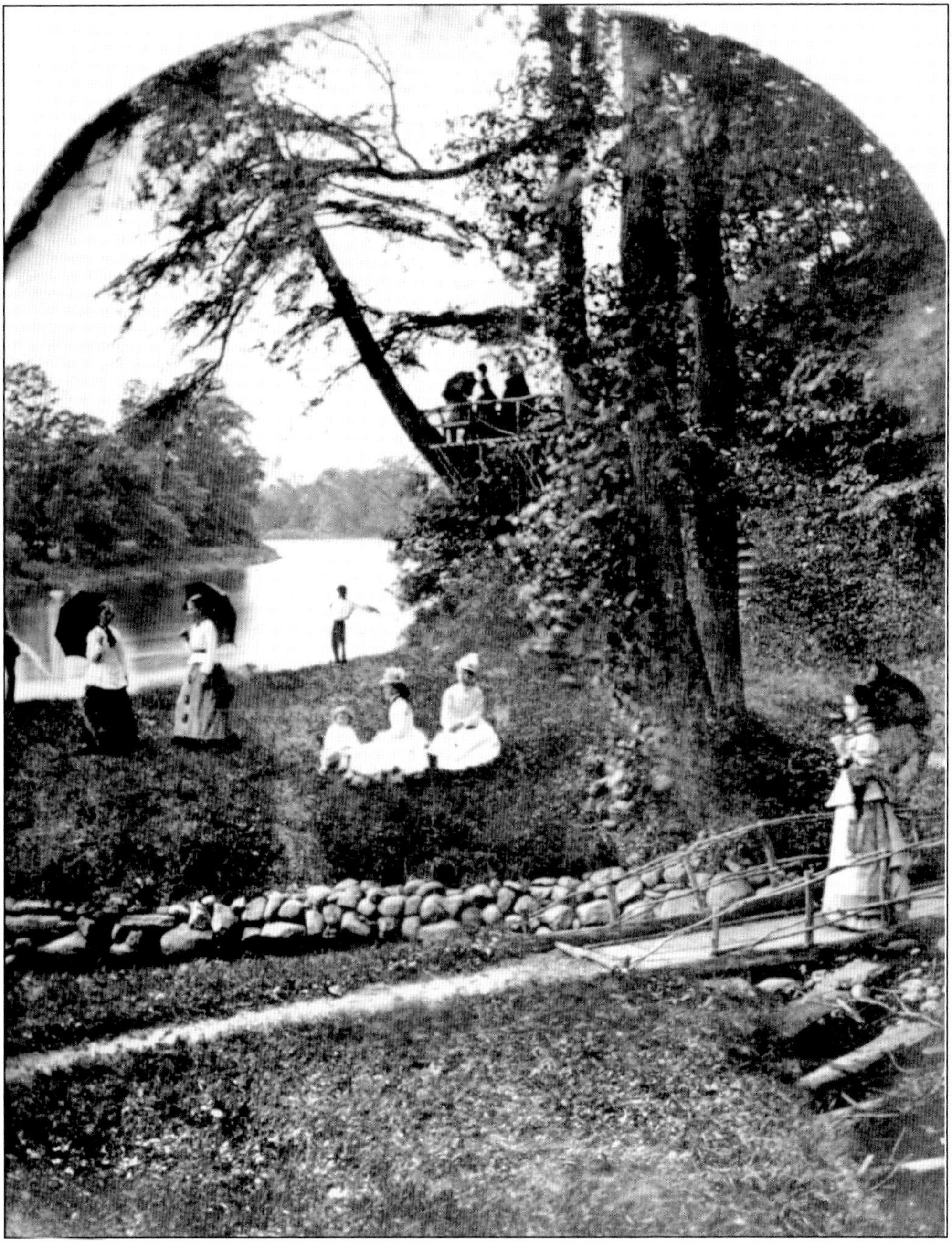

Stuart Perry, an inventor and a very successful butter and cheese dealer of Newport, wanted to share his good fortune with the community. He opened the beautifully landscaped grounds of his home to the public. Perry Park was used for concerts, picnics, and community functions.

On the cover: George and Fred Read operated a general store in Poland from the 1870s to the early 1900s. Pictured from left to right are Charlie Henry, John Knights, Grace Read, Reverend Hyatt, and George Read.

IMAGES
of America

KUYAHOORA TOWNS

Kuyahoora Valley Historical Society

ARCADIA
PUBLISHING

ISBN 978-0-7385-1205-1

Published by Arcadia Publishing
Charleston, South Carolina

Printed in the United States of America

Library of Congress Catalog Card Number: 2003104545

For all general information contact Arcadia Publishing at:
Telephone 843-853-2070
Fax 843-853-0044
E-mail sales@arcadiapublishing.com
For customer service and orders:
Toll-Free 1-888-313-2665

Visit us on the Internet at www.arcadiapublishing.com

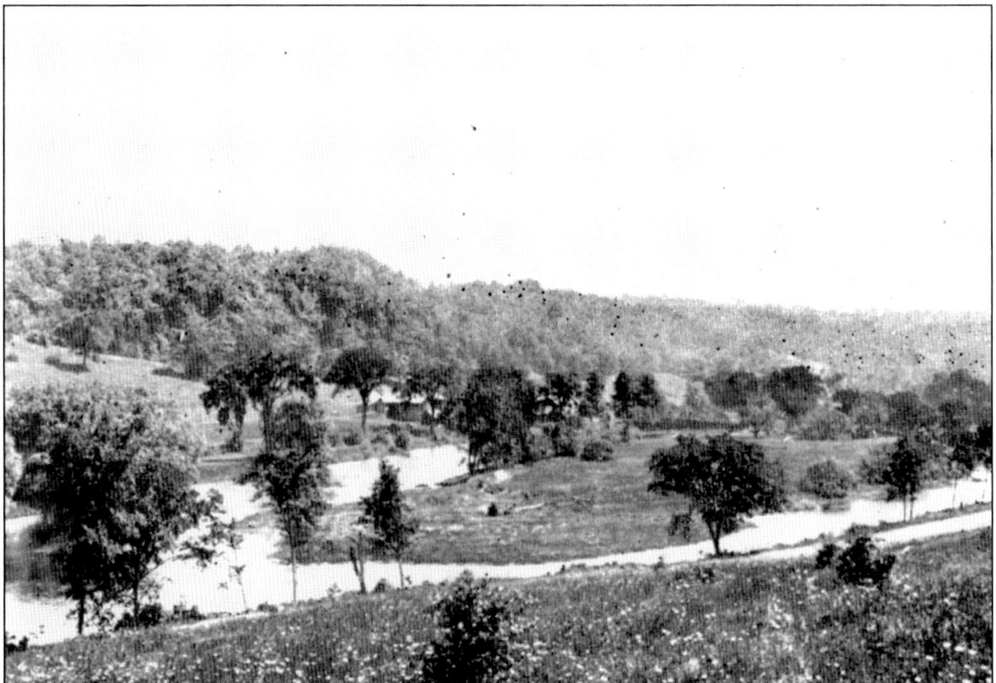

The stretch of the Kuyahoora from Poland to Middleville contains several islands. This view shows Sunny Island, outside of Poland.

CONTENTS

ACKNOWLEDGMENTS

We at the Kuyahoora Valley Historical Society are indebted to the following people and organizations for providing photographs and postcard images for this book: Nancy Crisino, Richard Tucker, Jack Carney, Brad Davis, Janet Burt, Joyce Murphy, Joseph Murphy, Ellen Harris, Helen Garlock, Muriel Fenner, Eric Newman, Barbara Seidel, James Fisher, Dr. John Reese, Paula Johnson (Town of Russia Historian) Helen Wheatley (Town of Norway Historian), Jane Dieffenbacher (Town of Fairfield Historian), the Newport History Center, the Herkimer County Historical Society and the Henry Blue collection. Many other local residents have allowed us the use of their images of their homes and businesses. Our researchers relied on the local histories of each town and village, along with files at the Newport History Center. A special thank-you is extended to all.

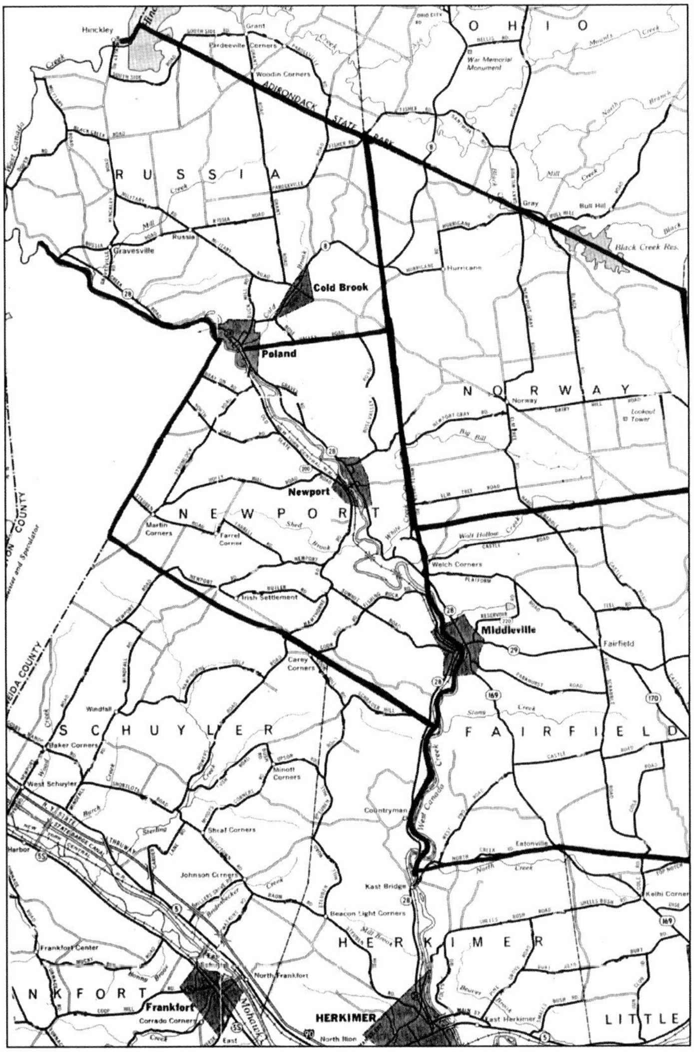

The valleys and uplands of the towns of Fairfield, Norway, Russia, and Newport surround the West Canada Creek as it winds its way from the southern Adirondacks to the Mohawk River in Herkimer. The villages of Fairfield, Norway, Gray, Cold Brook, Poland, Grant, Gravesville, Newport, and Middleville are located in these Kuyahoora towns.

INTRODUCTION

Maps show that before and shortly after the American Revolutionary War, the West Canada Creek was known as the Gayahora or Kuyahoora, a Native American word meaning "slanting waters." Although today the West Canada is known as a creek, in size and volume it is a much larger stream than some of the rivers in New York. *Kuyahoora Towns* explores the life and times and accomplishments of the early settlers in the four towns of Fairfield, Norway, Russia, and Newport.

No evidence of Native American settlements in the Kuyahoora area exists; however, Indians are believed to have used many of these lands for hunting and fishing. A few of the German Palatines from the Mohawk Valley made their way up the north hills before the American Revolution. The primary settlement of the region, however, came after the Revolution. Land obtained from the Mohawk Nation by Sir William Johnson, as well as lands granted to Johnson before the Revolution by the king of England, was confiscated by the state of New York after the defeat of the British. To offset the war debt, the royal grant lands were offered by the state of New York at cheap prices to entice New England settlers to the region.

Norway's first settlers arrived from Rhode Island in 1787. Five years later the town of Norway was organized. In those early years, Norway stretched nearly 150 miles to the St. Lawrence area and included what were to become some 35 towns, including Fairfield, Russia, and Newport. Johnson had located a few families in the Fairfield region in 1770. From 1785 to 1800, Fairfield grew rapidly, and it became a town in 1796. The town of Russia was formed from Norway in 1806 and was known for a few years as Union. The building of the State Road in 1806 fostered the settlement of the village of Cold Brook and the town of Russia. Like Russia, Newport was formed from Norway in 1806. Christopher Hawkins became the first permanent settler of Newport in 1791.

The first task of these early settlers was to clear the land and build cabins for their pioneer families. Much of the land was hilly, and the soil was rather poor and stony. In the early years, the settlers raised hay and grain and grazed a few animals. Wheat was a cash crop, but as settlers moved to western counties more suitable for growing wheat, the market for wheat was not as profitable in the Kuyahoora area. The agriculture endeavors gradually shifted to dairying, and the Kuyahoora towns became famous for their cheese production.

The settlers soon recognized the tremendous opportunities that lay in harnessing the waterpower of the many tributaries of the West Canada. Mills and factories sprang up along the streams and produced goods for both the pioneer families and for trade. Roads, canals, and railroads provided means to transport the settlers' agricultural and factory products to the cities and the expanding frontier.

The native limestone found in the Newport area was an important building material. It was used in the construction of bridges, roads, factories, churches, and homes. Many limestone architectural creations remain today as reminders of the heritage of the craftsmen of the Kuyahoora Valley.

Religion and education were very important to the early families. Long before they erected church buildings, settlers held religious services in cabins and homes, with the help of missionaries and circuit preachers. The earliest churches were frame buildings constructed in the New England meetinghouse style. One- or two-room schools offering elementary education were built throughout the area. Rev. Caleb Alexander, a missionary preacher, established the first school offering preparation for college in Fairfield in 1802. The Fairfield Academy gained an excellent reputation and attracted students from a wide area of New York and New England. A medical college was chartered at the academy in 1812. It was coeducational from the beginning, and more women were enrolled when the Ladies Seminary building was added in 1854. Teacher training and business subjects were later offered. Military instruction was added in 1891. The Fairfield Academy, Seminary, and Military Academy served as an institution of higher learning for 99 years. It closed in 1901 as a result of the growth of public high schools.

The 20th century brought dramatic changes to the area. The industrial age, the coming of the automobile, and the shift of population to the cities and to the west brought decline to the shops, factories, and businesses of the small towns. However, as the old way of life was disappearing, a new era of tourism was dawning. Today, the Kuyahoora area is well known for its natural beauty and its recreational opportunities. Hunting, fishing, hiking, boating, skiing, and snowmobiling attract visitors to the area. The Kuyahoora area includes a portion of the state's recently designated Scenic Byway of the Southern Adirondacks, for travelers heading to the Adirondack Mountains. A local initiative in Herkimer County, Gems Along the Mohawk, is showcasing the many tourist attractions of the area. Today's residents are proud of their heritage and welcome travelers and newcomers to share in the history and beauty of the region.

—Janet Burt
Kuyahoora Valley Historical Society

One

Working the Land

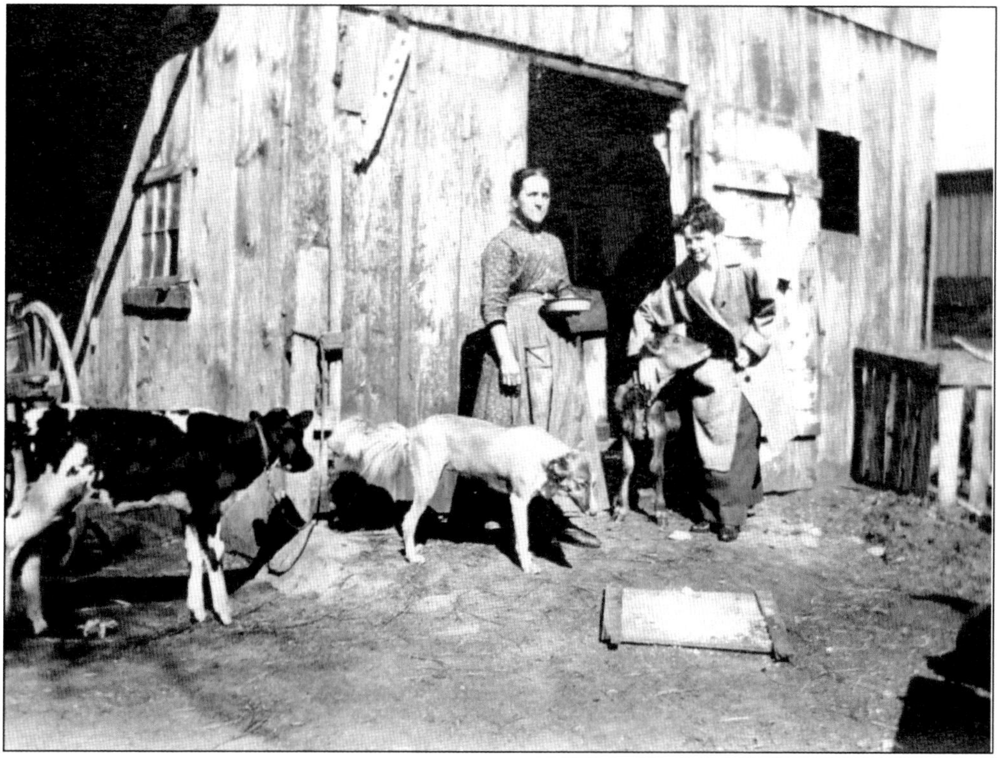

The early settlers cleared old-growth forests to provide space to grow crops and pasture their animals. The felled trees and brush were heaped into piles and burned. The dry ashes were then leached and boiled in kettles. The residue, called black salts, was taken to an ashery for refinement into potash. Many of the pioneers paid for their land with proceeds from the sale of potash. From the first settlements in the 1790s through the middle of the 19th century, farming evolved from the subsistence level to the production of food and animal products for market. Most families had sheep, hogs, and a few cows and made their own butter and cheese. By 1850, farming shifted from sheep and grain toward a dairy industry, producing milk for cheese factories. Improved roads and the coming of the canals and railroad provided the farmers with extended markets for their products. By 1900, milk plants were built to receive milk and ship it to large cities. Industrialization introduced machinery for tilling, planting, and harvesting. As tractors replaced horses and the size of farms increased, agriculture grew into a business. Every member of the farm family, women and children included, was involved in daily chores. This picture shows two women caring for young animals.

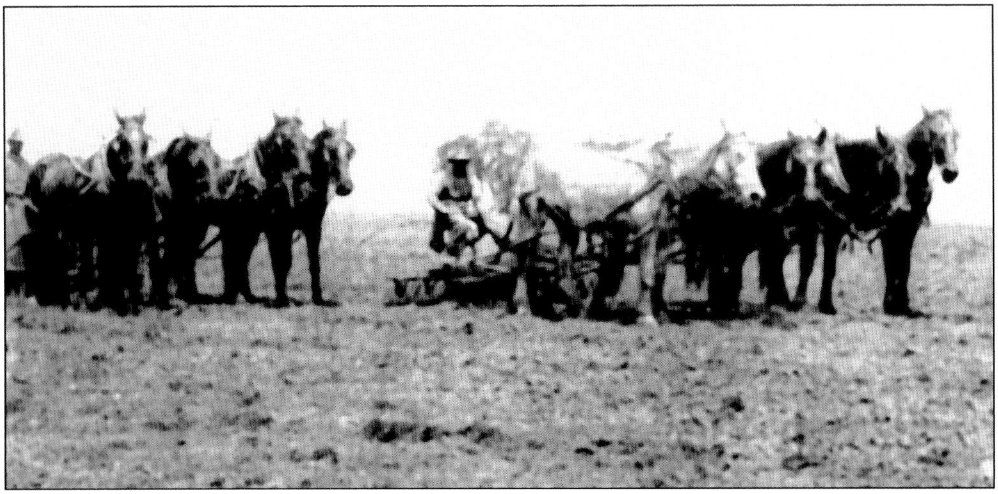

Fitting the land required a great deal of "horsepower." Here, teams of four horses are harrowing on the Robens farm on Cold Brook Hill.

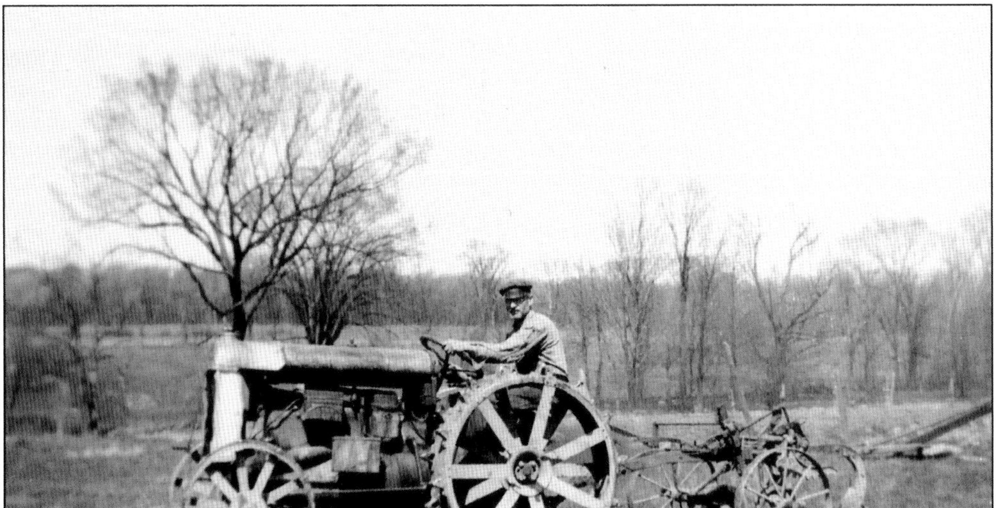

Horses were gradually replaced with tractors in the 1920s. Here, Dennis Murphy is plowing with a one-bottom plow and a Fordson tractor in the town of Fairfield.

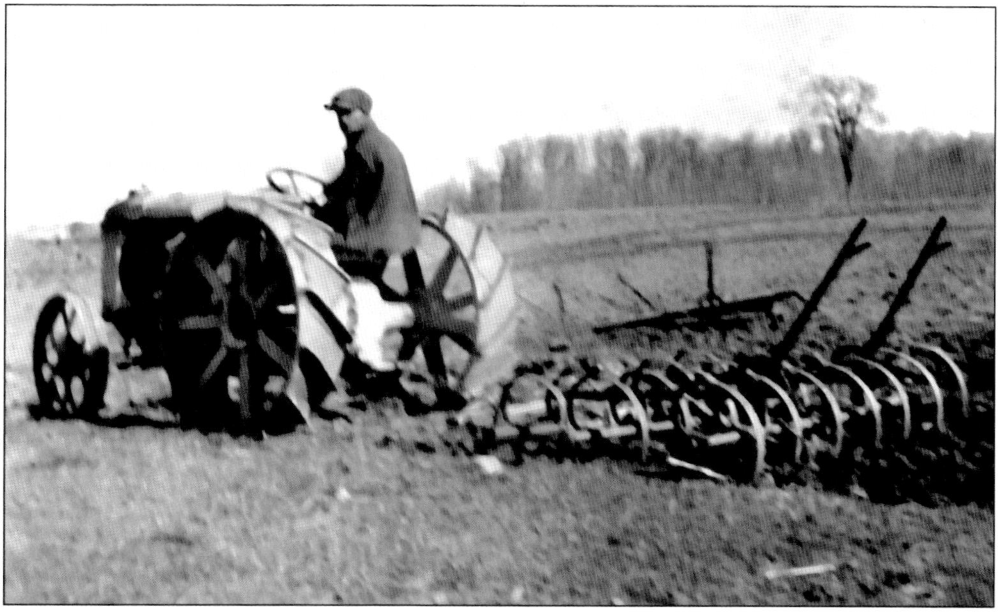

In preparation for planting, Zina Burt is harrowing a field with his new 1922 Fordson tractor in the town of Norway.

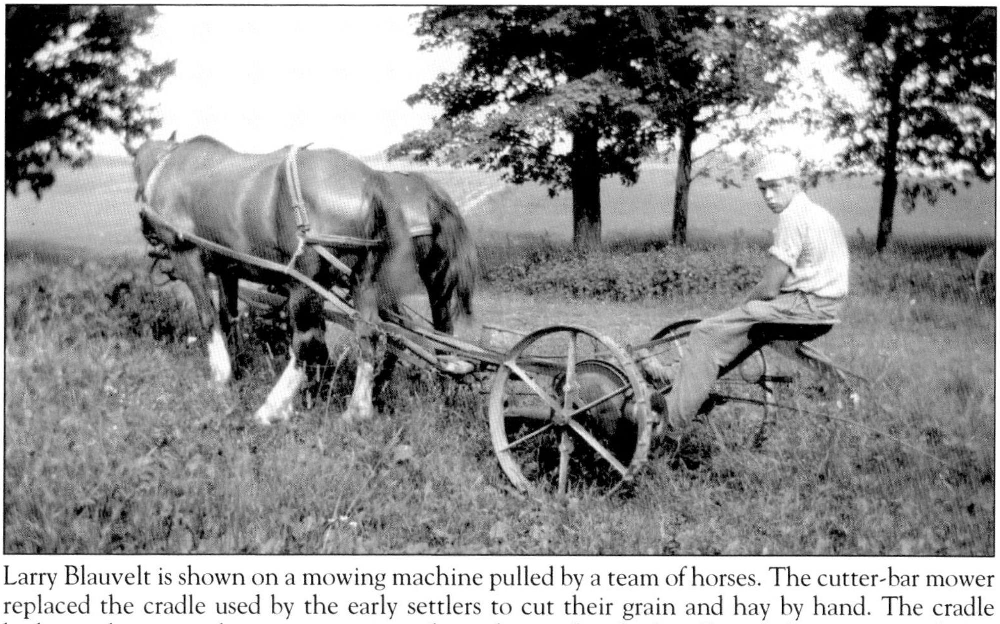

Larry Blauvelt is shown on a mowing machine pulled by a team of horses. The cutter-bar mower replaced the cradle used by the early settlers to cut their grain and hay by hand. The cradle had a scythe to cut the grass or grain and wooden teeth, which collected the cut material into bunches that were stood up to dry.

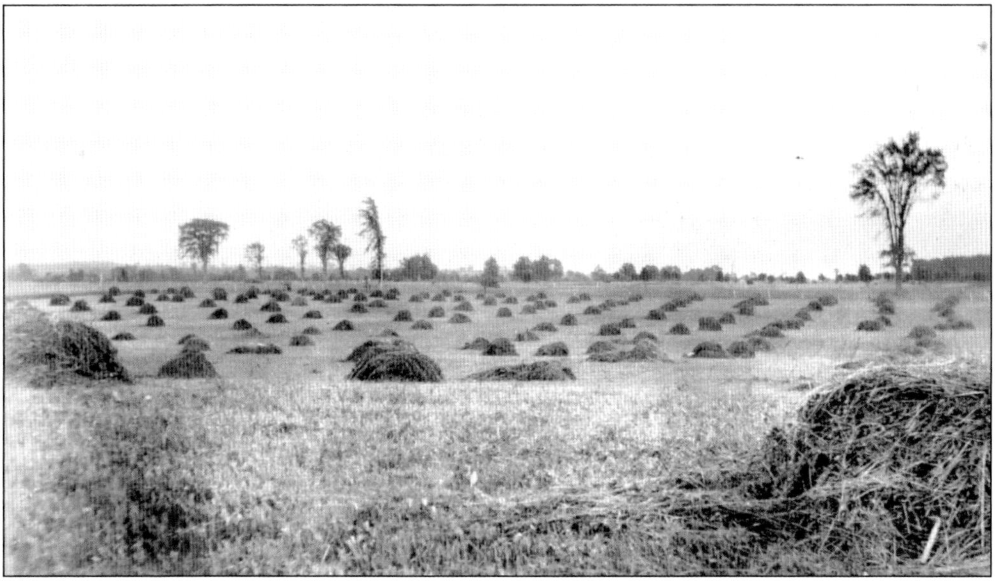

This scene shows cocks of hay drying in a Norway field.

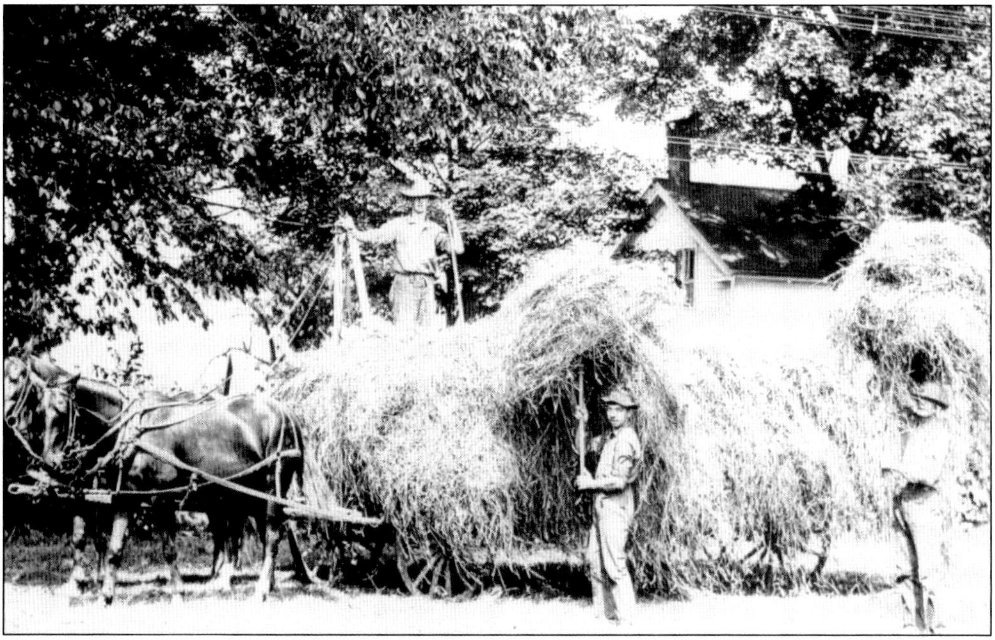

The hired man and Everad Fenner pitch the cocks of dried hay onto a wagon drawn by horses. On the wagon, Dean Fenner spreads the hay out on the load and takes care of driving the team of horses as well.

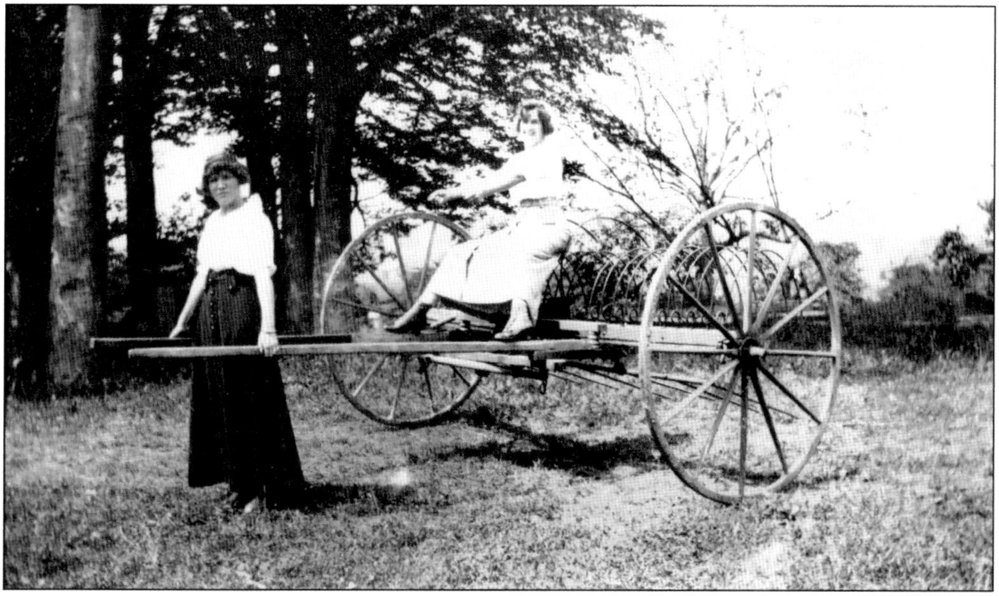

The dump rake gathered hay into windrows in the field. A single horse drew the rake, and the rider stepped on a lever when the rake filled with hay. Here, two women pose—one as the horse and the other as the rider.

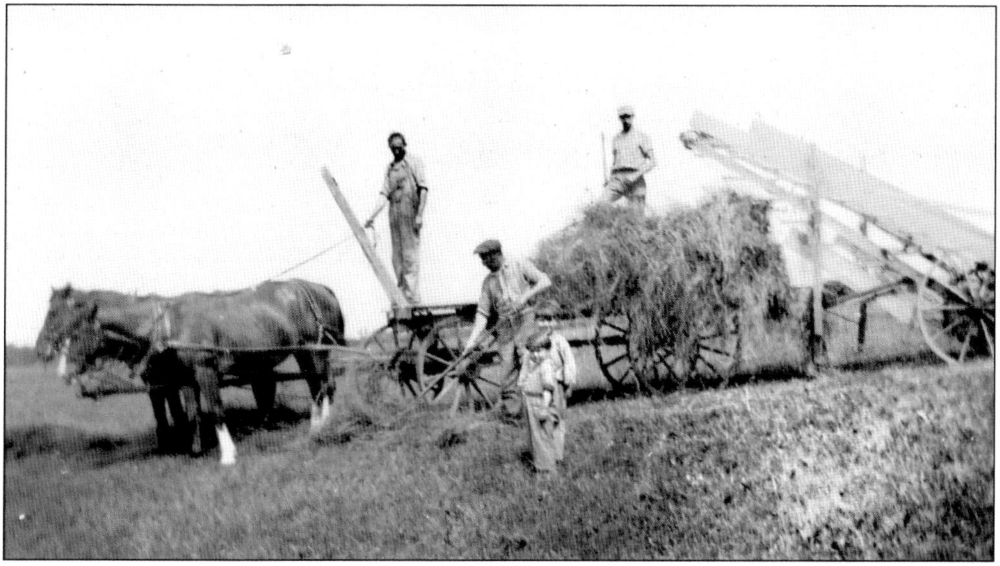

Another innovation was the hay loader. This team of horses on the Blauvelt farm in Russia drew the wagon and the attached loader over a windrow that had been raked. Teeth picked up the hay and elevated it onto the wagon. One of the two men on the wagon is driving the team, and the other is spreading the hay evenly on the load. The man on the ground is pitching up scatterings, the hay that the rake or loader missed.

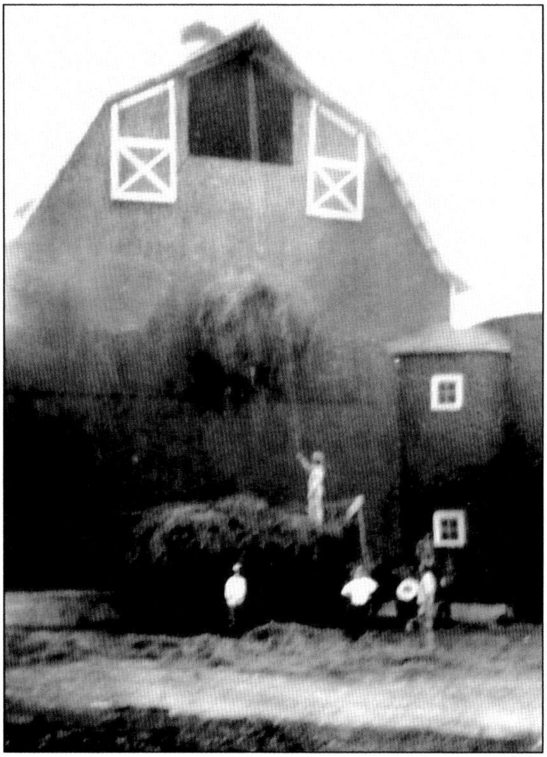

Once the wagon of hay was loaded, it was drawn to the barn for storage. The early method of unloading the hay was for men to pitch it off into a mow in the barn. This picture shows the method of unloading the hay by using a large hayfork attached to a rope and pulley. Either horses or a mechanical engine drew the rope through the pulley and lifted the hay up to the top of the mow before dumping it. The hay was then mowed away by men in the barn. Here, hay is unloaded at the Jean Clark Farm outside of Norway. This large dairy barn was built in 1917. It featured tongue-and-groove construction and had a gambrel roof.

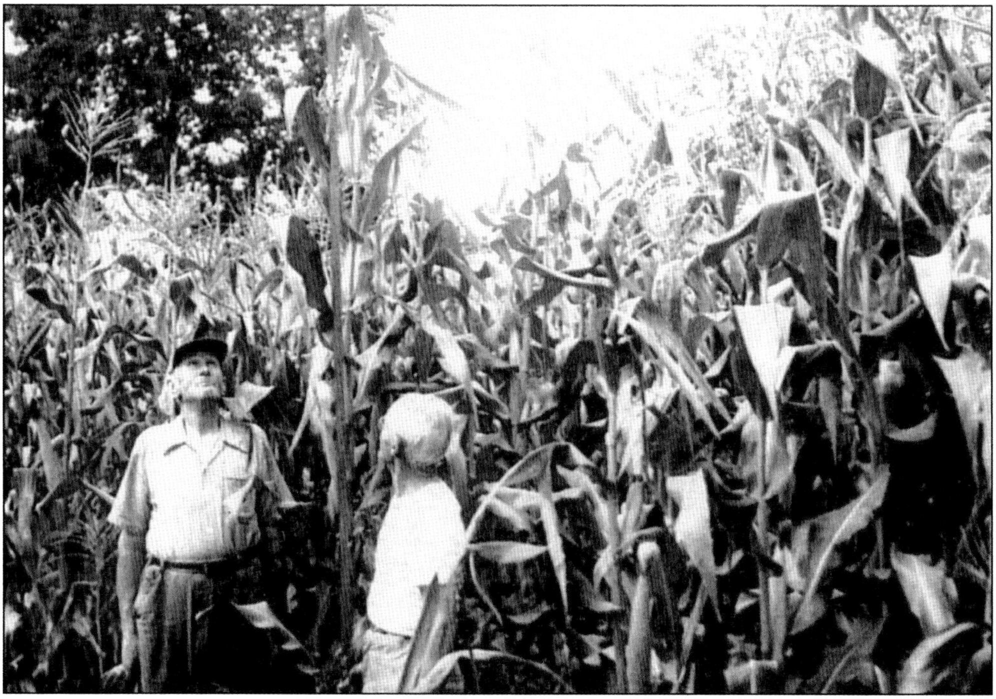

Corn was raised for silage for feed for the cows. George Seidel and his hired man are inspecting a field of corn on the Pearce farm, outside of Newport. The open pollinated corn of pre–World War II days grew much taller than the modern corn hybrids do.

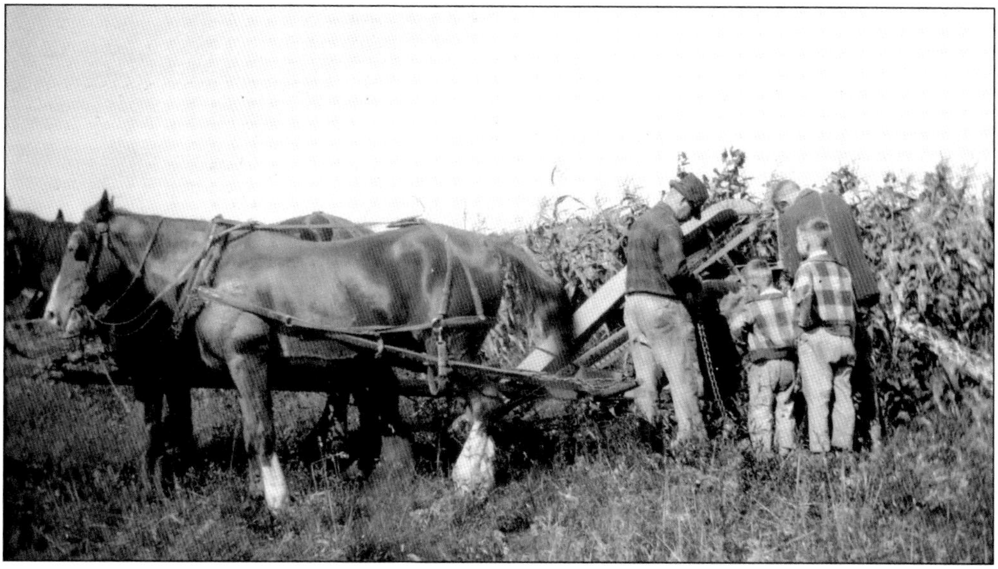

In the early days, corn was cut by hand with a sickle and piled in bundles to be loaded by hand onto a wagon. This horse-drawn corn harvester on the Blauvelt farm made the harvesting of the corn much easier. The corn harvester straddled a row of corn, and blades cut the stalks near to the ground. The stalks were then bunched and tied before being kicked out of the harvester onto the ground.

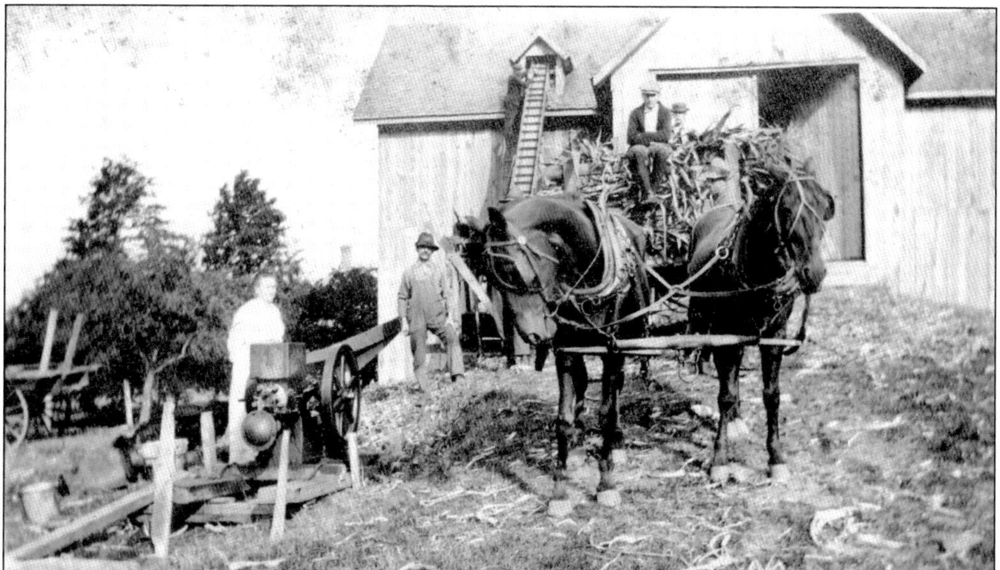

Once the corn was loaded, it was taken to the silo for storage. It was chopped into small pieces, before being conveyed to the top of the silo. A tractor or a stationary engine was used to power the chopper and blower or conveyor. This picture shows a unique inside silo on the Burt farm in Norway. The corn is being conveyed to the inside silo through a cupola on the roof.

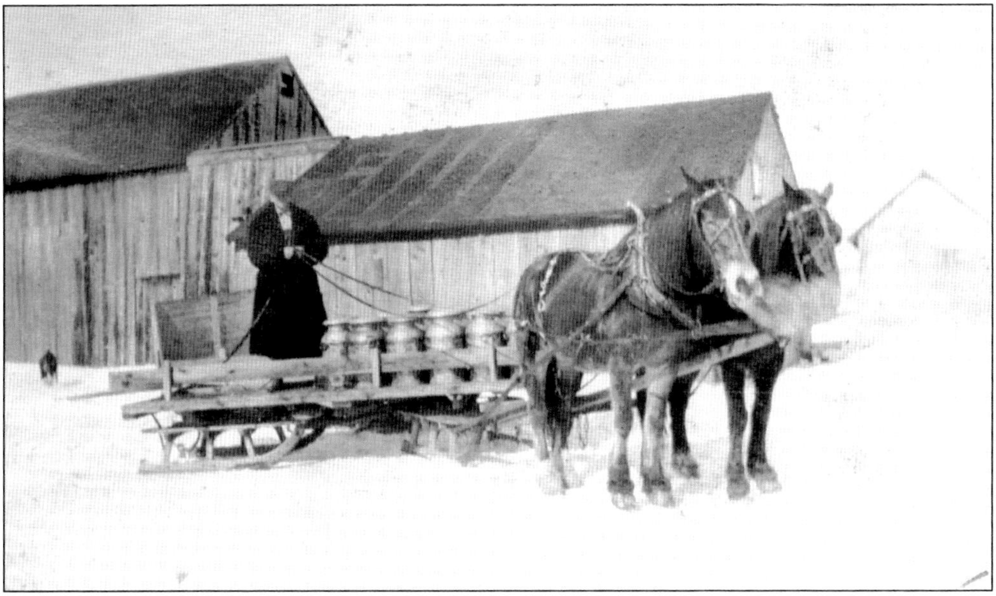

When farmers began to sell their milk to cheese factories or milk plants, they had to transport the milk in cans to the plant. Often a farmer drew neighbors' milk along with his own. This picture shows a team and sleigh with a load of 10-gallon cans heading for the market.

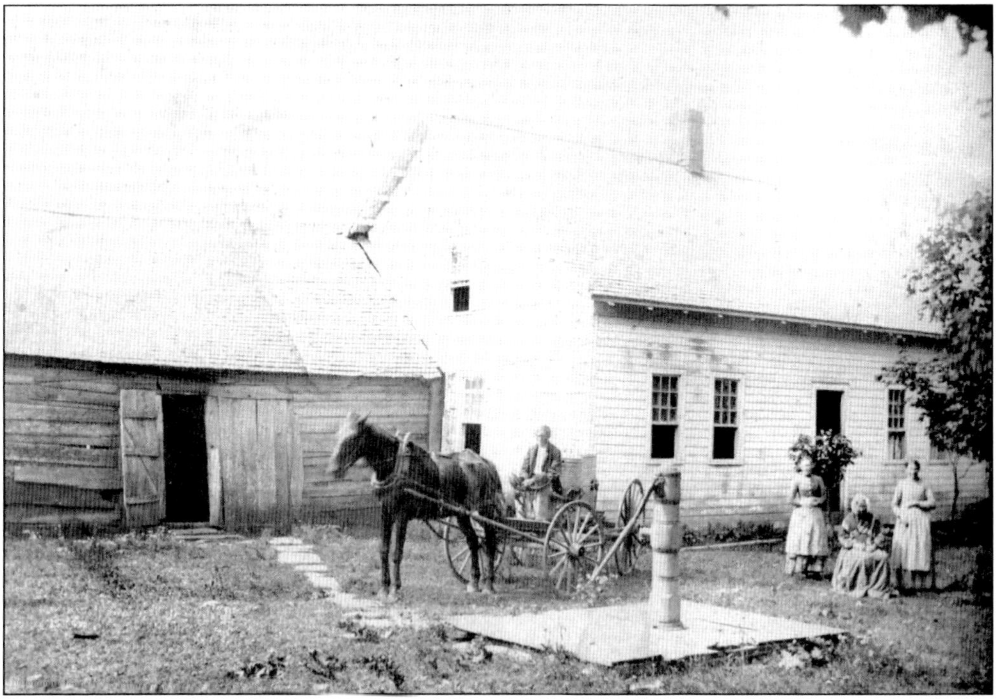

This photograph shows a single horse-drawn wagon leaving the James Ryan farm, on the Castle Road outside of Middleville. Note the large size of the cans on the wagon. Each can probably held 40 gallons.

Early farmers grew grain to feed their cows, sheep, and goats. They often took bags of grain to a gristmill for grinding. This 1920 picture shows Robert Burt in his Model T truck, returning from the gristmill with a load of ground feed in bags.

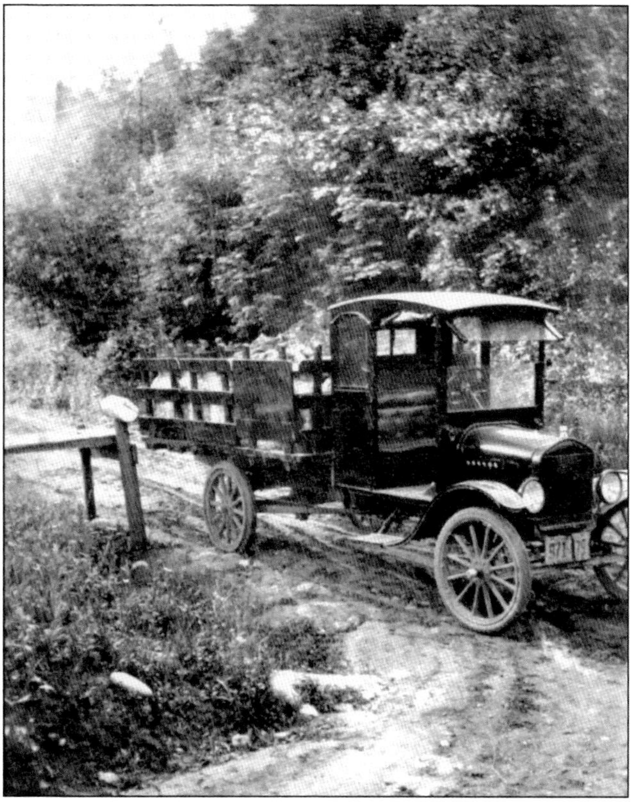

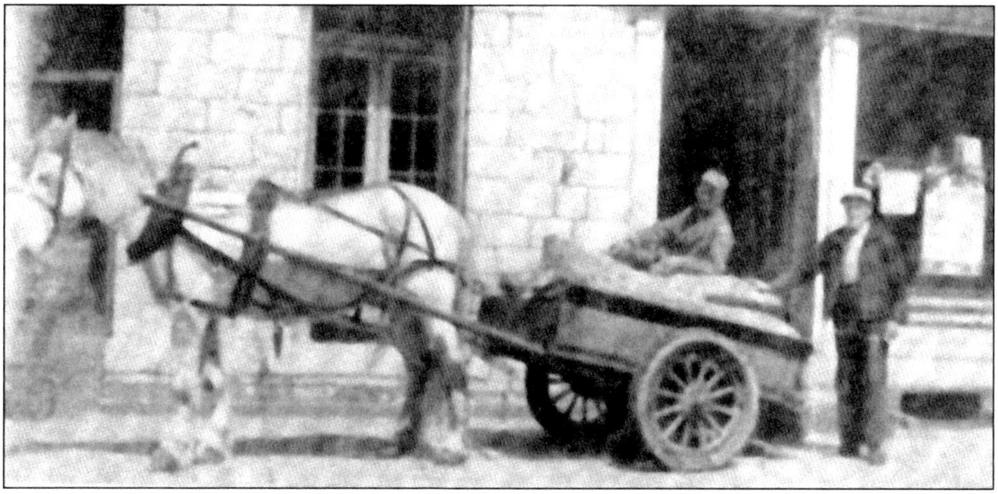

Feed stores sold blends of various grains for farm animal feed. Different formulas provided nutrition for cows, calves, horses, and so on. Here, Dean Fenner (left) has just finished loading his horse-drawn wagon with feed bags. Dan Boynton (right) was a Larro Dairy Feed dealer in Newport.

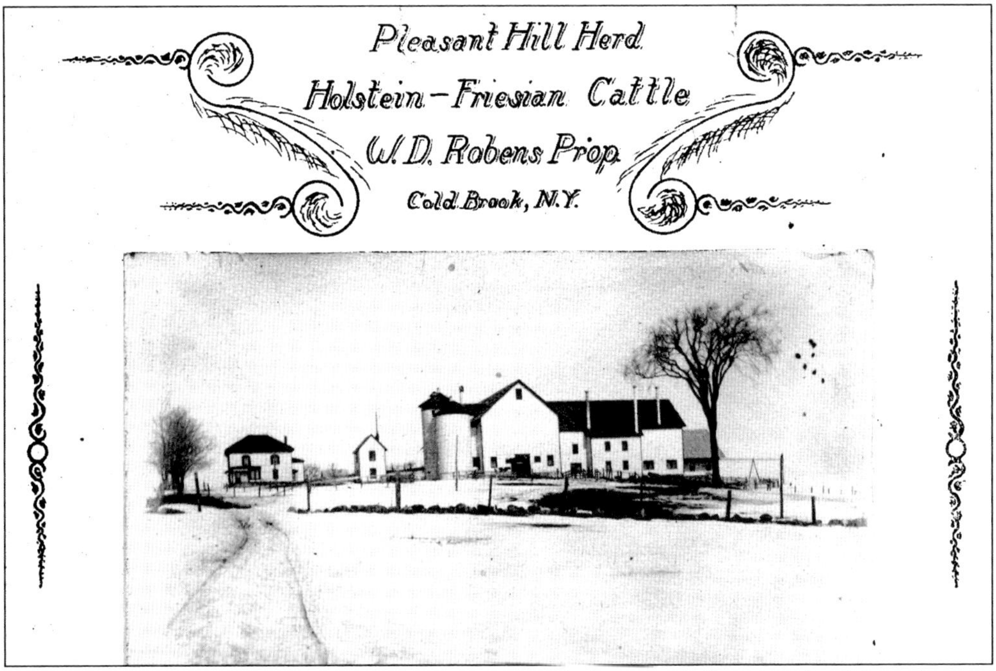

William Robens and his brother Reuben Robens settled on the hilltop north of the village of Cold Brook in the late 1790s. In 1823, Reuben Robens deeded land to Cold Brook to build a school, and in 1828 he leased land to the Methodist Society to build a church. William D. Robens (1874–1950), great-grandson of the early settler William Robens, was a breeder and promoter of Holstein-Friesian cattle, as well as a banker and investor in local businesses. His barns were constructed in 1907–1908.

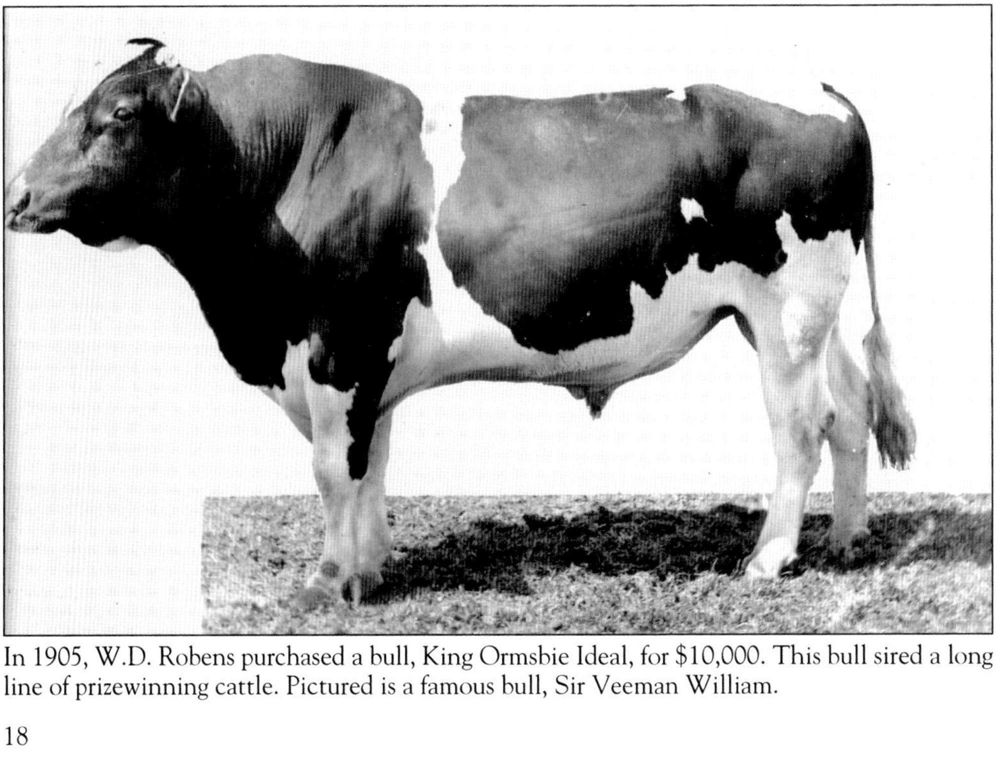

In 1905, W.D. Robens purchased a bull, King Ormsbie Ideal, for $10,000. This bull sired a long line of prizewinning cattle. Pictured is a famous bull, Sir Veeman William.

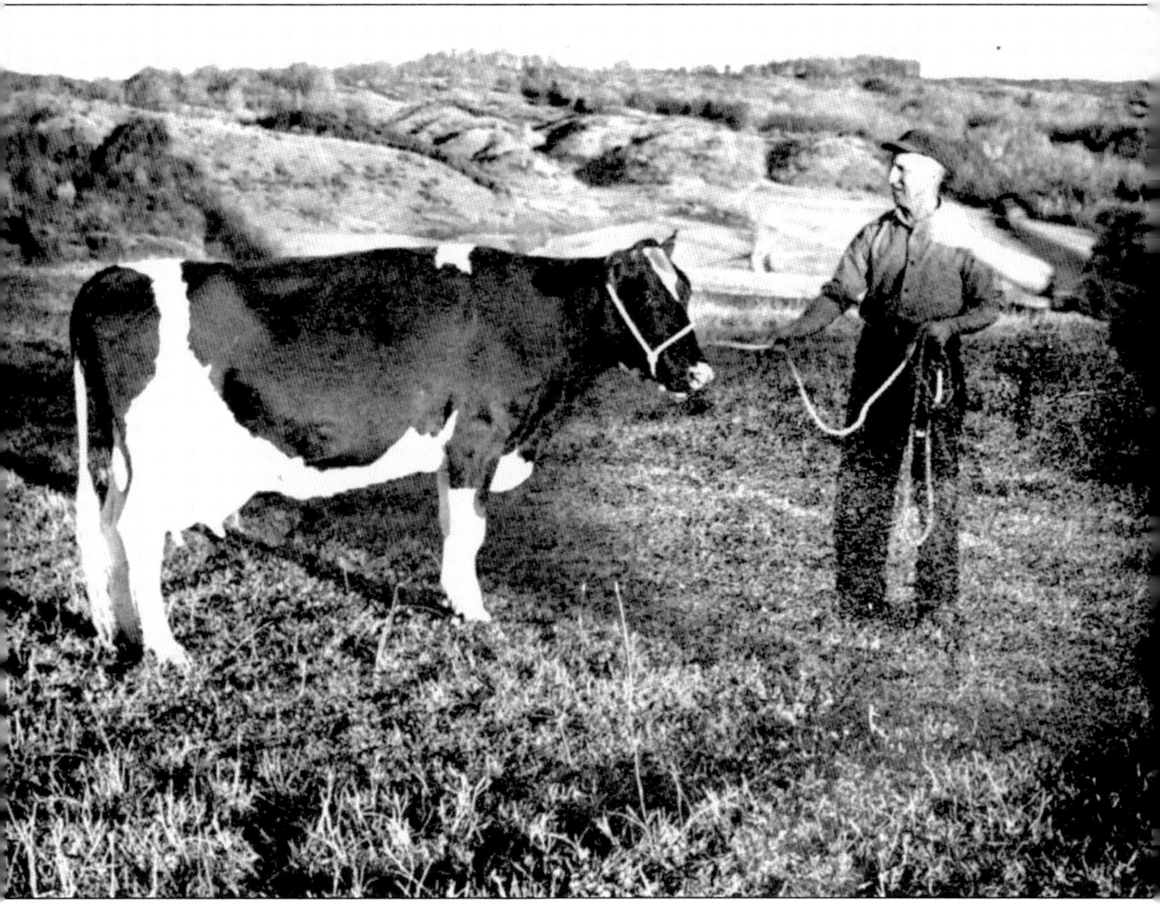

W.D. Robens's son, Glenn Robens, D.V.M., managed the farm and practiced veterinary medicine for 40 years in the Kuyahoora area. He is pictured with a prizewinning cow on the family farm. The Robens family continued the operation of the farm until 1965, when the property was sold to Henry Swartz. Brad Davis now operates it as Cold Brook Farms.

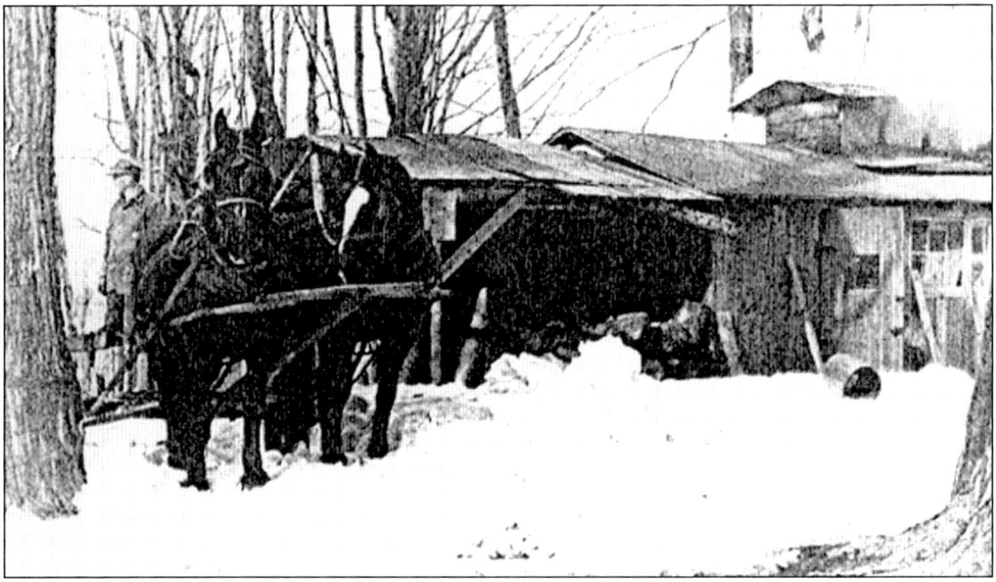

Cane sugar was not available to the pioneers; the only sweeteners were honey or maple sugar. The early farm families produced their own sugar from the sap of maple trees. Syrup making was a seasonal activity, occurring between the end of winter and the planting of spring crops. The season usually lasted four or five weeks in March and early April. By tapping 40 or 50 trees, the farmers were able to gather enough sap to make a year's supply of sugar for their families. In pioneer times, they boiled the sap into syrup in open kettles outdoors. Later, they used flat pans placed on a brick arch inside a building. Robert Burt is shown above with his team and gathering sled near the sugar shack in his woods. Note the milk cans on the sled for collecting the sap. Below, Burt and his uncle, Elmer Keller (lower right), oversee the steaming sap in the open flat pans.

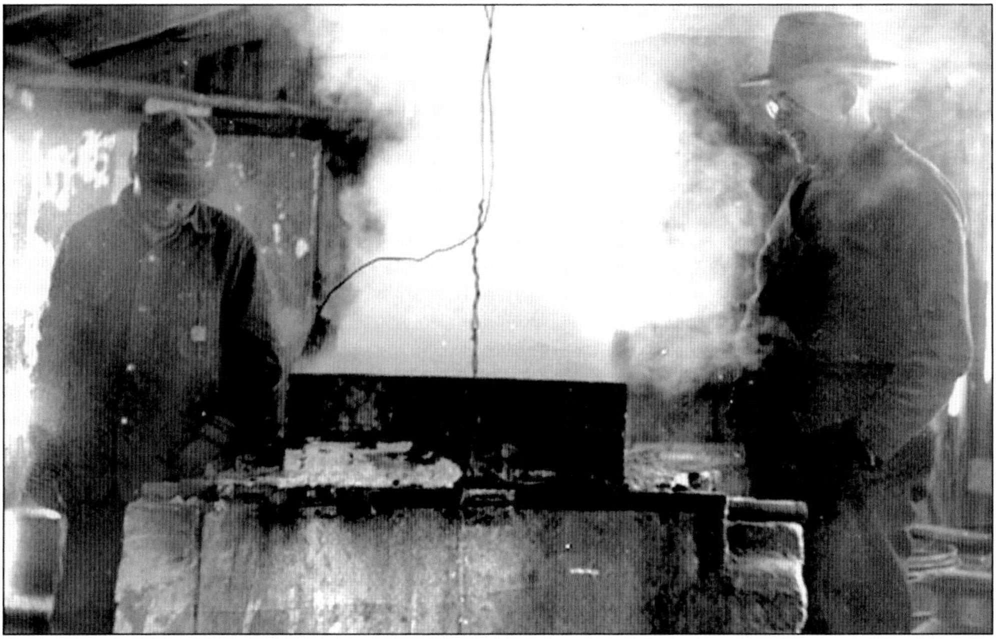

Two

WATERPOWER BRINGS INDUSTRY

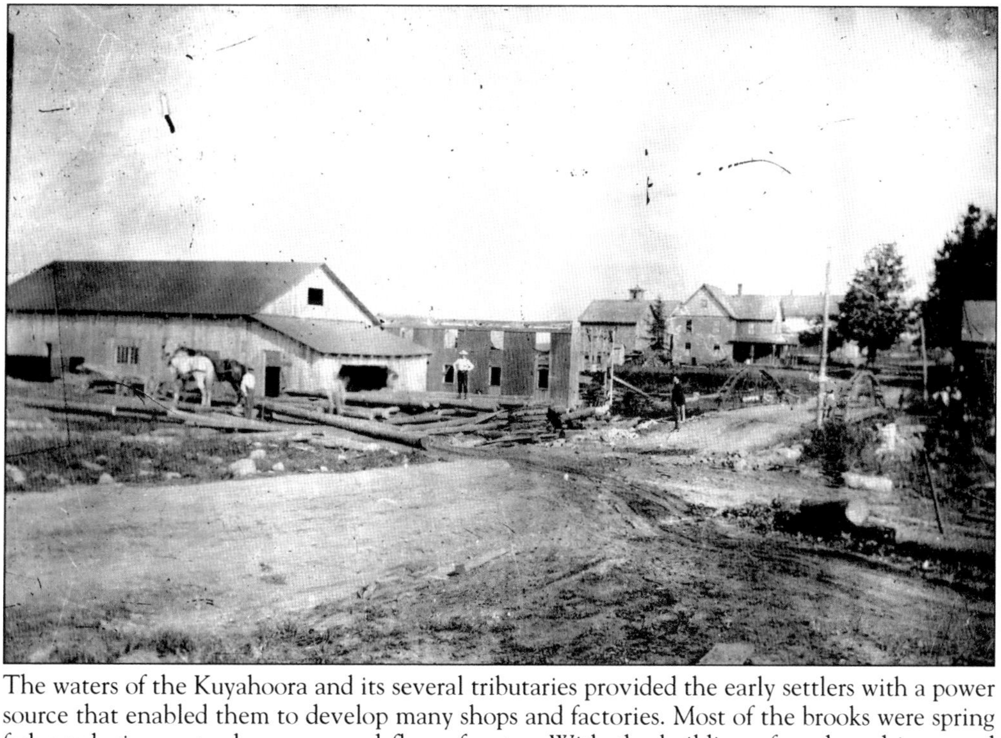

The waters of the Kuyahoora and its several tributaries provided the early settlers with a power source that enabled them to develop many shops and factories. Most of the brooks were spring fed, producing a steady, year-round flow of water. With the building of roads and improved transportation, more settlers arrived. Demand for goods and services increased beyond the subsistence level of early agrarian society. Wagons, sleds, tools to work the land and clear the forests, mills to grind grain for the animals, lumber to build houses and barns, furniture and household goods for the growing families—these all became necessities.This sawmill on the Black Creek in Gray sawed lumber from the huge supply of logs yielded by the clearing of the land. Near this site was a clothespin factory, which used the products of the mill. Owned by Charles Gray, the factory employed 18 women, who each were paid 75¢ for a 10-hour day. The factory closed in 1899.

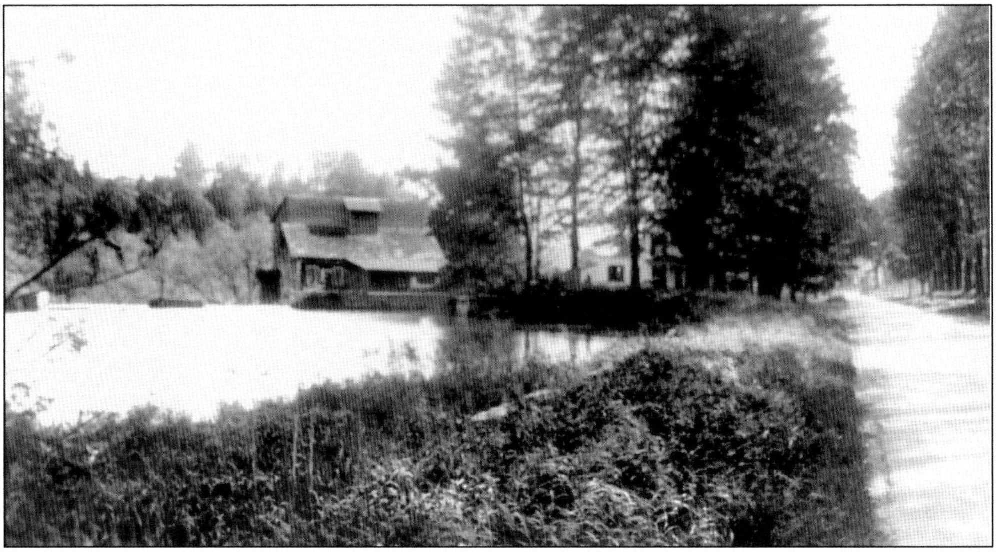

A dozen or more mills and factories were located along the Cold Brook stream, which runs several miles through the towns of Norway and Russia and the village of Cold Brook, and enters the West Canada Creek in Poland. This scene of the brook shows a dam that provided water to power the gristmill in the distance. The Old Flour Mill was built in 1857 and closed in the 1940s. After World War II, the historic mill was purchased by a local artist, Grace Paull, and operated as an antiques and gift gallery. In 1975, it was placed on the National Register of Historic Places.

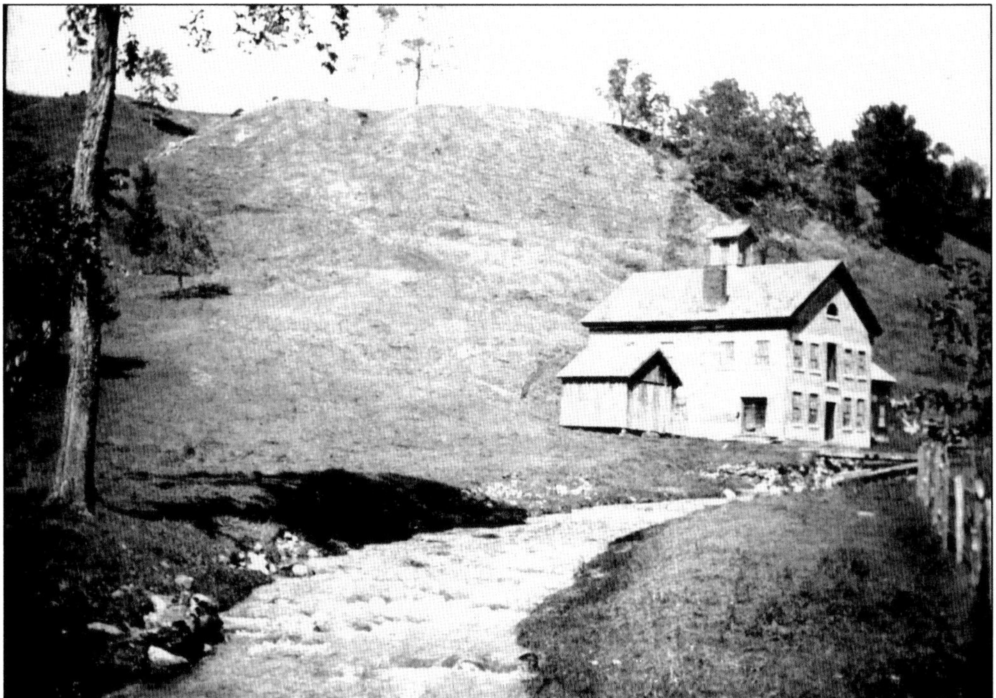

An axe-handle factory also was located along the Cold Brook stream at the southern end of the village. Operated by the Trask family, it was the only Cold Brook factory built of bricks.

Wooden buttons of various sizes were produced at Will Rhodes's button factory, located at the northern edge of Cold Brook. Hard maple logs were sawed into thin, narrow strips of lumber. After they were kiln dried, these strips were fed into a machine that punched out buttons of different sizes. Then another machine drilled two, three, or four holes in each button. It was reported that the drilling machines could turn out 72 buttons per minute. Will Rhodes sold his buttons throughout New York and New England. At clothing factories, the buttons were covered with cloth material or leather for women's and men's garments. This photograph shows a sampler of buttons.

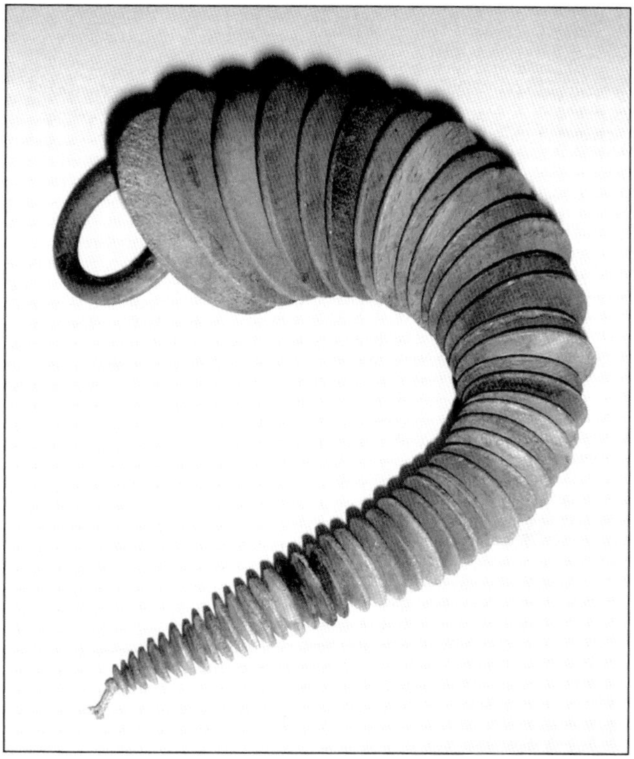

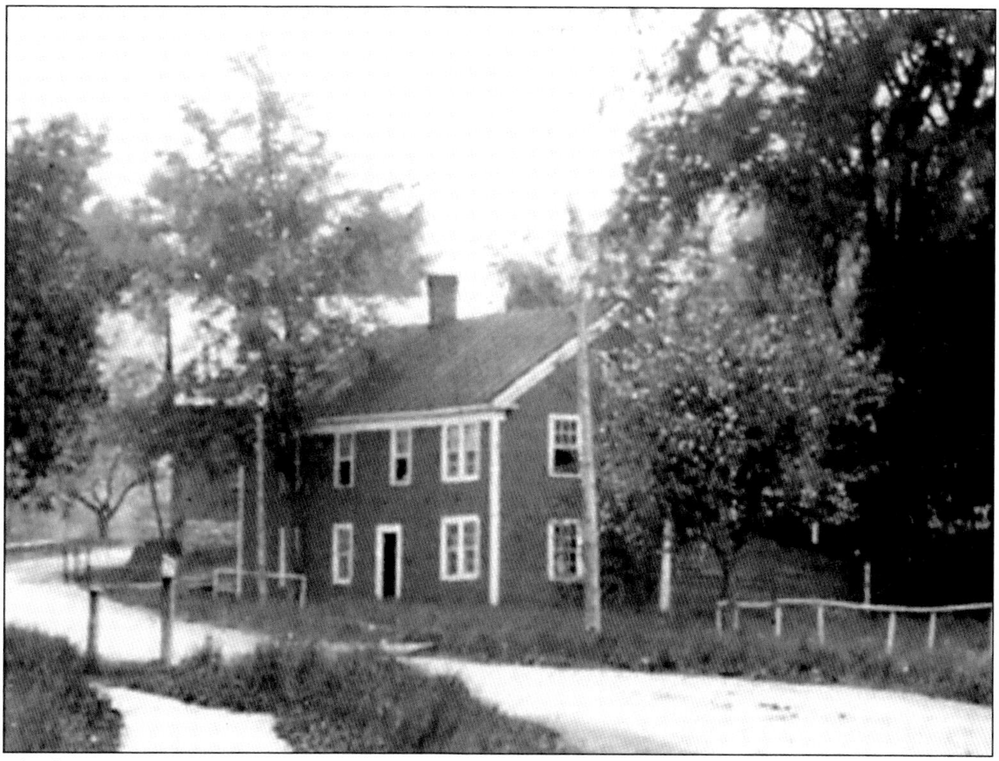

The button factory was situated near a small dam on the brook.

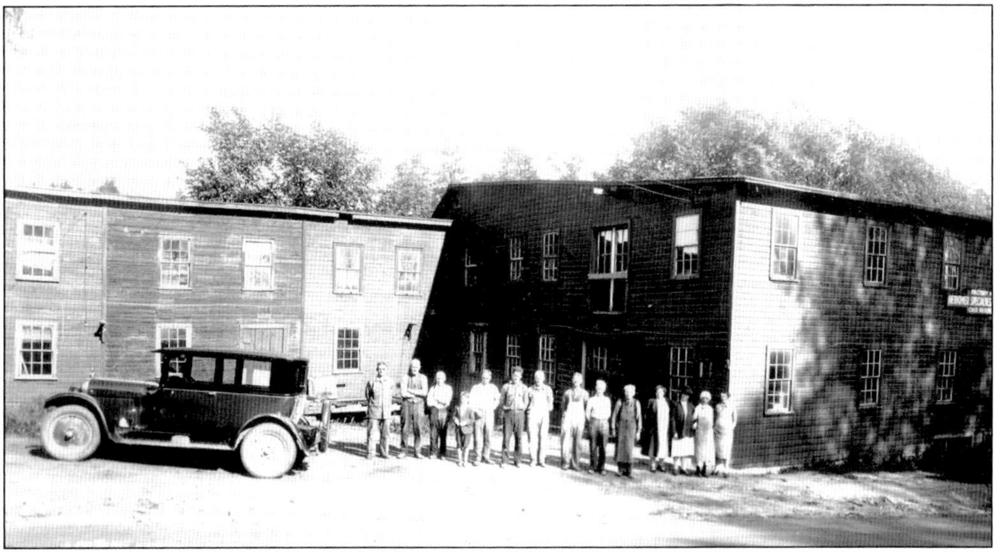

On the south end of Cold Brook, the "chair" factory became nationally known in the 1920s for its production of a service cart, advertised in *Good Housekeeping* magazine and sold throughout the United States. The factory was built in the mid-1800s by the Rhodes family to produce sashes and blinds. Later, it manufactured card tables, service carts, and wooden folding chairs. Many of the wooden slatted chairs made at the factory are still in use in community and church halls. In later years, the factory operated under the name of the Herkimer Specialities Company. It was destroyed by fire in 1933.

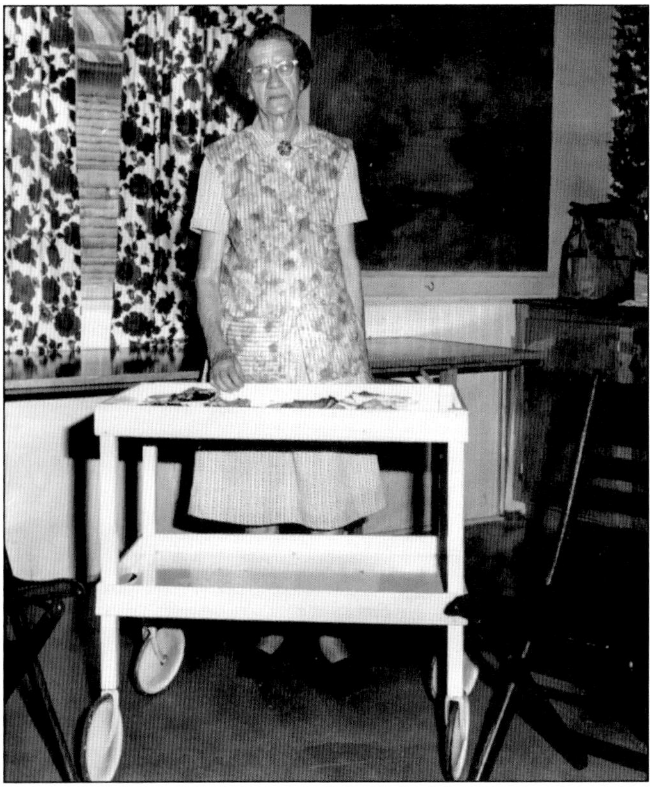

Juva Christman, born in the early 1890s, was a former employee of the chair factory. She recalled dipping the stained chairs in a hot varnish and hanging them over vats to dry. She also installed the rubber tires on the metal wheels of the service carts. She is pictured here in the Cold Brook church with a tea cart and folding chairs.

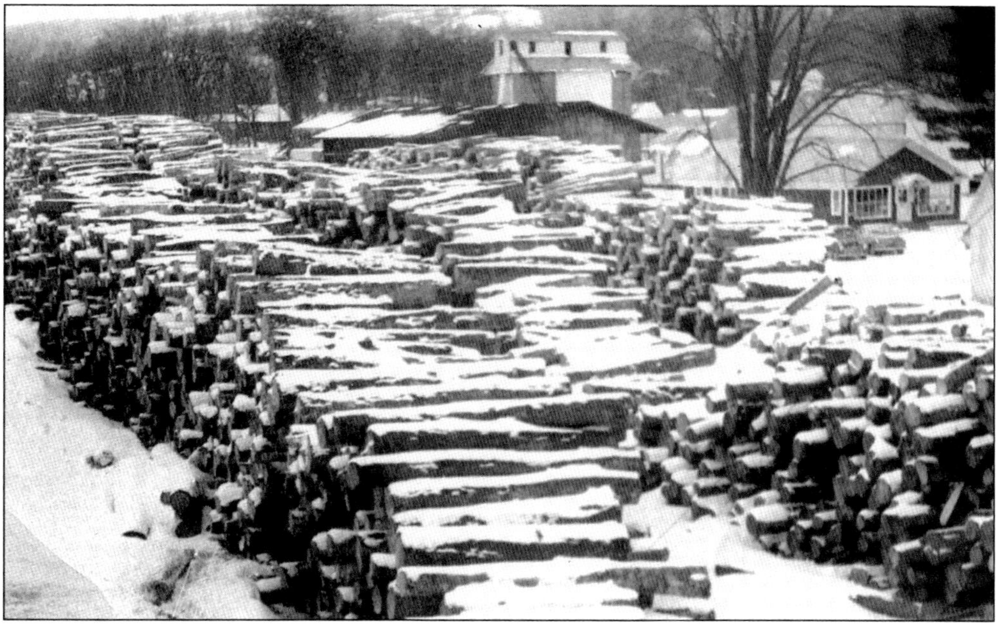

In the 1920s, a sawmill was built between the West Canada Creek and the New York Central Railroad in Poland. The mill employed up to 50 men and specialized in sawing softwood lumber obtained from the extensive logging operations in the southern Adirondacks. As a result of the depletion of the supply of logs, the mill closed in 1938, but it was reopened in 1945 as the Northern Lumber Company. The mill was remodeled, and a dry kiln and a planing mill were added. The company specialized in hardwoods. The Northern Lumber Company and its sister mill in Riverside sawed into lumber more hardwood than any other sawmill in the United States. The company was sold to C.C. Canada in 1972. Furniture manufacturers found excellent maple, cherry, and birch hardwoods readily available from C.C. Canada. The log yard of the Northern Lumber Company is shown above. C.C. Canada's office, located in a completely remodeled early-19th-century trading post and cheese factory along the bank of the West Canada Creek, is shown below.

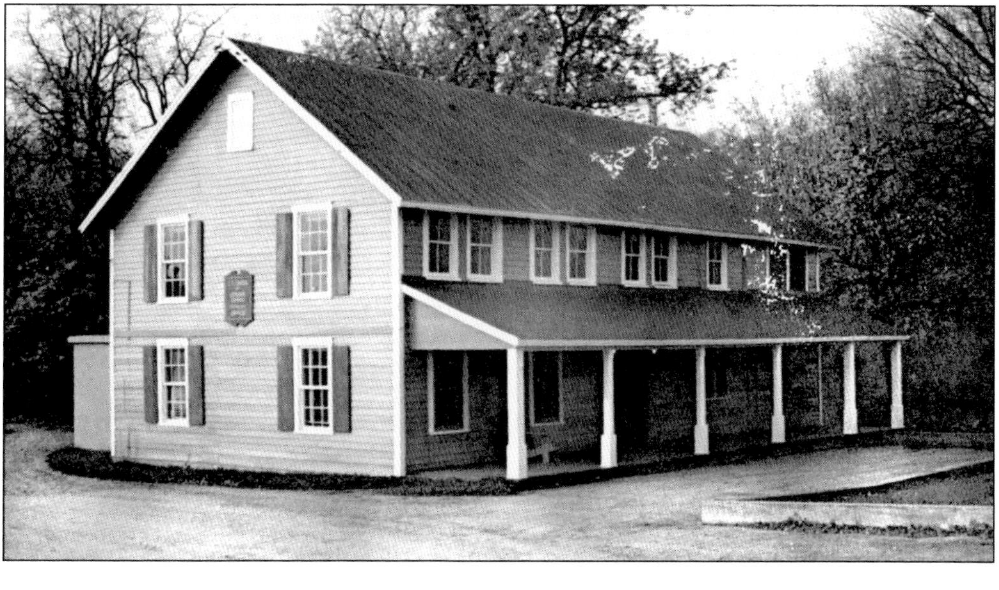

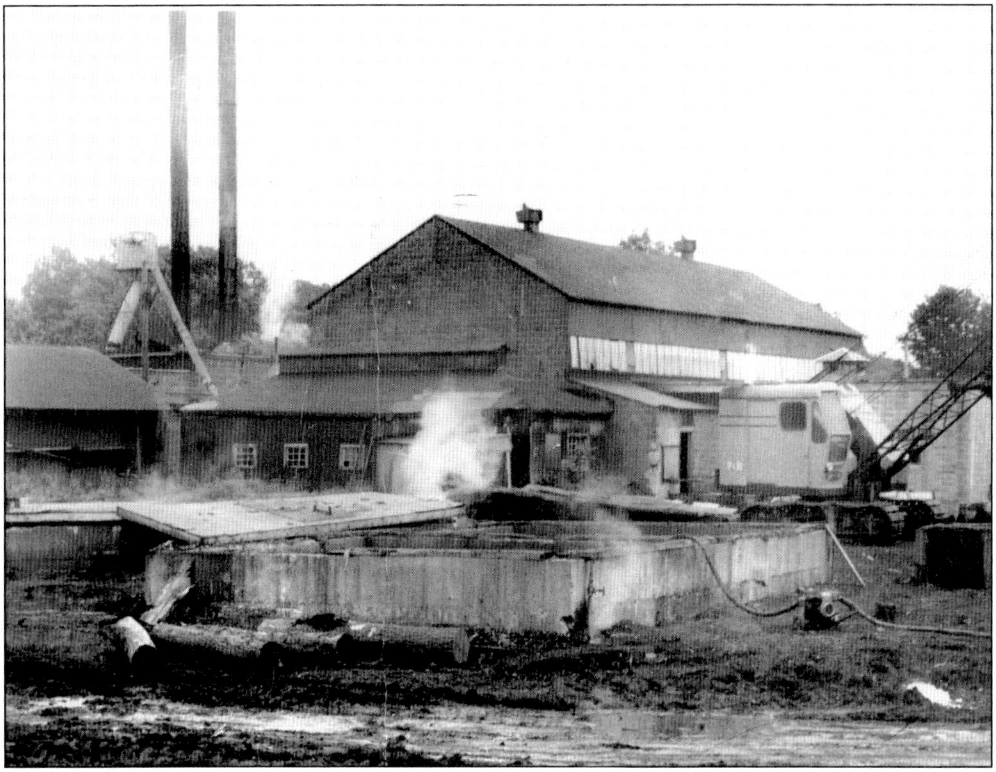

The Jamestown Veneer and Plywood Corporation of Jamestown acquired property from the village of Poland in 1925 and built a mill to produce thin veneer for furniture and flush doors. Its product also was laminated into plywood and sold to large companies, such as Georgia Pacific. The complete operation was performed at the plant: from birch log into finished laminated plywood. At its peak production, the mill employed 130 people and shipped two railroad cars of veneer and plywood each week. The influx of foreign imports forced the mill to close in 1969.

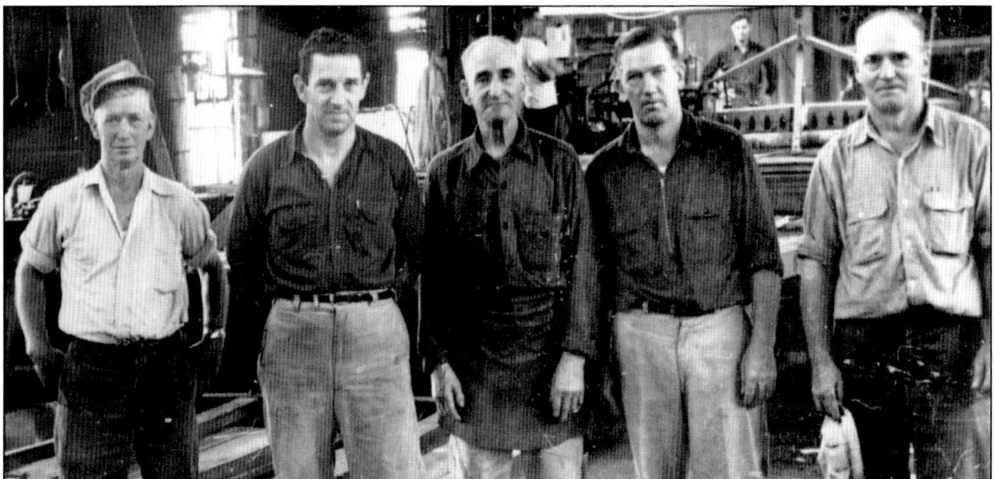

Employees of Jamestown Veneer, from left to right, are Charles Johnson, Milbury Charlton, Harold Thayer, Fred Weakley, and an unidentified worker.

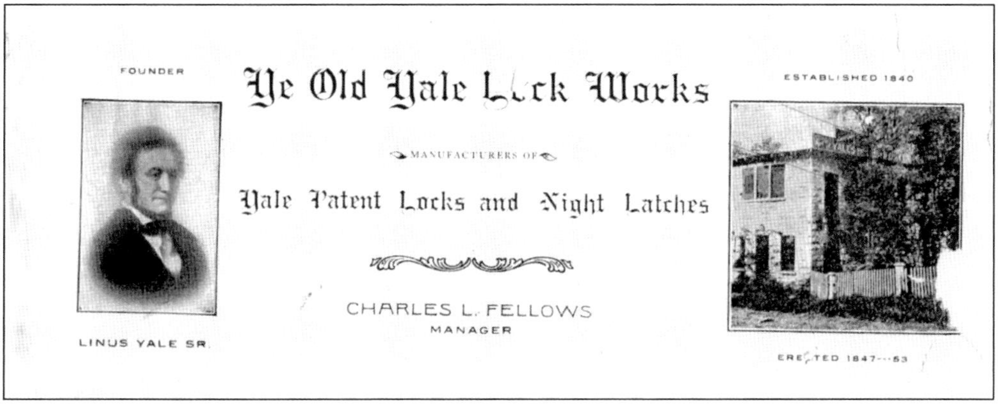

In 1847, Linus Yale purchased land and water rights on the northern edge of Newport and built a stone factory building on Knights Brook. In his shop he invented several forms of locks for bank vaults and safes for both businesses and homes. He held several patents for his locks and invented other items such as a threshing machine and sawmill machinery.

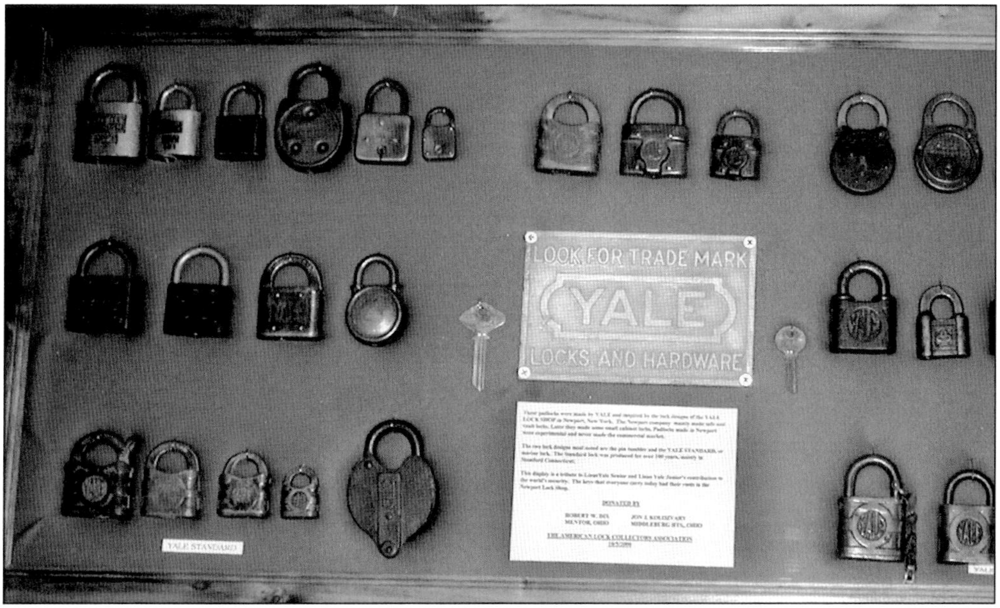

This collection of Yale locks was donated to the Newport History Center by Robert Dix of Mentor, Ohio.

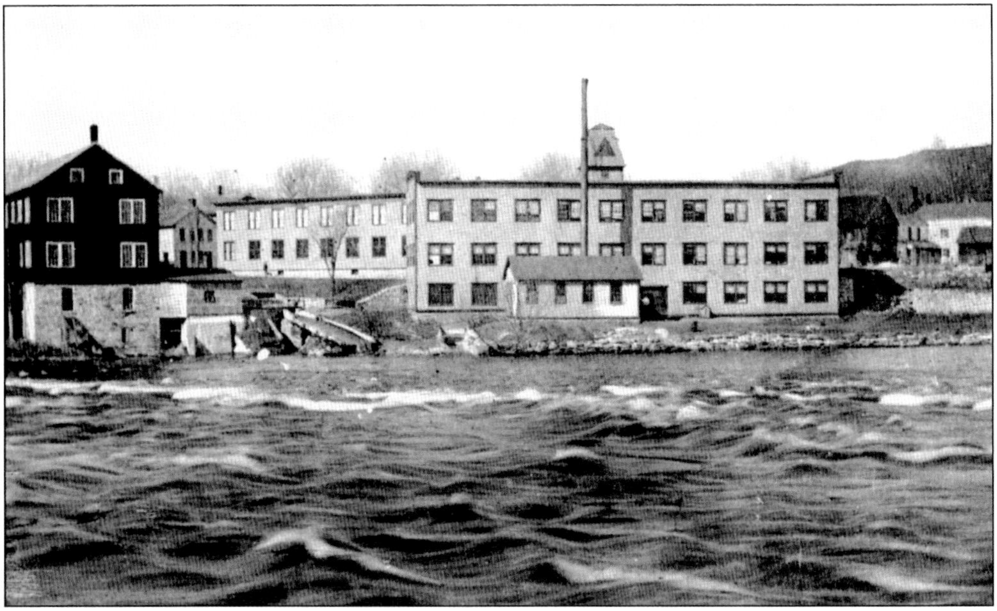

In 1900, a large two-story mill was built on the bank of the West Canada Creek in Newport. The Newport Knitting Mill included modern machinery for up-to-date manufacturing of knitted goods.

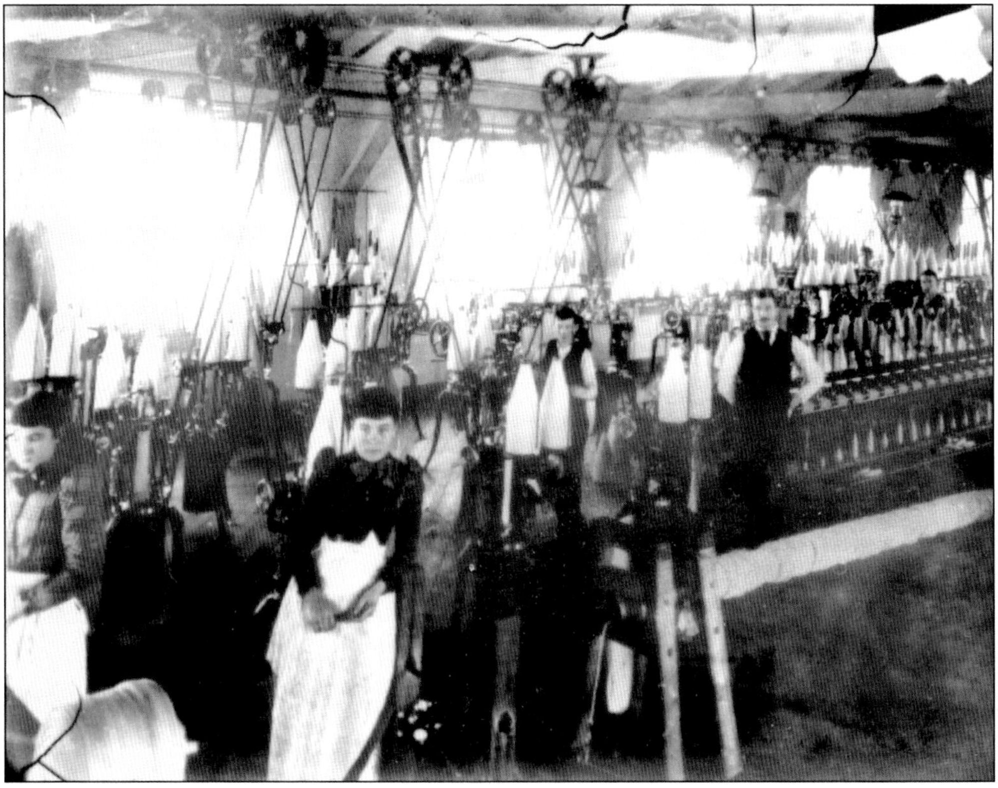

The mill employed about 100 men and women, and the mill's production reached 70,000 dozen undergarments during the first year of operation. Shown here is an interior view of the mill.

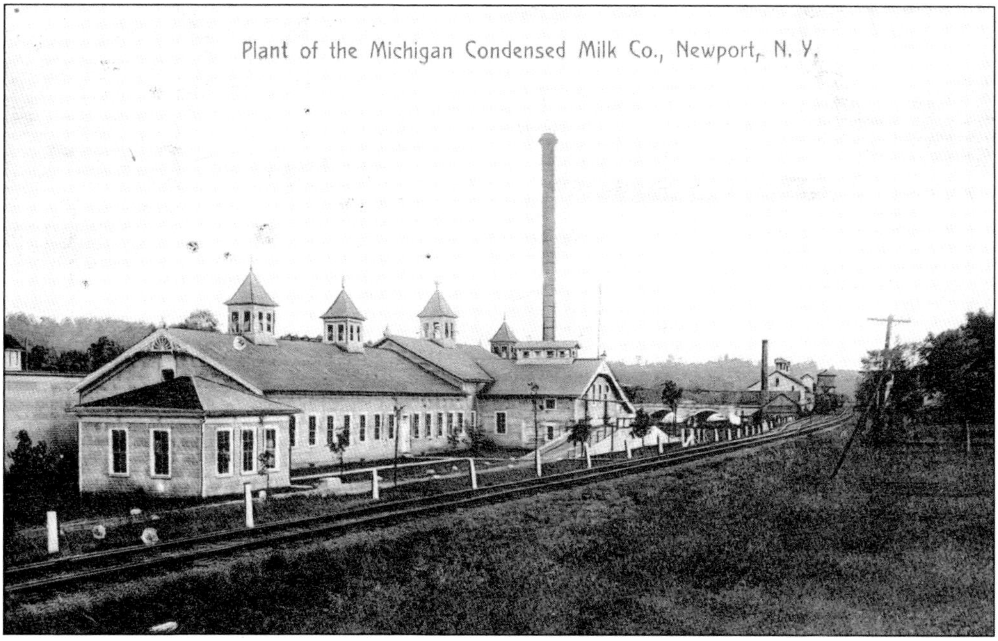

The Michigan Condensed Milk Corporation purchased the old Clover Leaf Creamery in 1904. After improvements were made to the property, farmers drew milk to the Newport Condensery from 1907 through the 1930s.

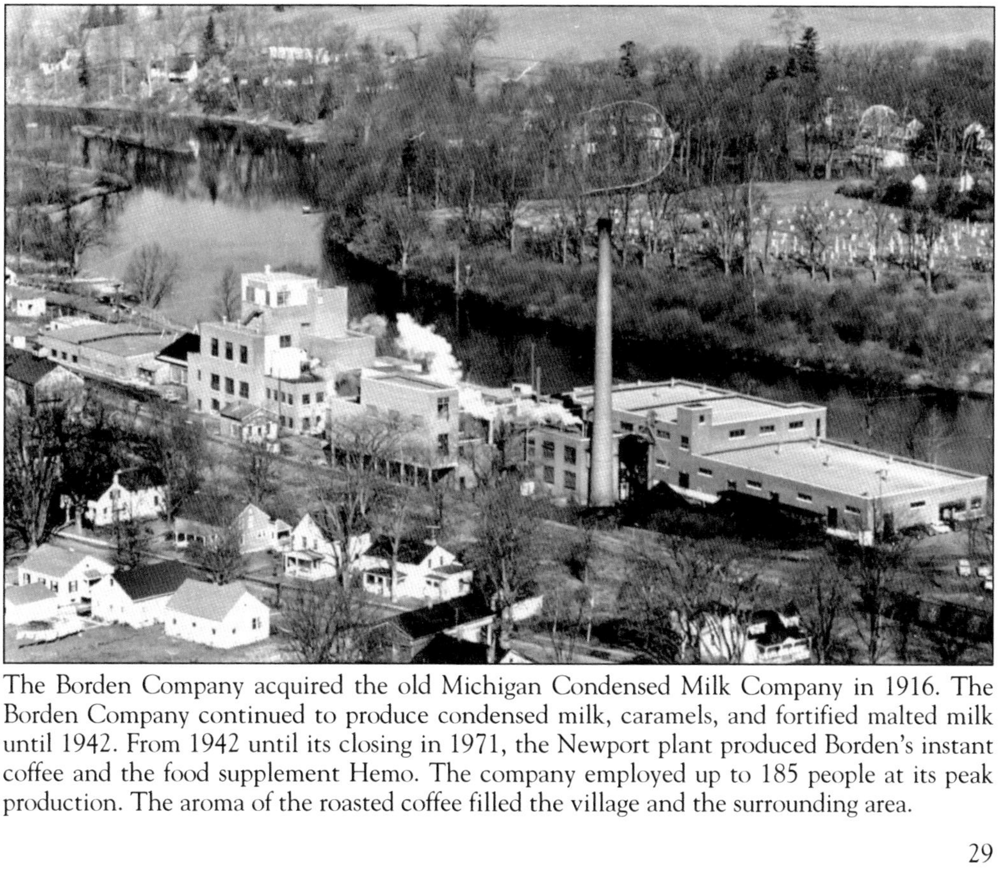

The Borden Company acquired the old Michigan Condensed Milk Company in 1916. The Borden Company continued to produce condensed milk, caramels, and fortified malted milk until 1942. From 1942 until its closing in 1971, the Newport plant produced Borden's instant coffee and the food supplement Hemo. The company employed up to 185 people at its peak production. The aroma of the roasted coffee filled the village and the surrounding area.

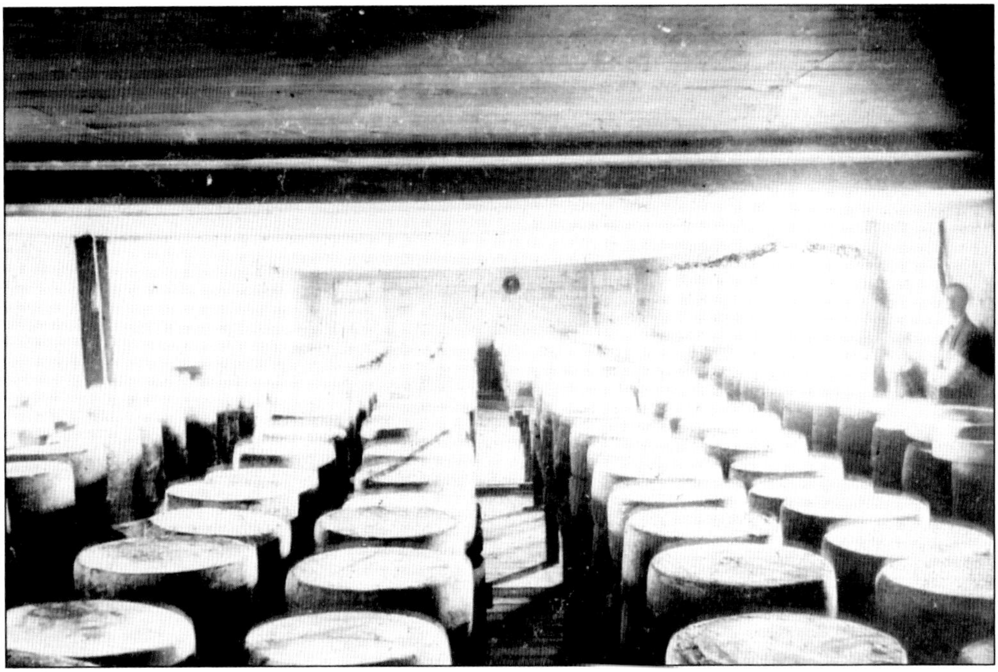

In the early 1800s, nearly every farm made butter and cheese. After 1850, cheese factories were built and the farmers sold their milk to the factory. This picture shows the curing room in the Carpenter Cheese Factory, on the Military Road between Cold Brook and Russia. Much of the cheese was sold at the cheese market in Little Falls.

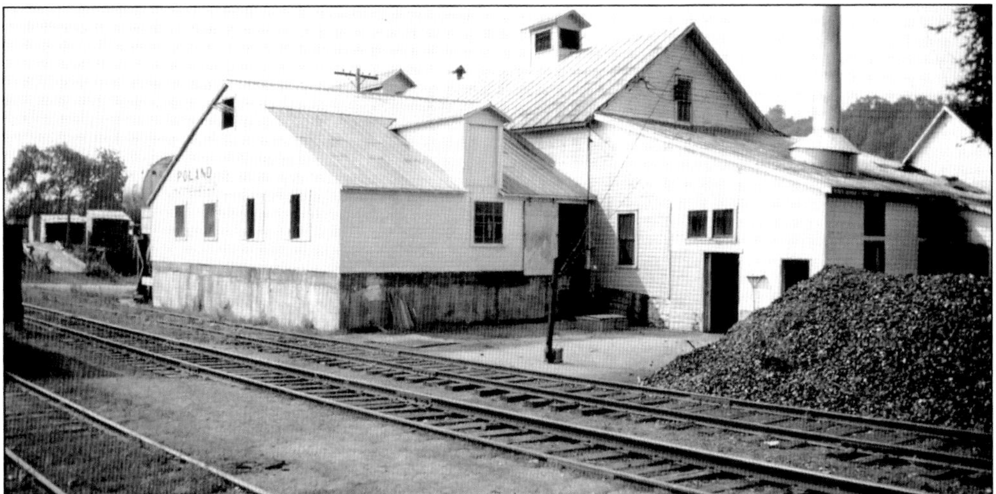

The Poland Milk Producers' Co-op was located by the railroad in Poland. It was formed in the 1930s by a group of farmers who wanted to get a better price for their milk, by handling and processing it themselves. Most of the area farmers became members. In 1933, when the cooperative faced a surplus of milk, the group revived cheese making. By 1950, the Poland Co-op had a membership of 157 and became a rival to the Wisconsin cheese industry, producing several million pounds of cheese a year and doing $3 million worth of business. In 1958, the Poland Co-op bought its first bulk tank. By 1976, as farmers were going out of business, the membership had dwindled to 32 and the milk was trucked to other markets.

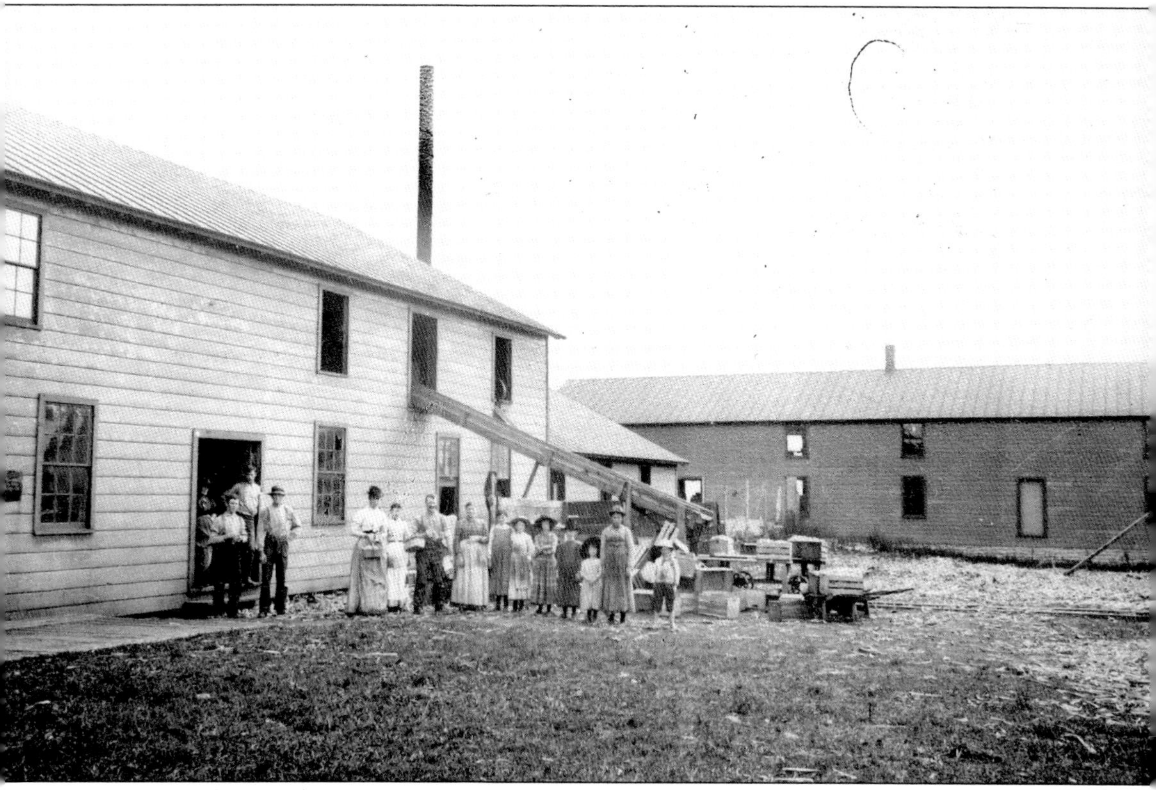

Canning was done in this Newport factory as a seasonal business from 1888 to 1890. Employees were women, boys, and girls, or anyone who had spare time and wanted to earn extra money. After the corn was husked, it was cut from the cob, put through a screen, cooked, and then put into cans, which were sealed by soldering. The cans were then cooked for another 50 minutes by steam. Pumpkin also was canned here. Note the husks on the ground.

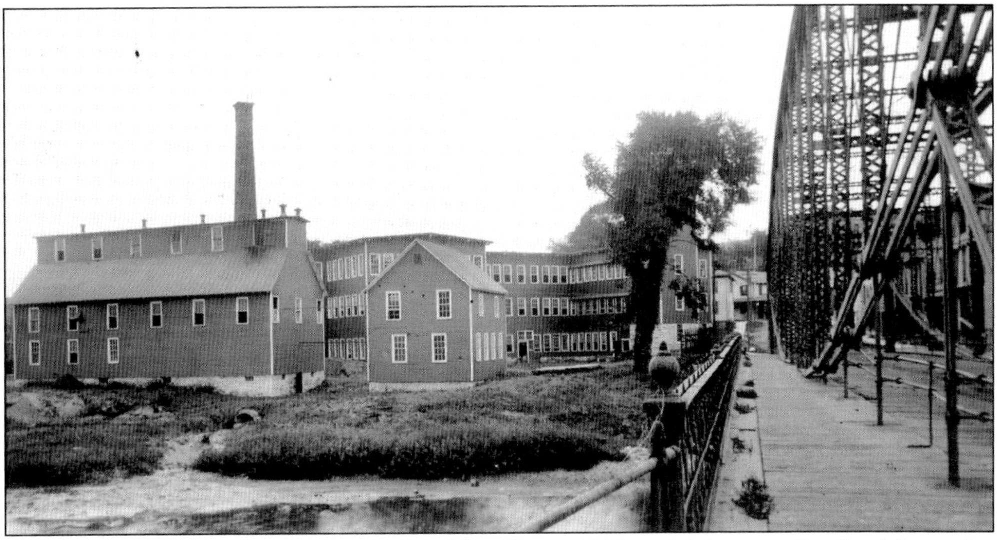

John Wood built the first tannery in Middleville in 1814 on Maltanner Creek. After a fire destroyed the tannery, a new one was built on the West Canada Creek, to capture more waterpower. The second tannery burned in 1902 and was replaced on the same site. The same family ran the business until after World War I. Later owners included George Thomas, E.C. Mills, A.C. Lawrence, William Haight, and Martin and Deichsel Leather Company. A decline in the leather business and state-mandated wastewater treatment led to its closing in 1973.

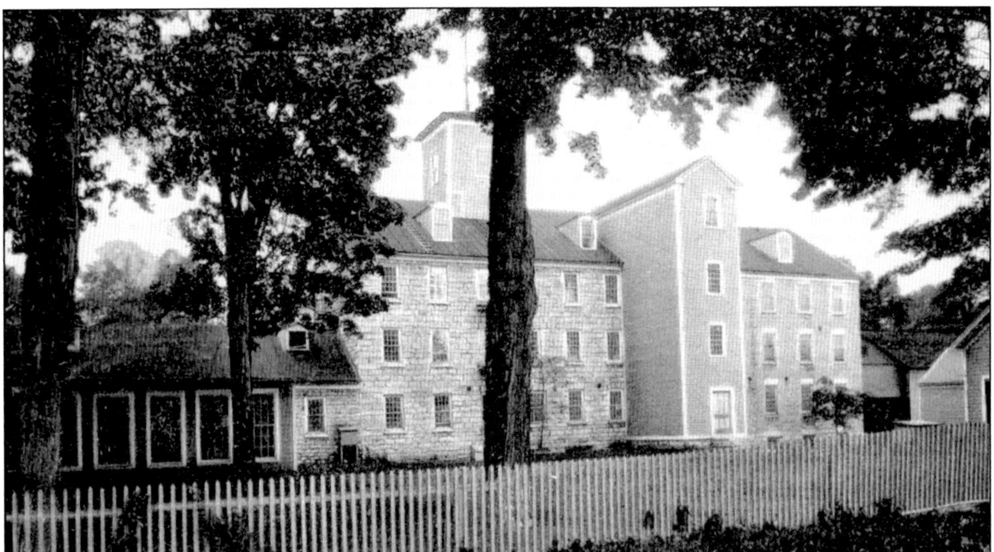

The Herkimer Manufacturing Company, organized in 1814, built a five-story stone building, with a two-story wing, on the west side of the West Canada Creek in Middleville. Cotton sheeting, bed ticking, bunting, scythes, axes, pitchforks, and hoes were manufactured there. The business was dissolved in 1834. The mill was operated by various owners—Harry Ellison, John Farrington, Simeon Osborne, Varnum Kenyon, W.W. Montgomery, and B.W. Nichols—until 1866, when E.J. Nelson and William Lansing purchased it and fitted it for a knitting mill. In 1902, it became the Nelson-Dedicke Felt Company. The building was razed in 1932.

Three

FROM CABINS TO MANSIONS

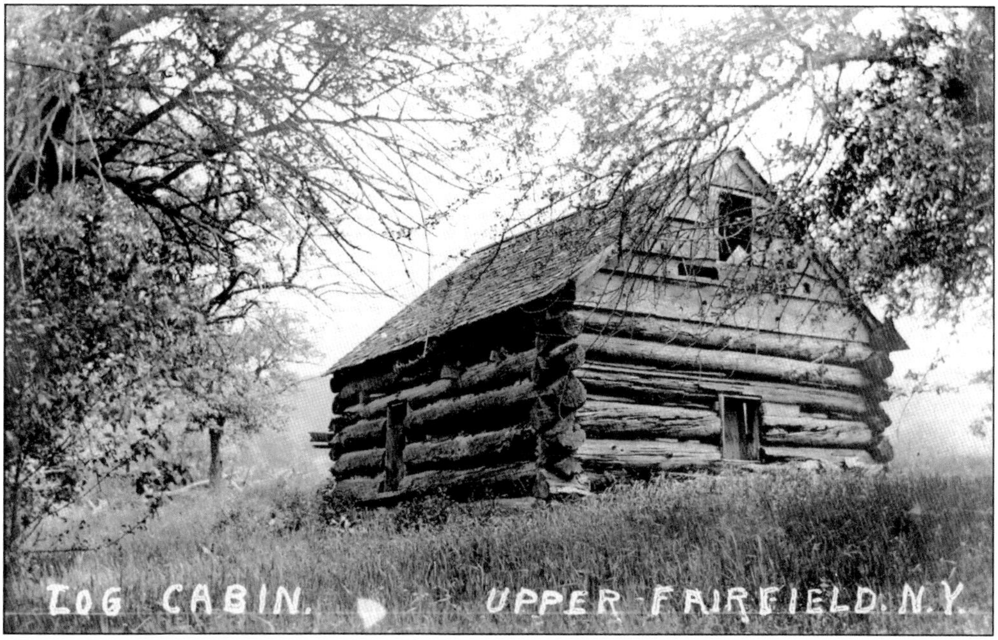

The earliest pioneers constructed simple log cabins with timber from the virgin forests of the area. These humble homes served the growing families for several years as they established their homesteads, growing crops and gardens to feed themselves and their animals. In the early 1800s, simple two-story homes, similar to those in Massachusetts and Rhode Island at the time, replaced the log cabins. These homes were most often constructed in the Federal plank style, using lath and plaster techniques. Many of them featured an elaborate front door. By the 1830s, several limestone homes had been constructed in the Kuyahoora Valley from the abundant native limestone. The Greek Revival style of the 1800s was followed in the 1900s by Italianate and Victorian styles. Double-gabled homes were popular in the villages at the beginning of the 20th century. The Victorian houses varied in style from those with simple steep-pitched roofs to those with elaborate ornamentation around the roofs, windows, and porches. The log cabin shown here was located in Fairfield.

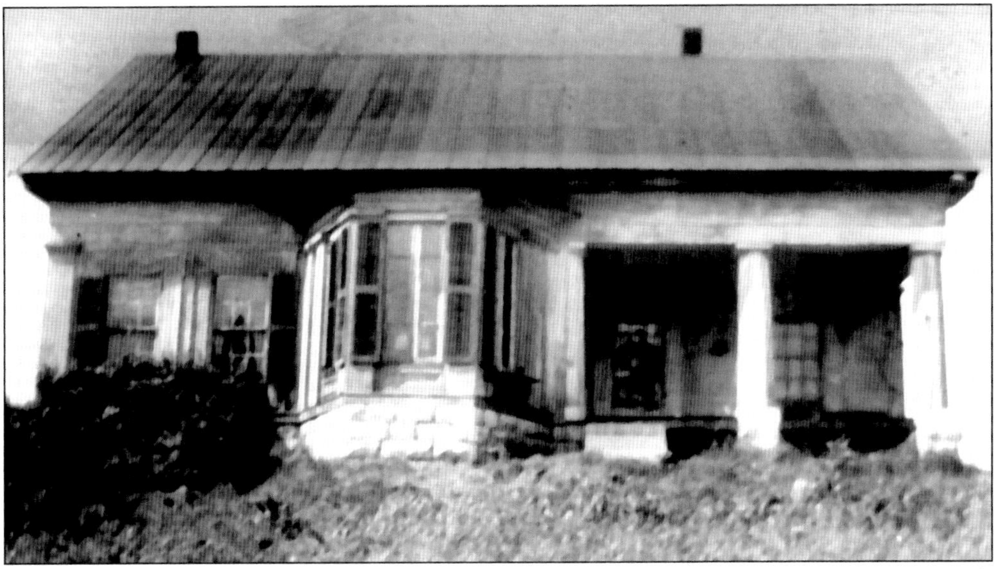

Samuel and Sarah Sherman from Rhode Island settled in Norway in 1793. They located north of the village and became well-to-do farmers of their day. The Shermans and their 11 children originally lived in a log cabin, which was replaced by this farmhouse in 1814. Samuel and Sarah Sherman and several of their children are buried in a plot along the hedgerow separating the Sherman land from the roadway. The deed that conveyed the Sherman property to Benjamin Hurd in 1835 reserved the burying ground for the Sherman family.

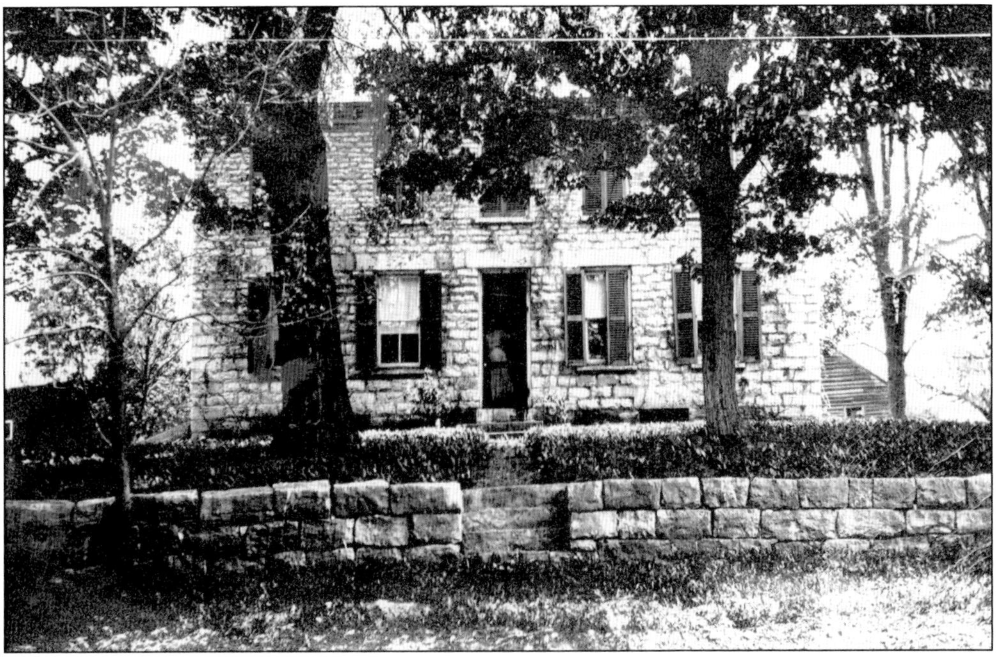

Noble Ross built this limestone farmhouse between Norway and Newport in 1825. The limestone came from the quarry in Newport. Ross was a well-known builder. He constructed many of the houses in Norway, as well as the Union Church. In 1854, Ross sold the farm to the Jackson family. It is still an operating farm.

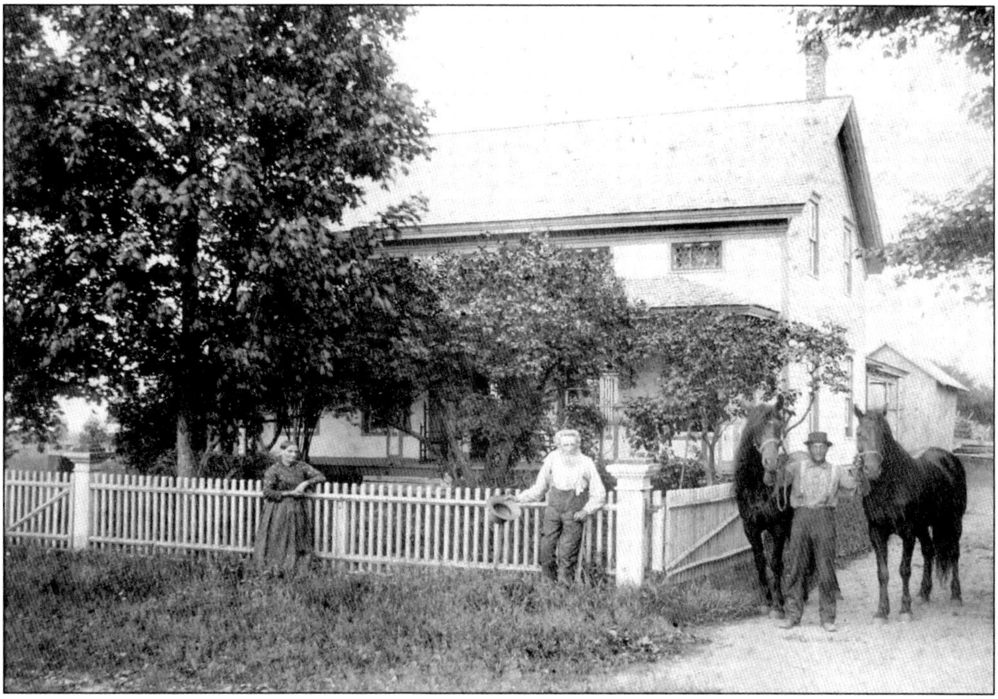

American Revolutionary War soldier Lt. Seth Smith and his two sons settled *c.* 1794 in Norway. Smith used his soldier's pension to buy land four miles north of Norway in the area known as the Hurricane. His wood plank house was built there in the early 1800s. Smith raised sheep and grain and hay for his son's tavern in Norway. Rev. Seth Burt, a Presbyterian circuit rider, came to Norway in 1817 to preach at the Union Church. He married Smith's granddaughter, Jennett Smith, and the Burts moved to the farm in 1840. Their son, Henry Burt, added the large front section of the house in 1865. This picture, taken in 1890, shows Caroline and Henry and their son Zina. The current owners of the homestead are Zina Burt's grandchildren.

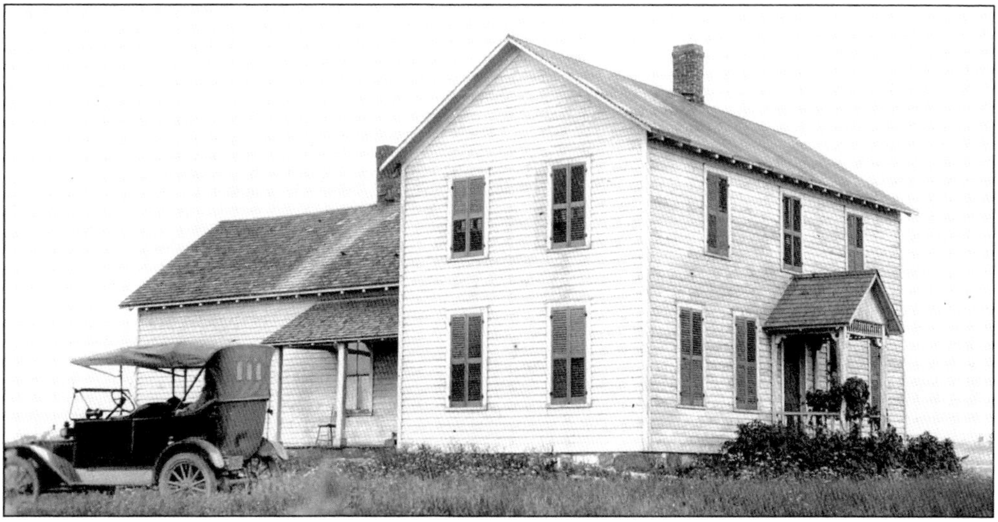

This farmhouse is located on Dairy Hill in Norway. At one time it was the home of Ackland Salisbury. It later became the Shibnah Nicholas farm.

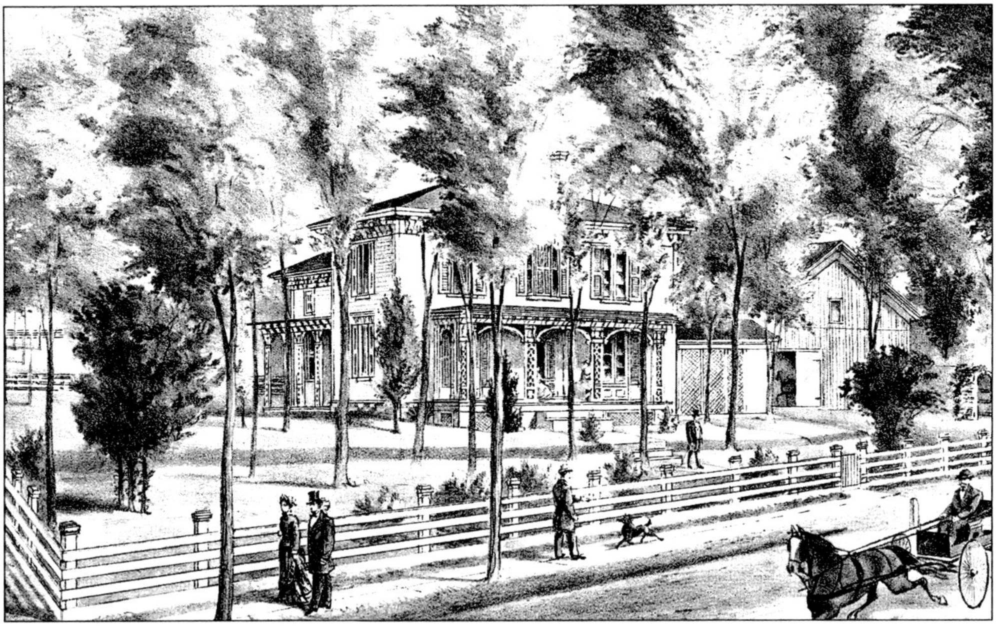

The Thomas Rice house, at the crossroads in the village of Fairfield, is believed to have been built from a pioneer store operated by Smith and Daniels. This fine home was a short distance from the Fairfield Seminary. For many years, it was the Van Auken home, and at one time it was a rest home operated by the Foster family. The present owners are modernizing the home.

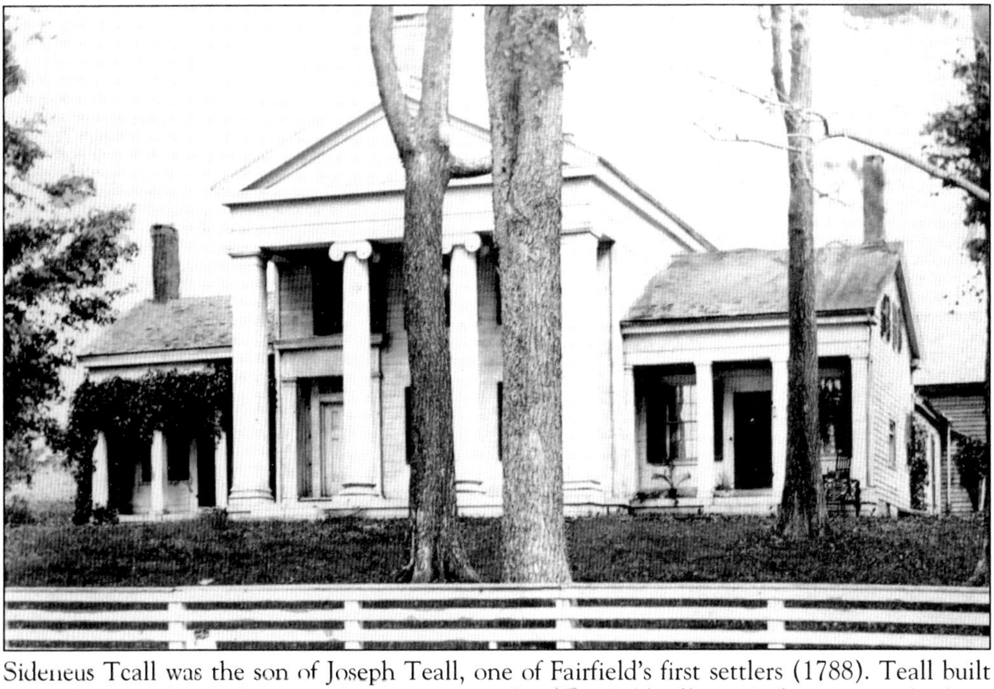

Sideneus Teall was the son of Joseph Teall, one of Fairfield's first settlers (1788). Teall built a Greek Revival–style house with 20 rooms north of Fairfield village. A sheep raiser, he later became a dairyman and supervisor of the town of Fairfield. The home remained in the Teall family until the 1930s.

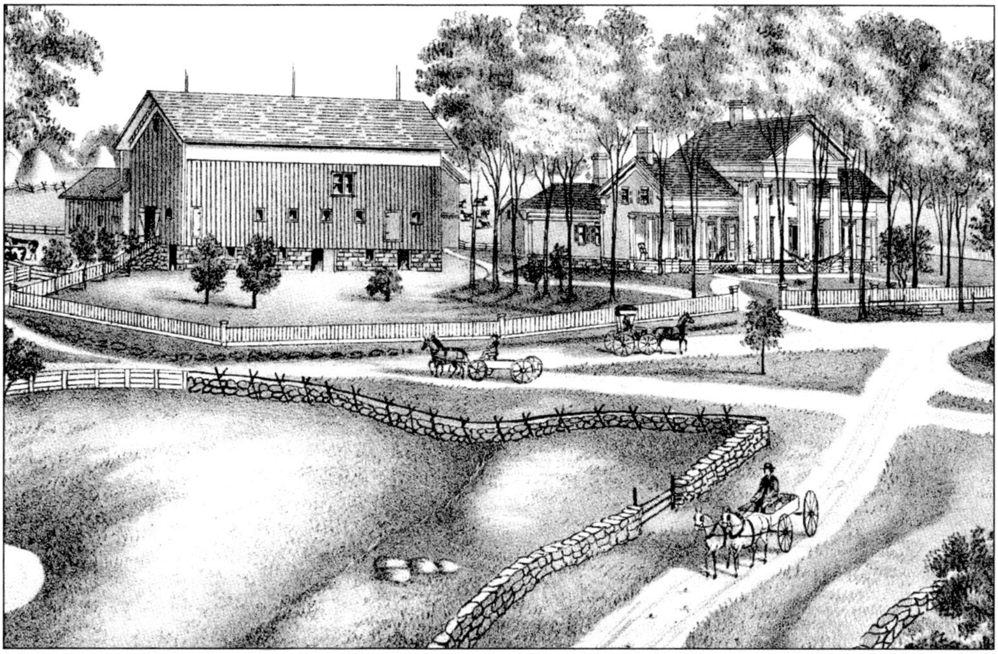

William Buck came to the Cold Brook-Poland area from Massachusetts in 1827. He brought with him oxen, a log chain, and a stone boat. He proceeded to work in the business of constructing stone walls. In 1833, he married Susan Millington and eventually became a large landowner. He built this large home on his 275-acre farm, at the top of a hill above Poland. This "wood stove" house had no fireplaces. A stairway from the servants' attic quarters led down into the dining room. For many years the farm was owned and operated by the Fitch family. Maria and Robert Eisenhower purchased this home in 1979.

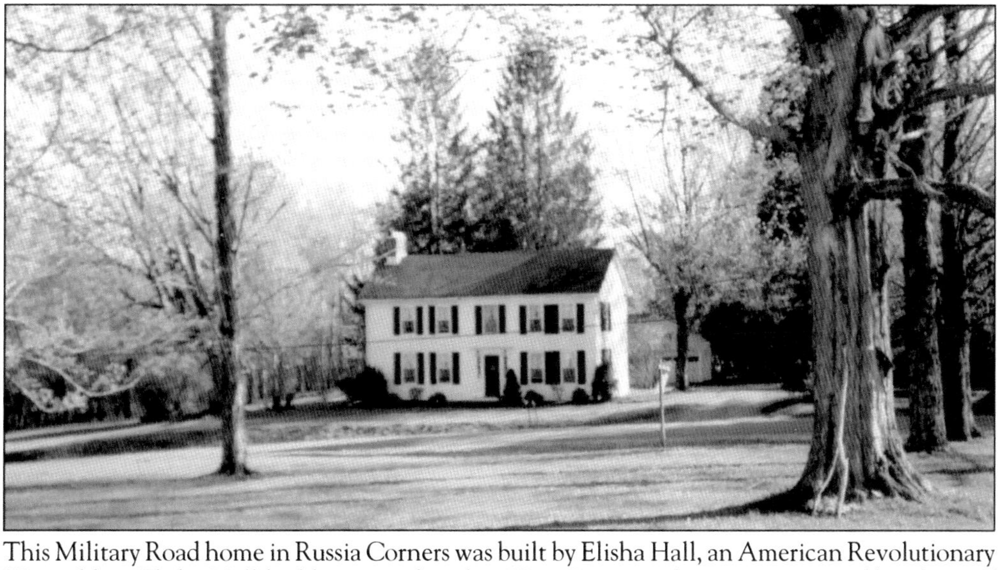

This Military Road home in Russia Corners was built by Elisha Hall, an American Revolutionary War soldier. Elisha Hall had been employed at West Point in the construction of bomb-proof forts. The house is Federal style in design, with plank and plaster walls. The first-floor fireplace has a beehive brick oven. The present owners have restored the house, keeping as much of the "old" as possible.

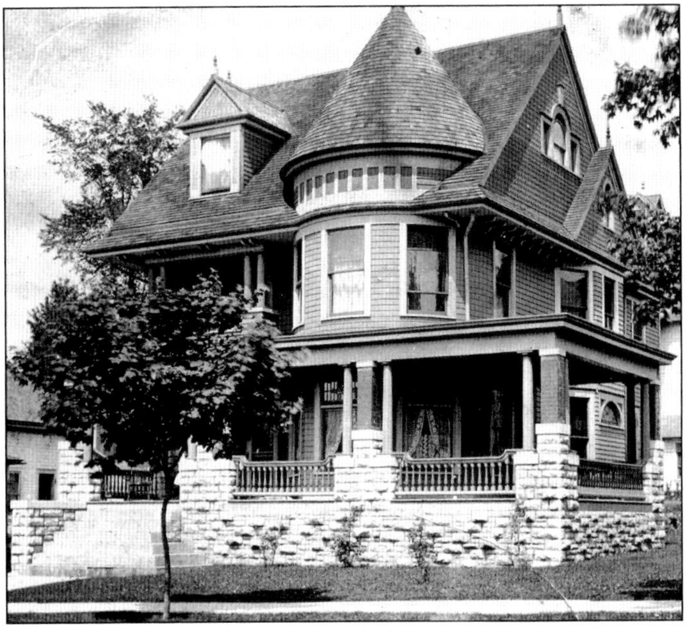

Firman Ouderkirk was a lumberman who also owned a gristmill. In 1900, he built one of the finest homes in Cold Brook. The woodwork on the first floor is quartered oak, and on the second floor it is cherry. The leaded windows are made of plate glass. For many years, it was the home of Poland school principal Ellsworth Buck and his wife, Dorothy Buck.

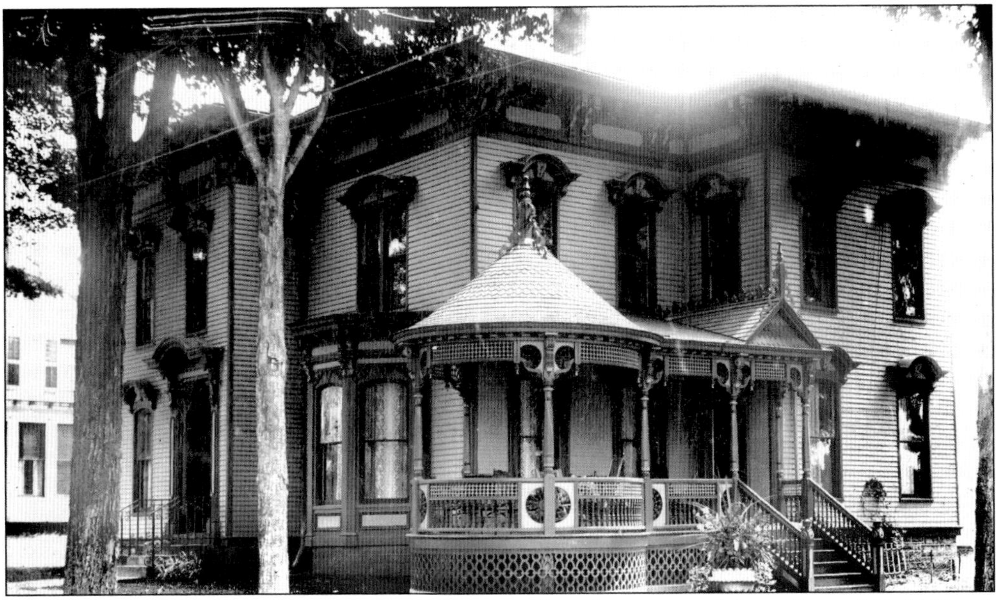

Alfred B. Coonradt built this house in 1872 on land in the center of the village of Cold Brook that he acquired from his father-in-law, Cameron Moon. The house had three floors, with a kitchen, pantry, cellar, furnace room, and storage room on the basement level. A dumbwaiter serviced the first-floor dining room from the basement kitchen. There were four bedrooms on the second floor, and the master bedroom featured a fireplace. There was a copper-lined cistern on the second floor as well. The bathroom on the first floor had a wooden copper-lined bathtub, the first bathtub in Cold Brook. At Fourth of July celebrations, speakers and dignitaries used the circular part of the porch as a podium.

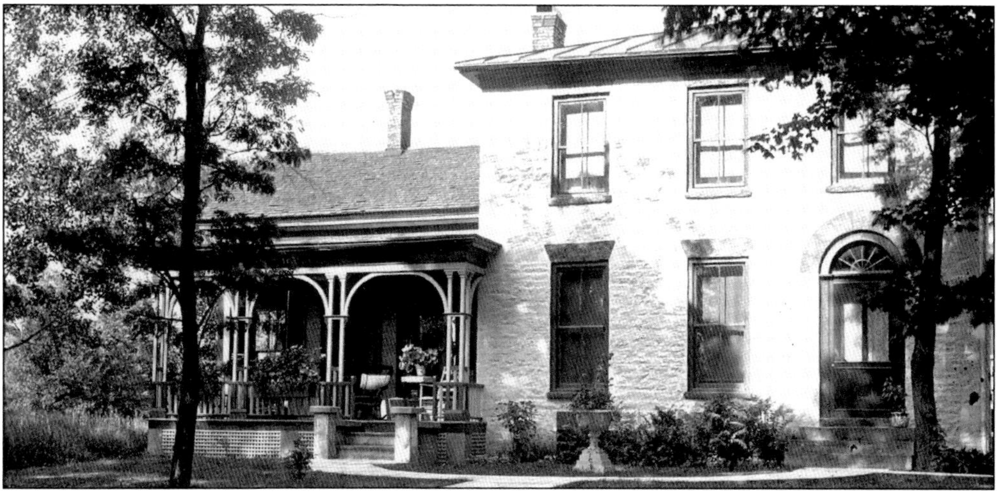

Nathan Burwell built this white stone house in 1820 on South Main Street in Poland. Originally a forge was operated in the front yard. From 1830 to 1840, Samuel Giles operated an inn in the house. It is believed that the building consisted of two open rooms, one downstairs and one up. In those days, travelers carried their own bedrolls and spread them out in a common room. The remains of a brick Dutch oven in the cellar indicate that the kitchen was located there. Tradition claims that in 1834, Nat Foster, on his way to Herkimer to stand trial for having killed a Native American, was held overnight in a room in the cellar. Over the years, the Westerns, the Firths, and the Seidels have owned the property. The Seidels operated a dairy farm on the land in back of the house. Tito and Pat DiTata purchased the house in 1965.

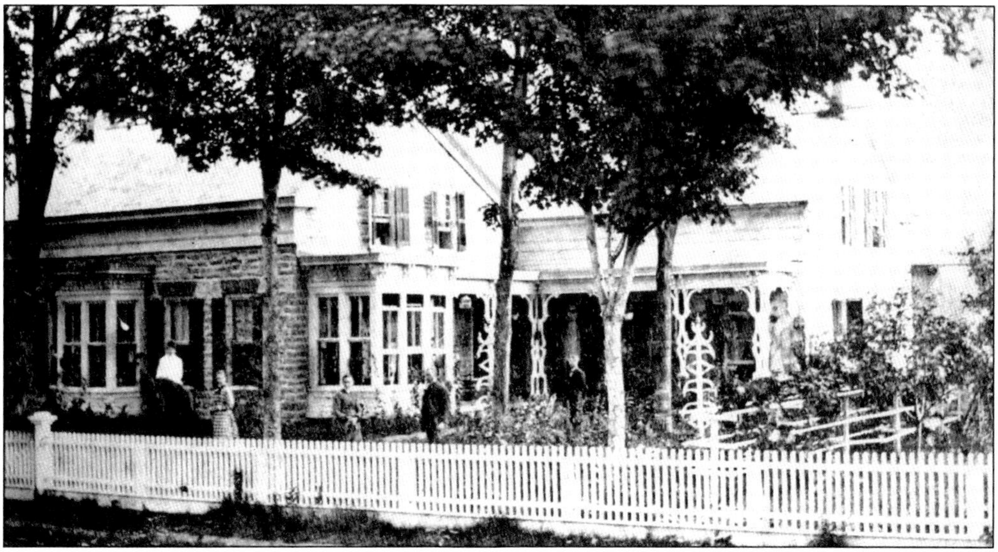

This Poland limestone home was added to an original wooden building in the 1830s. The house is a combination of Federal and Italianate styles in design. The walls are two feet thick, giving the house notably wide windowsills. Wide moldings were routed out of many layers of wood. Bubbles and ripples show in the glass of the two-over-two windows, which were replaced in the late 1800s. At the time the home was built, window panes were usually set six over six or eight over eight. Ornate posts on the porch show much imagination in their design and are possibly the work of the Potter brothers. Ivy covers much of the front and sides of the stone house, which from 1945 until recently, was owned by the Storandts.

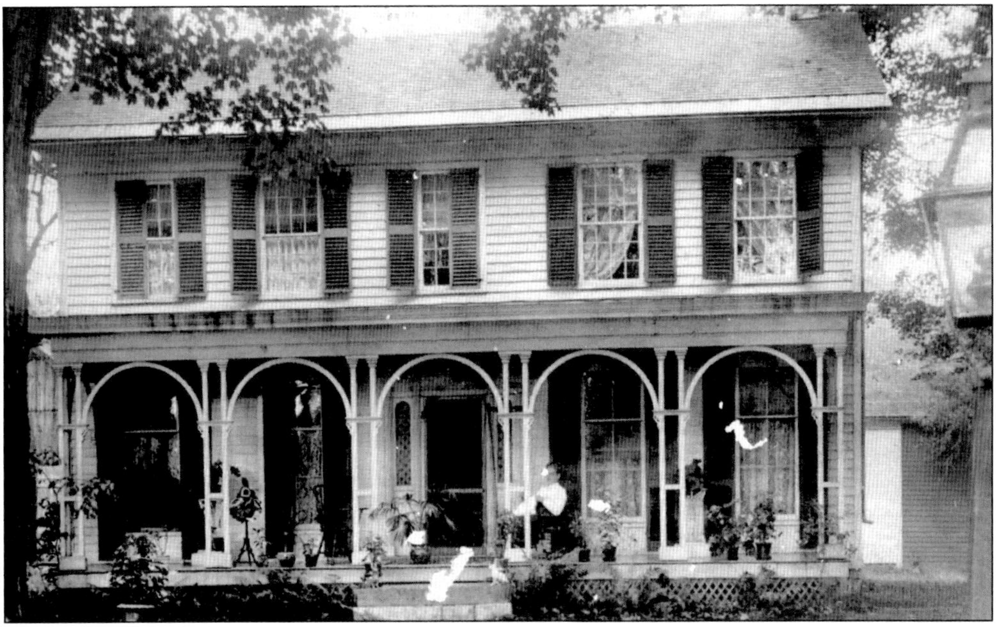

Known as the Blue home for many years, this Poland house was built by Chauncey Eddy in 1841. A large apple orchard occupied the site of the next-door Wiatr home. The porch, which has since been removed, typifies a popular style of porches in the area. A section from the rear of the house was removed for a garage.

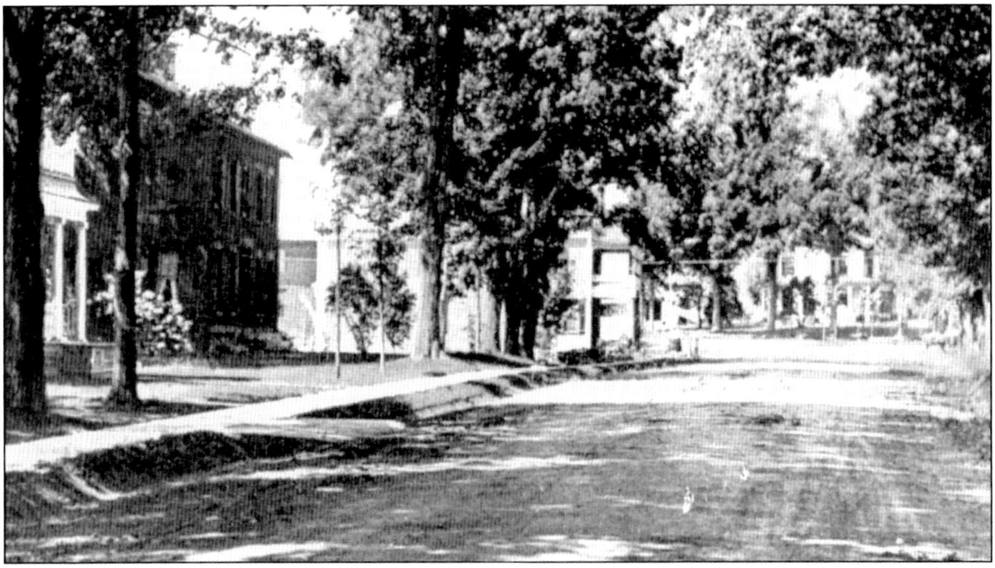

This Main Street view in Poland is looking north toward Haver's Store and Dr. Stephen Millington's home. To the left is the large brick house built by Jenks Benchley in 1836. Benchley, a brickmaker, had a brickyard on the Oxbow on the West Canada Creek. This is the only brick home in Poland. Designed with elements of the Greek Revival and Federal styles, its walls are a foot thick. The spacious grounds included a fountain and pond on the brook side and formal gardens with beds of flowers on the other side. People of distinction from Europe, as well as the United States, visited this house. Frances Erb made the home into two apartments. The present owners are renovating the house.

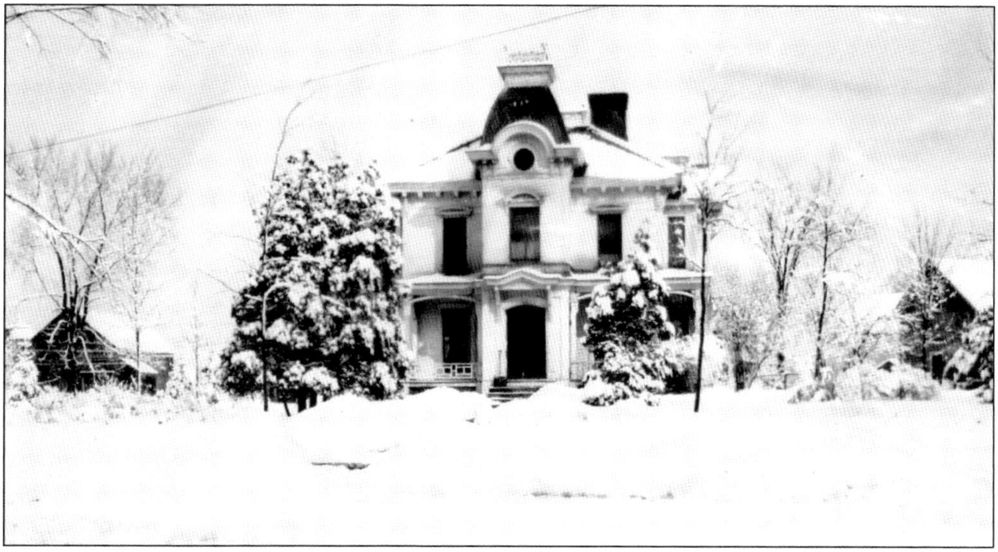

Dr. Stephen Millington moved from Norway to Poland in 1860. His home is notable for its French-style mansard roof. This house was originally rectangular in shape. The tower was added later.

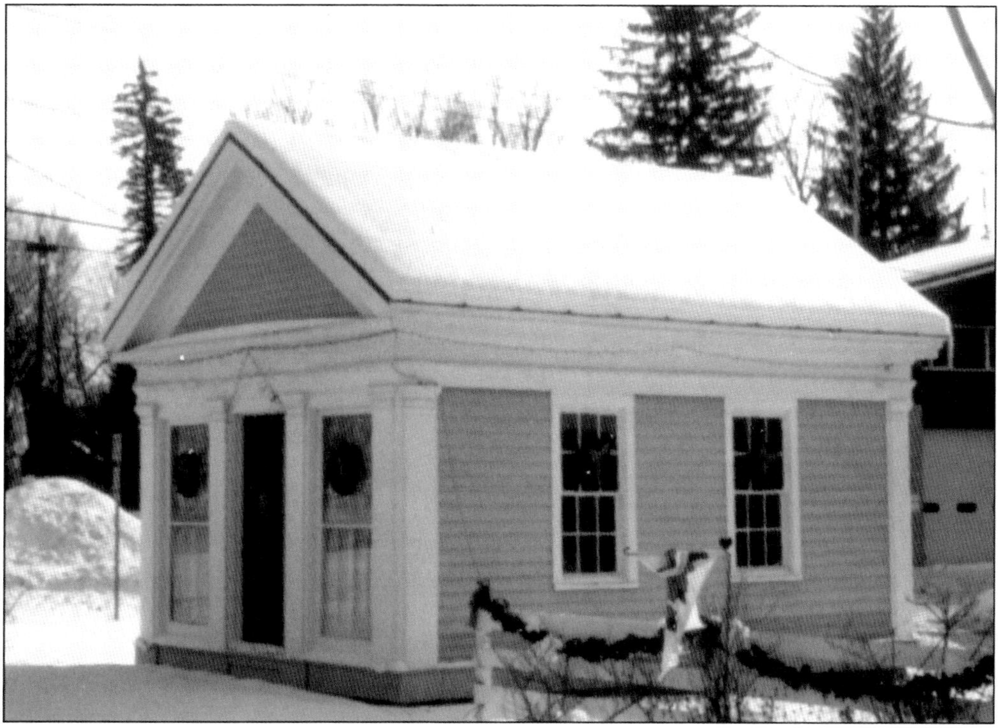

This small, Greek Revival–style building was built *c.* 1860 as an office for Dr. Millington. He was one of the organizers of the Bank of Poland. When Millington retired in 1872, the office was moved across the street and became the first bank building. In 1995, Mr. and Mrs. Stephen Olney moved the building to the corner of Main and Case Streets. They restored it as an example of business buildings of the late 1800s. An iron stove connected to a stub chimney in the roof provided heat for the office.

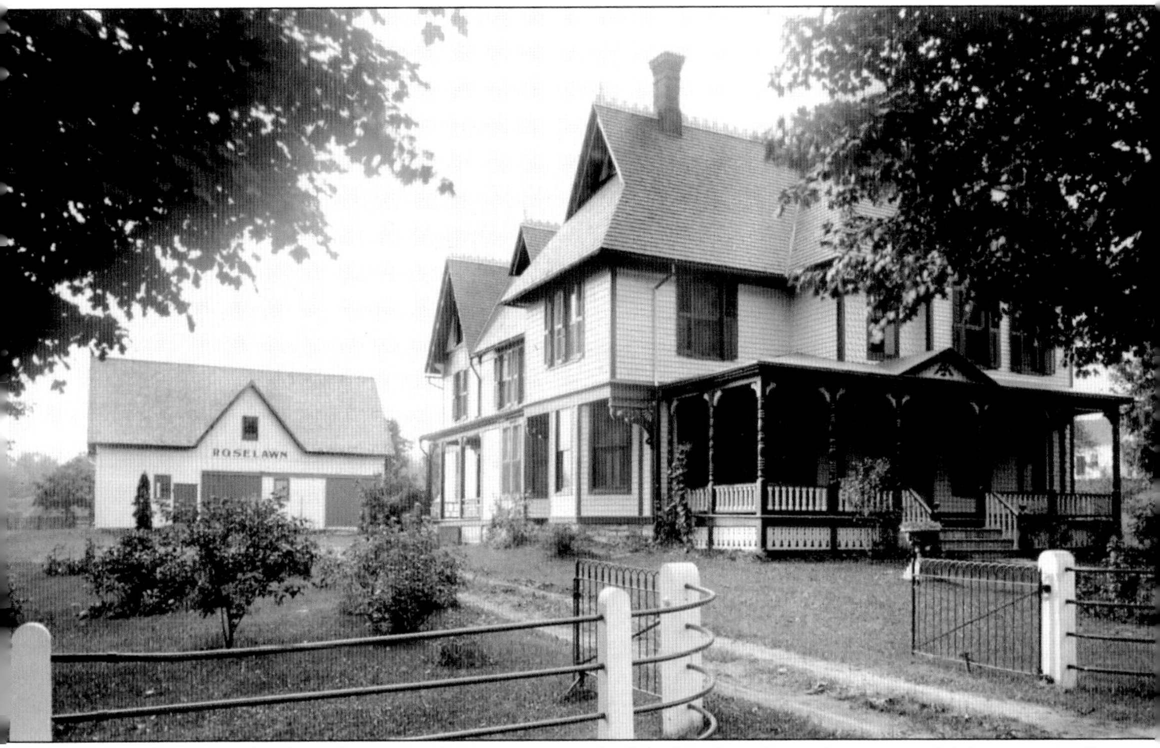

Roselawn was built in the early 1860s on a parcel of the Nathan Daniels estate, which comprised a large part of Poland (earlier known as Danielsville). The two-and-a-half-story house has three fireplaces, nine bedrooms, two large kitchens, a living room, a dining room, a library, and servants quarters. A total of 51 windows and 40 doors provide adequate light and circulation throughout. The attic has four rooms, one of which is 25 feet by 50 feet, and a 10-foot-high ceiling, finished in tongue-and-groove pine. Rumor has it that the first owner, Hoxie McNeil, wanted to build a house larger and grander than the Millington residence. The home was in the Buck family from 1865 to 1934, when the Holcombs purchased the property. The Bucks planted roses throughout the property, giving it the name of Roselawn. Michael and Martha Kraeger purchased the house in 1984.

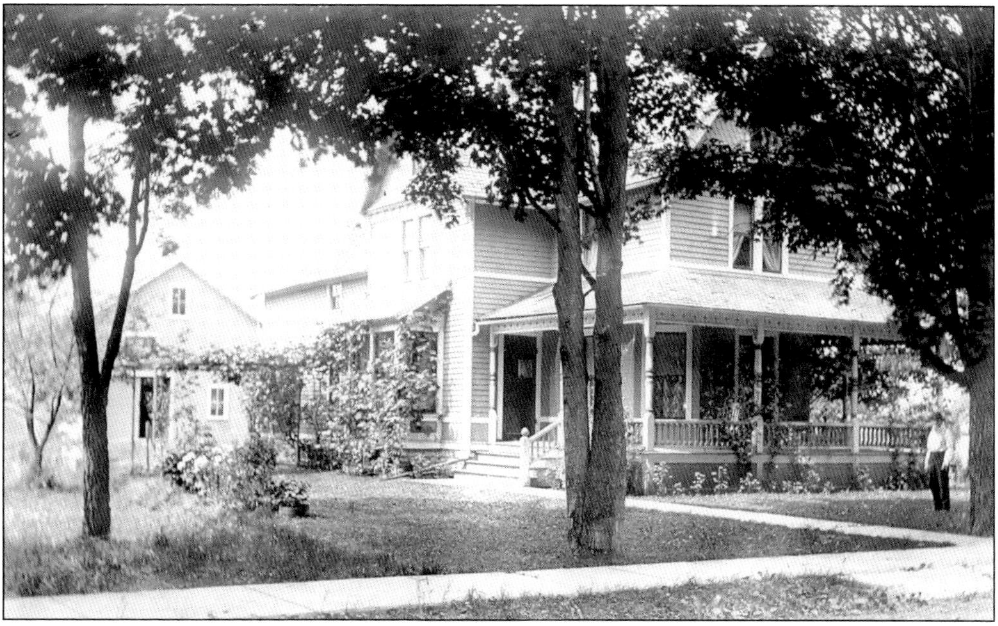

In 1890, Cornelius Schermerhorn built this Victorian double-gabled home with $450 worth of lumber from the Potter brothers. Schermerhorn, a cheesemaker, went to England, France, and Holland in 1870 to help people there build cheese factories. This Poland home remained in the Schermerhorn family for more than 100 years.

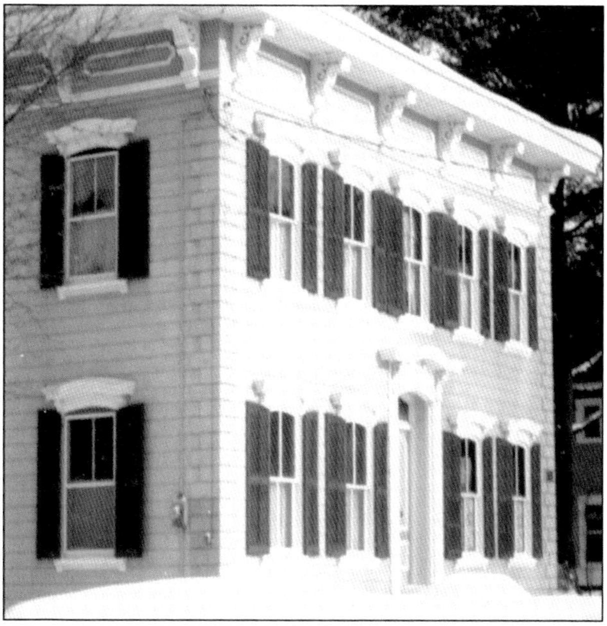

Deeds show that the land for this Poland Main Street home was purchased in 1871. Pardon Sanders built the Italinate-style house for Ralph Biblow, who owned a hardware store and a tin shop. Sanders studied architecture at Fairfield Academy. The rooms on the first floor have 10-foot-high ceilings. The rooms were heated with iron stoves, as the house had no fireplaces. The ceilings on the second floor were originally made of pressed metal. The unusual exterior features wood planking that was scored to look like stone block. Woodwork that was cut in the Potter brothers' shop can be found in many of the lovely homes in Poland.

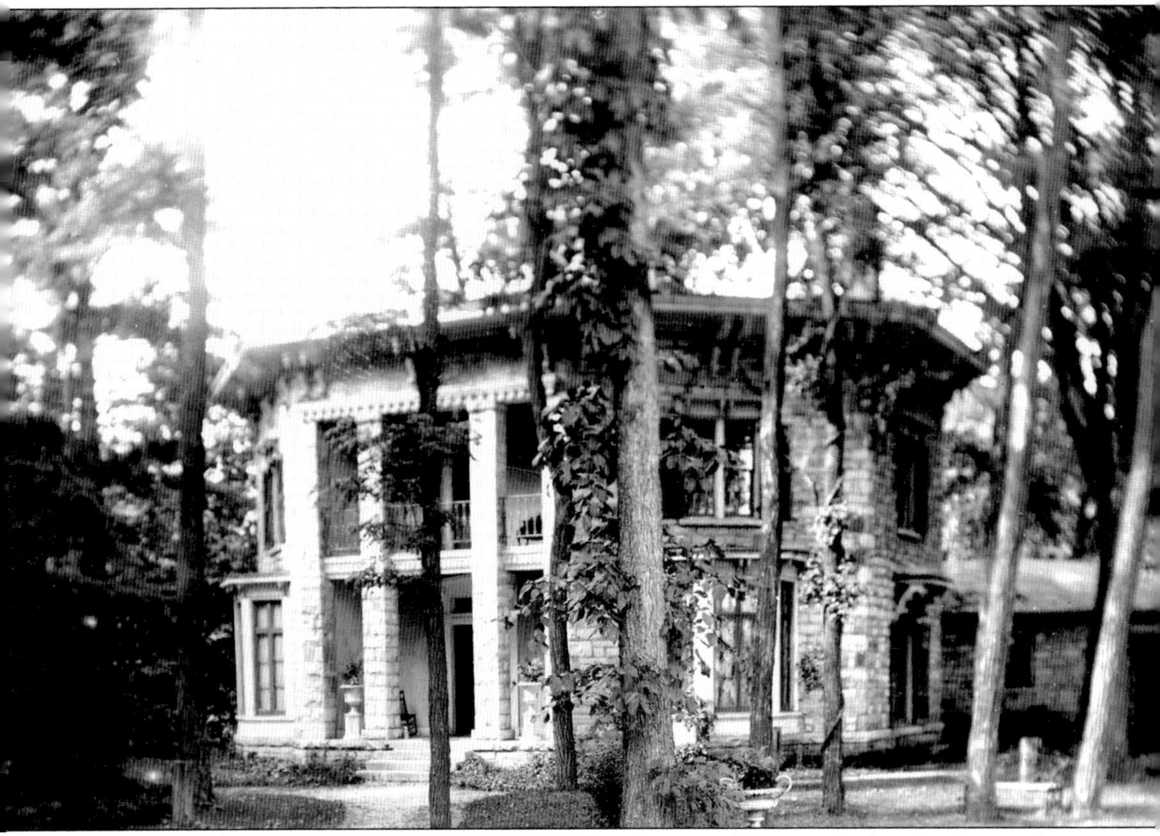

Linus Yale had the Octagon House built on Main Street in Newport for his daughter and son-in-law, Chlotilda and Ira Cady. Built in 1849–1850 from native limestone, it is one of five stone houses in Newport. This eight-sided house with a two-story recessed porch has a rare, hanging spiral staircase. The staircase leads to a cupola that has a 360-degree view of the surrounding countryside. There are no four-sided rooms in the house, and every room has a lock and key on the door. Clara Jones inherited this property in 1903 and lived here for 50 years. The property was then deeded to her grandson and his wife, Mr. and Mrs. Lawrence Evans, and it remains in the family today. A historical marker was placed on the Octagon House property in 1932.

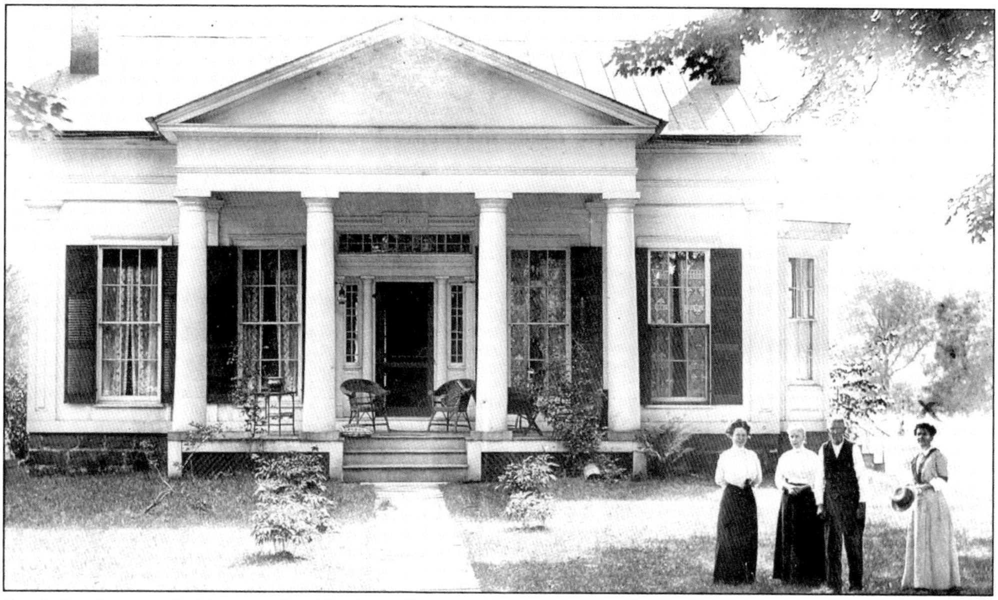

Built by Jeremiah Fenner for Nathan Bowen in 1836, this home is one of six Greek Revival-style houses in Newport. It has a Doric portico, 12-foot ceilings, 8-foot windows, and hand-carved woodwork. Bricks form the insulation between the outside plank walls and the interior lath and plaster. On the front door is the second lock made by Linus Yale. After Nathan Bowen died in 1872, his son Tom Bowen continued to live in the house. Dr. Croft conducted his practice here from the end of World War I to his death in 1934. George Parsons, manager of the Northern Lumber Company in Poland, and his wife, Marie, an artist known for her sketch of the Universalist church, were the next owners. D.B. Sanford and his wife, Ruth, purchased the home in 1947.

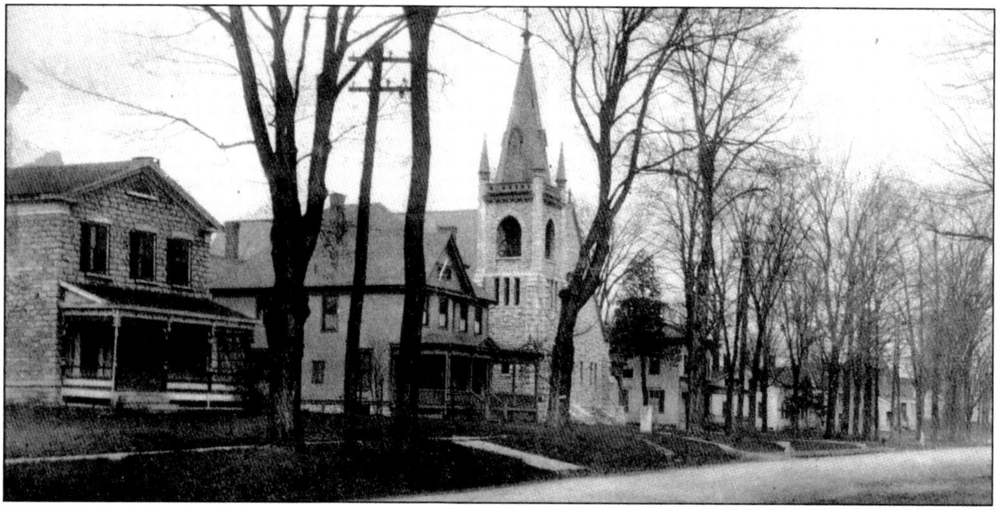

The Newport home on the left in this Main Street scene was built *c.* 1820. Linus Yale, the inventor of the Yale lock, acquired it for $1,500. Built of native limestone, the house is Federal style in design, with a fan window in the gable end. Two additions have enlarged the original structure. Victorian-style changes that are evident include the ornamental design on the porch and a bay window that has replaced a chimney on the south wing. Dr. Charles Huxtable purchased the home in 1926 and lived there until Beth and John Snyder acquired it in 1967.

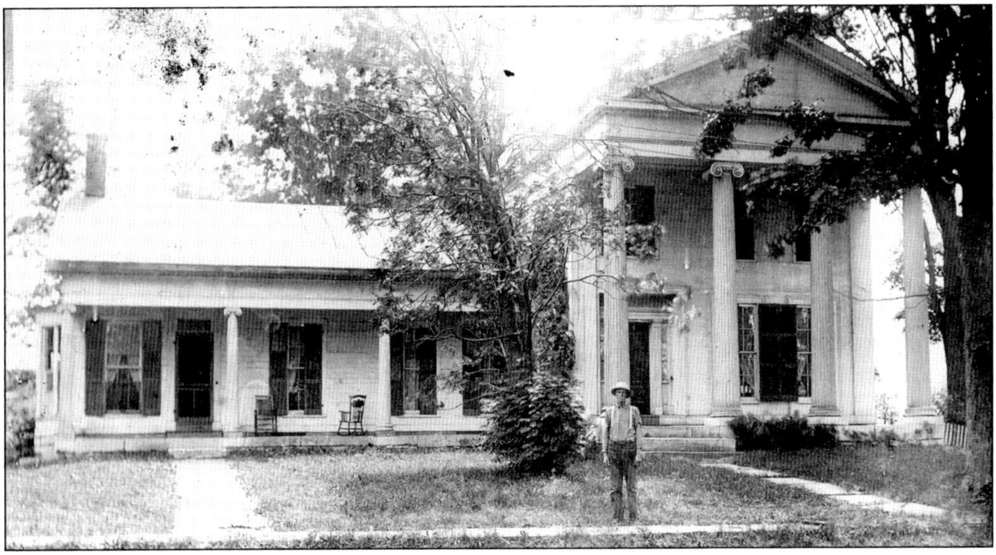

Everad Fenner is pictured in front of the Fenner homestead. This Greek Revival house looks down upon the West Canada Creek. Note the Ionic columns beneath the pediment. This is the only example of the use of Ionic columns in the Greek Revival homes of Newport. The limestone around the porches came from the stone quarry on the Fenner property.

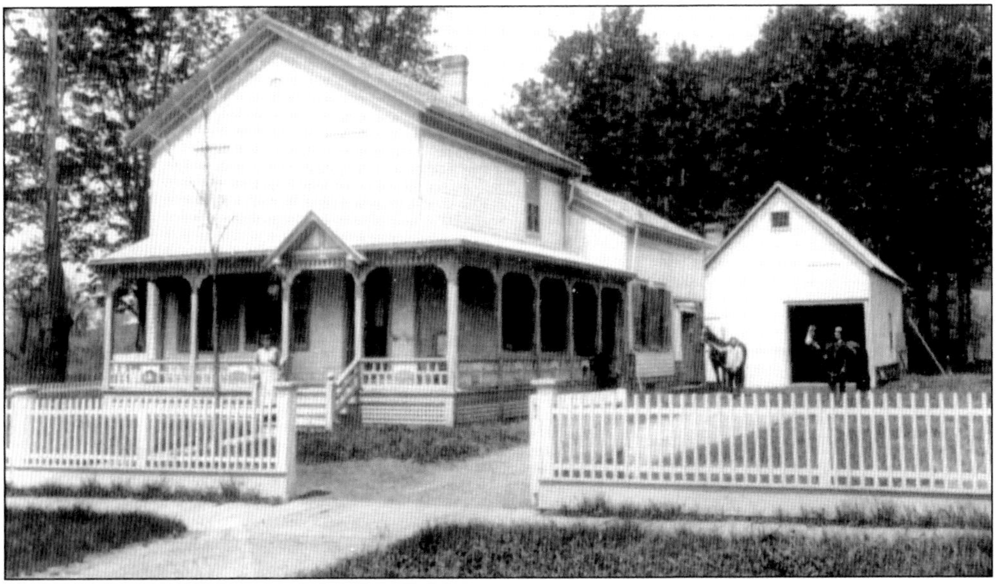

This was the North Street home of Millard Pearce, a local merchant who made his wealth buying and selling horses. Pearce completely remodeled this house in the late 1800s. The rebuilt home was a double house, with separate living areas on each side of a central hall. One side was for Millard and his wife, Kate; the other side was for Kate's widowed sister, Elva. The addition included a large carriage house connected to the horse barn. A special place with a slatted floor above a drain was built for washing the horse buggies. A rope lift was used to raise the buggies for the winter. In the barn, which was connected to the carriage house, there were horse stalls made of cherry wood, caretakers' quarters, and a harness room. Today, high peaks on three sides and an attractive rounded porch on the front distinguish this home.

This home at the top of Christian Hill in Newport was built by Norman Smith in the 1830s. Built three bricks thick, it is a classic Greek Revival. Eight-inch beams support the second story and the roof. Facing the front, the gabled end has a fan window. Norman Smith had a large and profitable distillery business. His son, Algernon Emery Smith, was born here. He became a hero at the age of 33, taking part in the battle known as Custer's Last Stand. Changes to the house through the years have included a wooden addition of three rooms on the north side. Art and Torrey Felio purchased the property in 1975 and completely restored this beautiful old home.

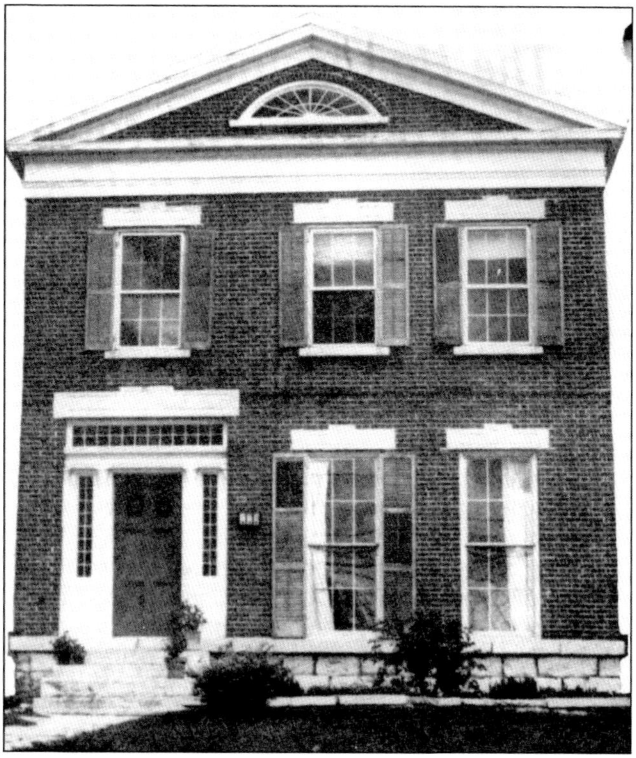

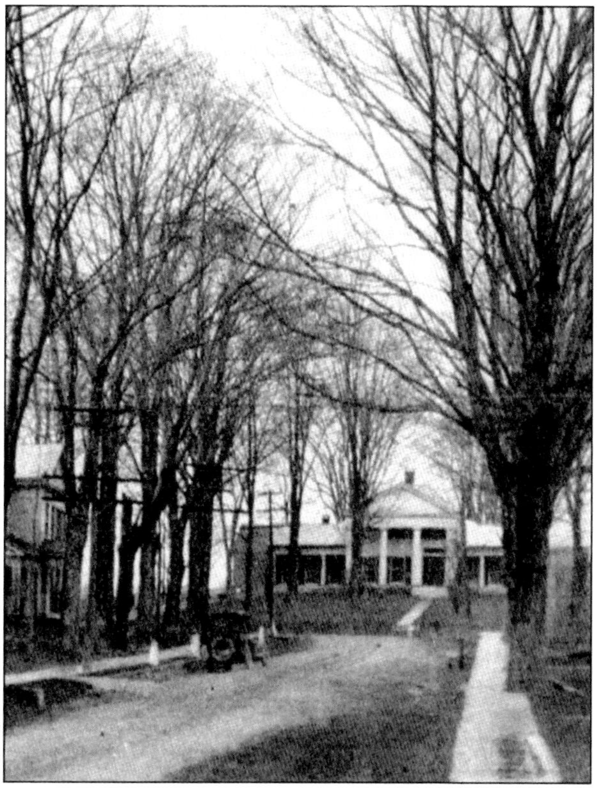

The large home at the head of Norway Street on East Street in Newport was built c. 1843 by J. Curry. Seymour Bowen purchased the house, and his daughter Nettie Bowen married Algernon Emery Smith here. Nettie Bowen often followed her husband by military wagon, and she became a friend of the wife of Gen. George Armstrong Custer. Elizabeth Custer visited here. She was often seen sitting on the Bowen front lawn writing her book, *Boots and Saddles*. In 1905, Seymour Bowen sold the property to Perry Kimball, owner of a local meat market. The present residents are his great granddaughter and her daughters, making this a family home for five generations.

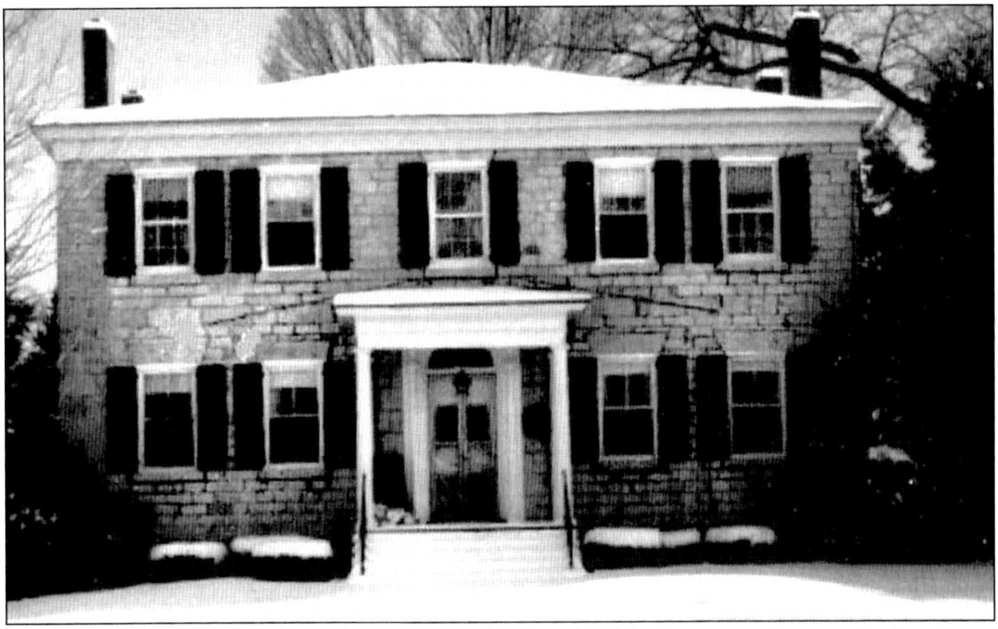

The residence known as What Cheer Hall was built in 1812 by Benjamin Bowen, the founder of Newport. Bowen came from Newport, Rhode Island, and built a dam and sawmill on the West Canada Creek. His home was a Federal Georgian, four square in design, built of native limestone. The front is dressed limestone, and the north, south, and east sides are field limestone. Other 19th-century buildings on the 24-acre property included those constructed to house animals and a smokehouse. The James Fisher family purchased the property in 1995 and converted it into a bed-and-breakfast. What Cheer Hall is listed on the New York State and the National Registers of Historic Places.

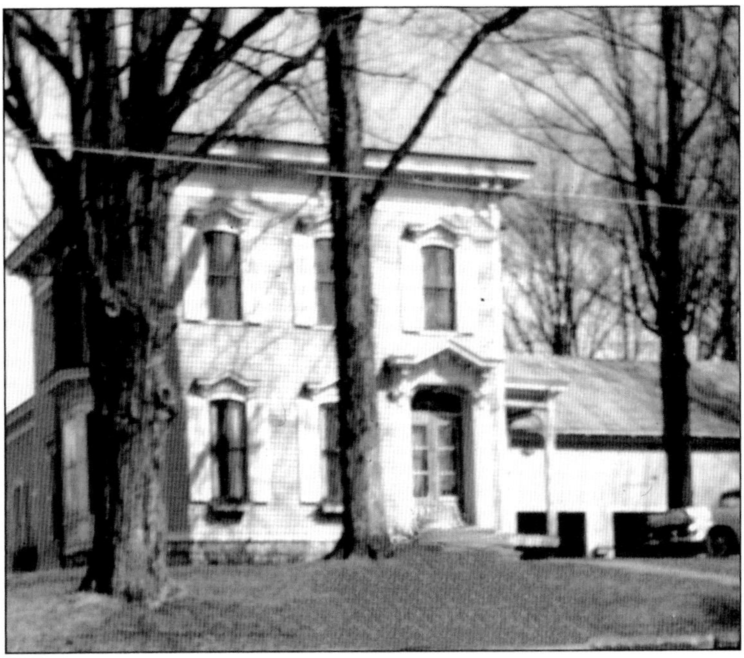

The contractors for this Italianate home on East Street were the Potter brothers of Poland. The interesting door and window treatments resemble those of other buildings the Potters constructed. Above the double door are a transom window and a pointed pediment. The arched windows have similar decorative pediments.

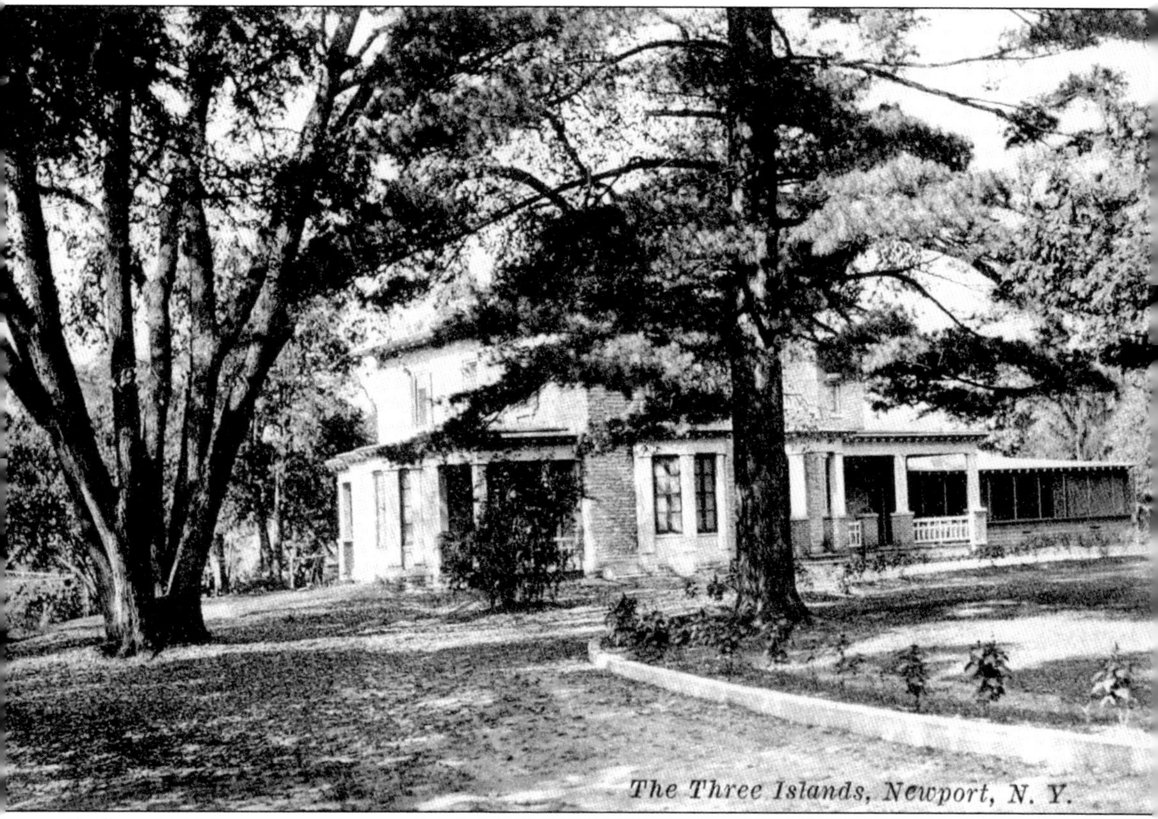

Built in 1848 from native limestone, this Italianate villa in Newport was designed by Alexander Jackson Davis, a noted American artist of the 1850s. The home was built for Stuart Perry, a butter and cheese dealer and inventor of the hay tedder. Riverview was known for its beautiful grounds. Mr. and Mrs. Daniel McCarthy purchased the home in 1920 and opened a restaurant called Three Islands on the porchlike addition. It was a popular dining place in the area, with many customers coming from Utica for wedding receptions, banquets, and parties. In recent years, Donald and Joni Chizzonite purchased and restored the house and grounds as closely as possible to Perry's original Riverview.

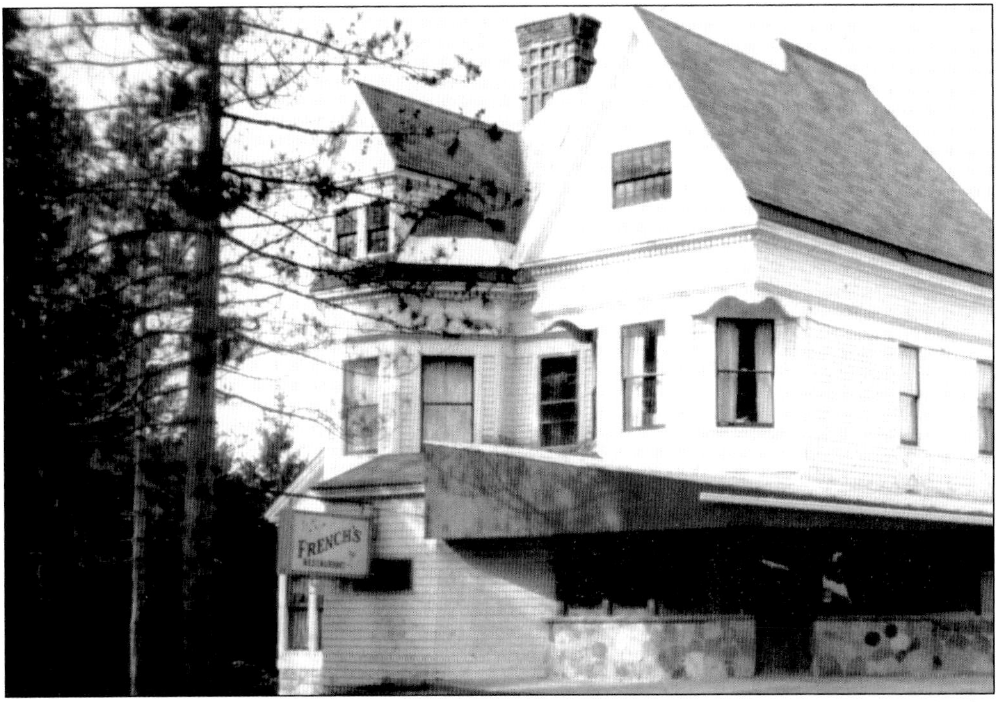

This elegant Victorian home on North Main Street in Middleville was built by Charles Wooster, president of the Newport National Bank in 1883. It was noted for its seven fireplaces and cherry wood staircase and paneling. In the late 1930s, Lottie Kazlowski converted the home into a restaurant called Lottie's. Following World War II, Robert Balch bought the restaurant and operated it as Balch's until 1983, when it became known as French's. It now operates under the name of Wild River Inn.

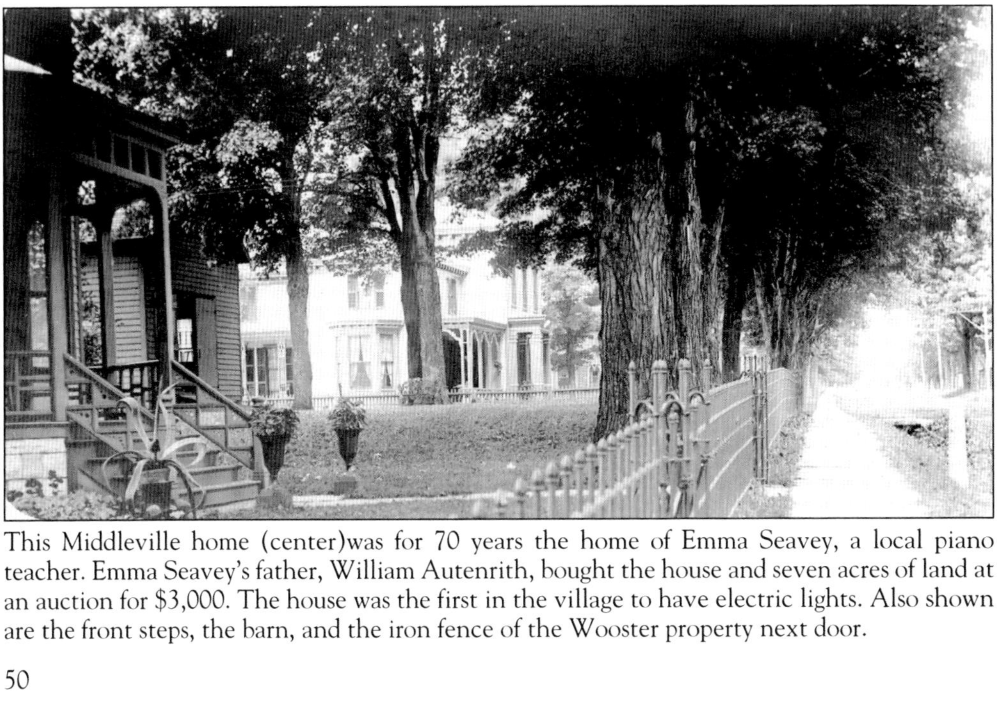

This Middleville home (center)was for 70 years the home of Emma Seavey, a local piano teacher. Emma Seavey's father, William Autenrith, bought the house and seven acres of land at an auction for $3,000. The house was the first in the village to have electric lights. Also shown are the front steps, the barn, and the iron fence of the Wooster property next door.

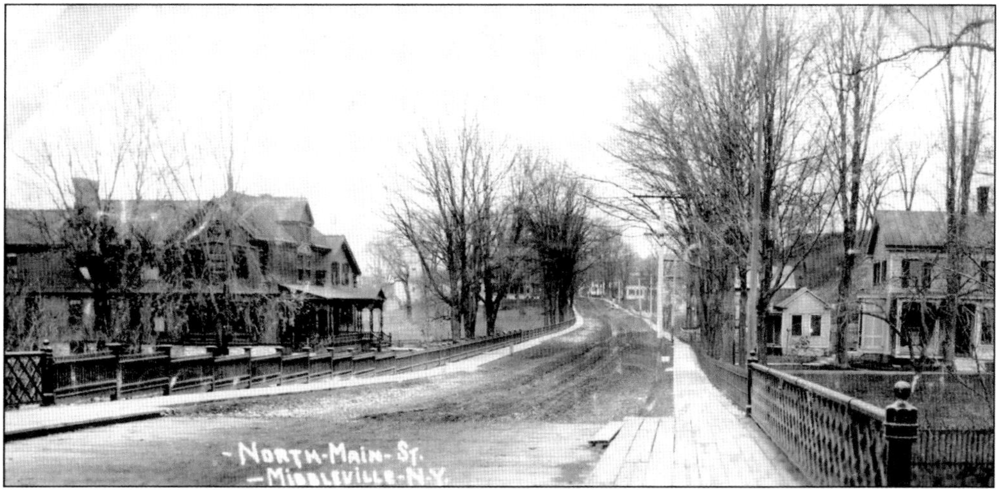

This street scene shows the home of Maj. Burns, a partner in the Middleville tannery during the later part of the 19th century. Albert Carlough, president of the Middleville bank, and his wife lived here for many years. Today it is the Middleville Rest Home. On the right is the home of Dr. C.W. Hamlin, who started his medical practice in the village in 1870. The small white building next to Hamlin's home was his office. Unusual and ornate iron fences lined both sides of the street.

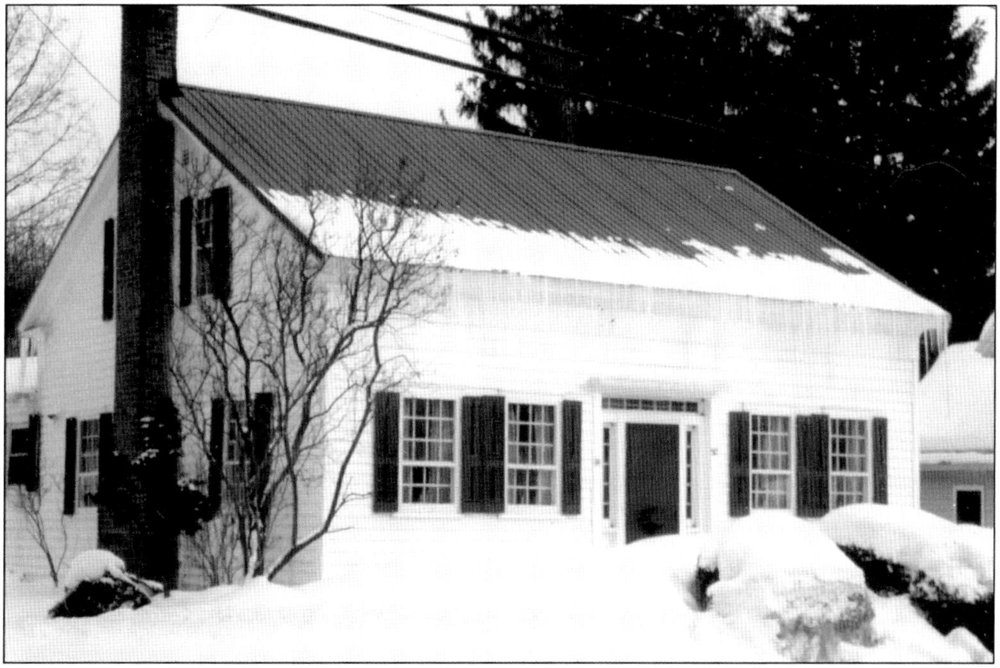

One of the oldest homes in Middleville is the *c.* 1807 Bernard Carney home on North Main Street. It was part of a farm owned by Samuel Stevens. Because several adjacent house lots from the farm were sold, this home has a narrow frontage. The walls are constructed of plank and covered with lath and plaster. The 12-over-8 windowpanes are uncommon for this period. A springhouse behind the main house covered a pool of water that flowed all year. It is said that a pipe from this spring fed a fountain near the center of the village, several hundred feet away. The home has been in the Carney family since 1942.

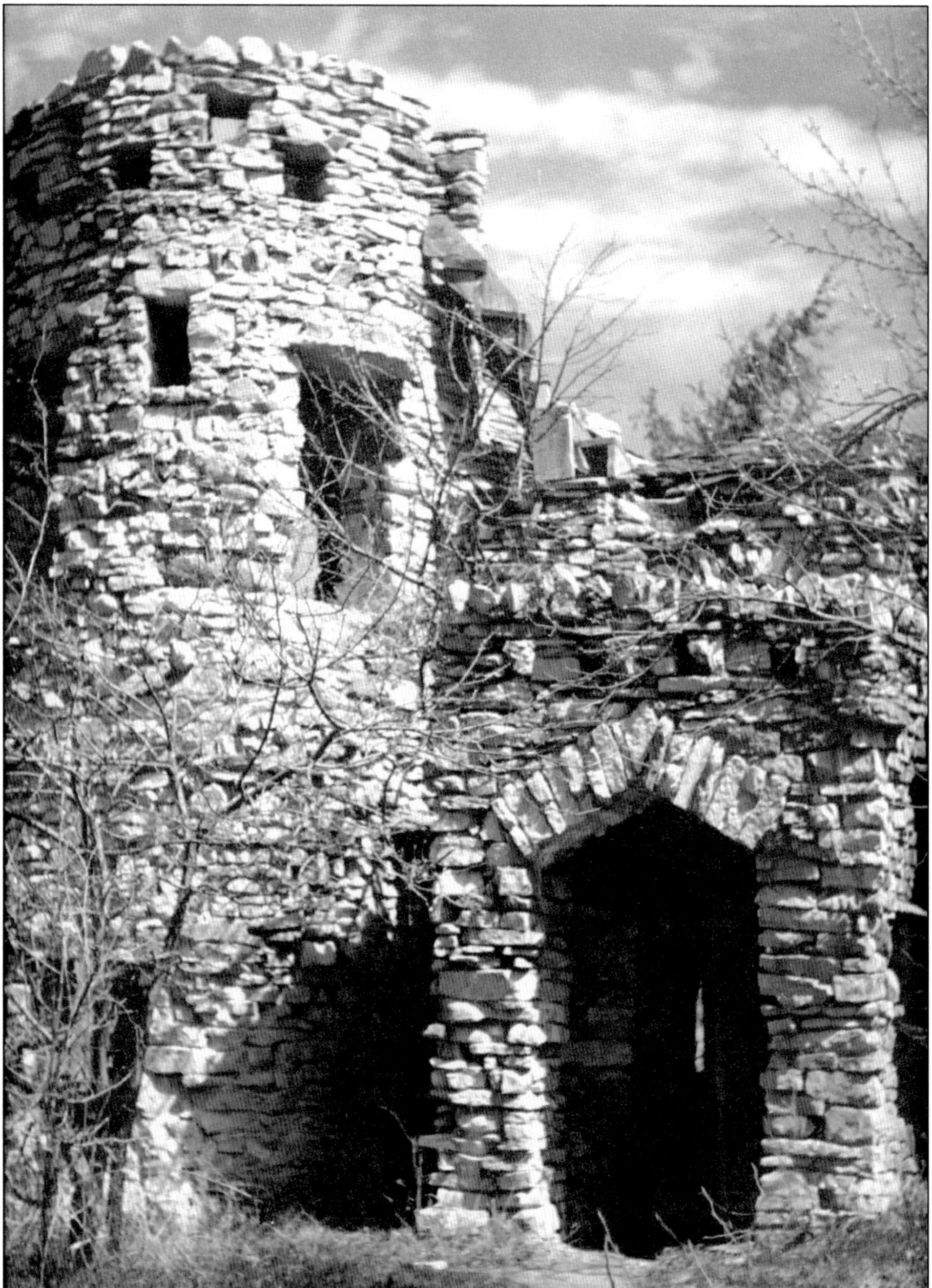

In 1926, Marklove Lowrey, a Utica landscape artist, planned a limestone home overlooking the cascade of falls on Mill Creek between Newport and Middleville. He used the cut limestone from several abandoned buildings to construct walls that were a foot thick. Beams and timbers also came from these abandoned buildings. Lowrey pulled the plans out of his head as he walked in the area, sometimes marking site lines with a stick. The building attracted much attention and eventually vandalism. Discouraged, Lowrey abandoned the idea of having his castle here. Instead, he purchased the small white house on Castle Road near his beloved spot.

Four

The Three R's

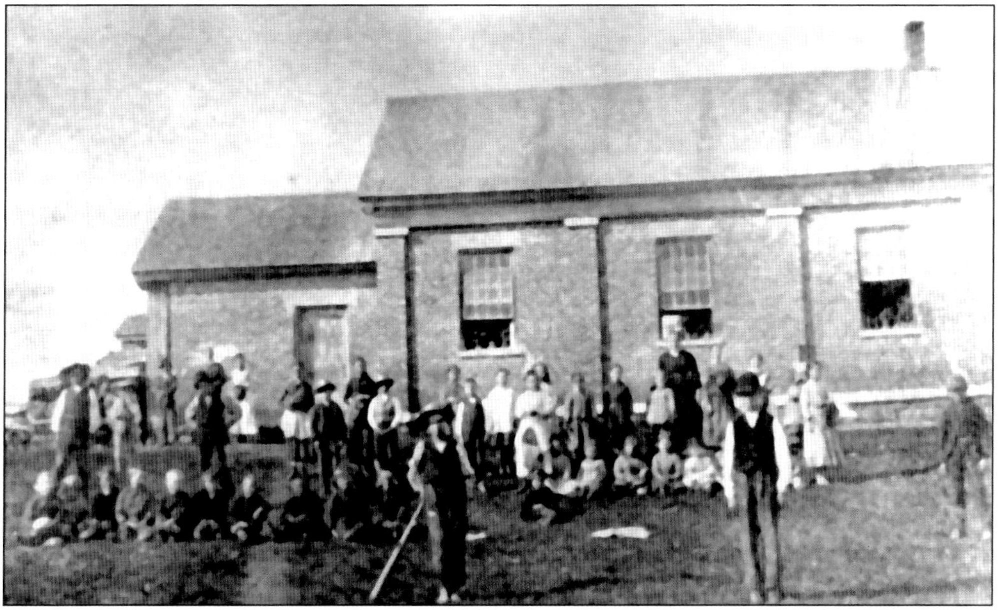

There were settlers in the Cold Brook area prior to 1800, but the opening of the State Road from Albany to Sacketts Harbor promoted the rapid growth of the village in the first decade of the 19th century. The earliest record of a schoolhouse is a brick building constructed on the crest of Cold Brook Hill on land deeded by Reuben Robens in 1823. Some sort of school undoubtedly existed before this, possibly a log building. This photograph dating from 1870 shows approximately 40 children of all ages. These one-room schools taught the basics of reading, spelling, grammar, writing, and arithmetic, through the eighth grade. Note the woodpile at the end of the building. Teachers were responsible for much more than academic instruction. Keeping the room warm by firing the wood stove was part of their daily chores.

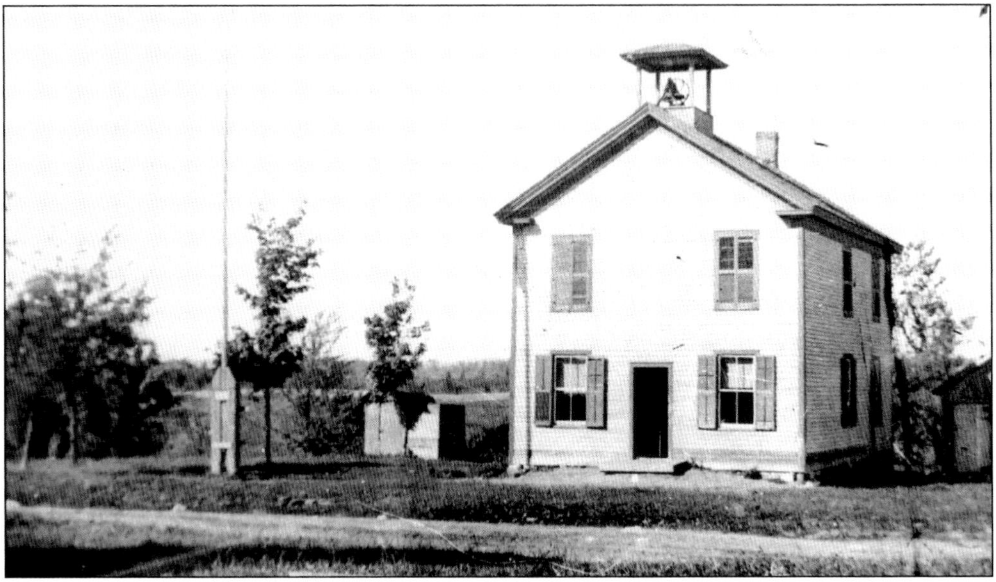

The Gray School was built in 1871 across the road from the Methodist church. During the early years, classes were held both upstairs and down. The school closed in the mid-1930s, after the centralization of the Poland School district. The building burned in the 1980s.

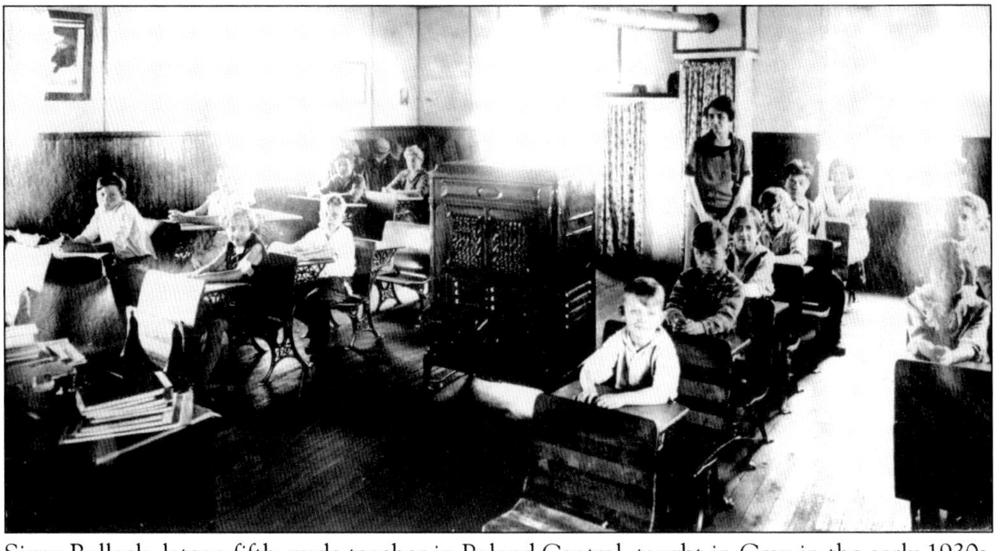

Signa Bullock, later a fifth-grade teacher in Poland Central, taught in Gray in the early 1930s. Her students are identified as follows: (row 1) Art Shafer, Elnora Comstock, Hubert Farber, and Charles Burke; (row 2) Florence Becraft and Charles Bullock; (row 3) Walter Bullock, Reynold Turner, Elsie Becraft, Francis Burke, Frank Darrow, and Anna Marko; (row 4) Ola Shafer, Philippa Comstock, Bart Comstock, Catherine Darrow, and John Becraft.

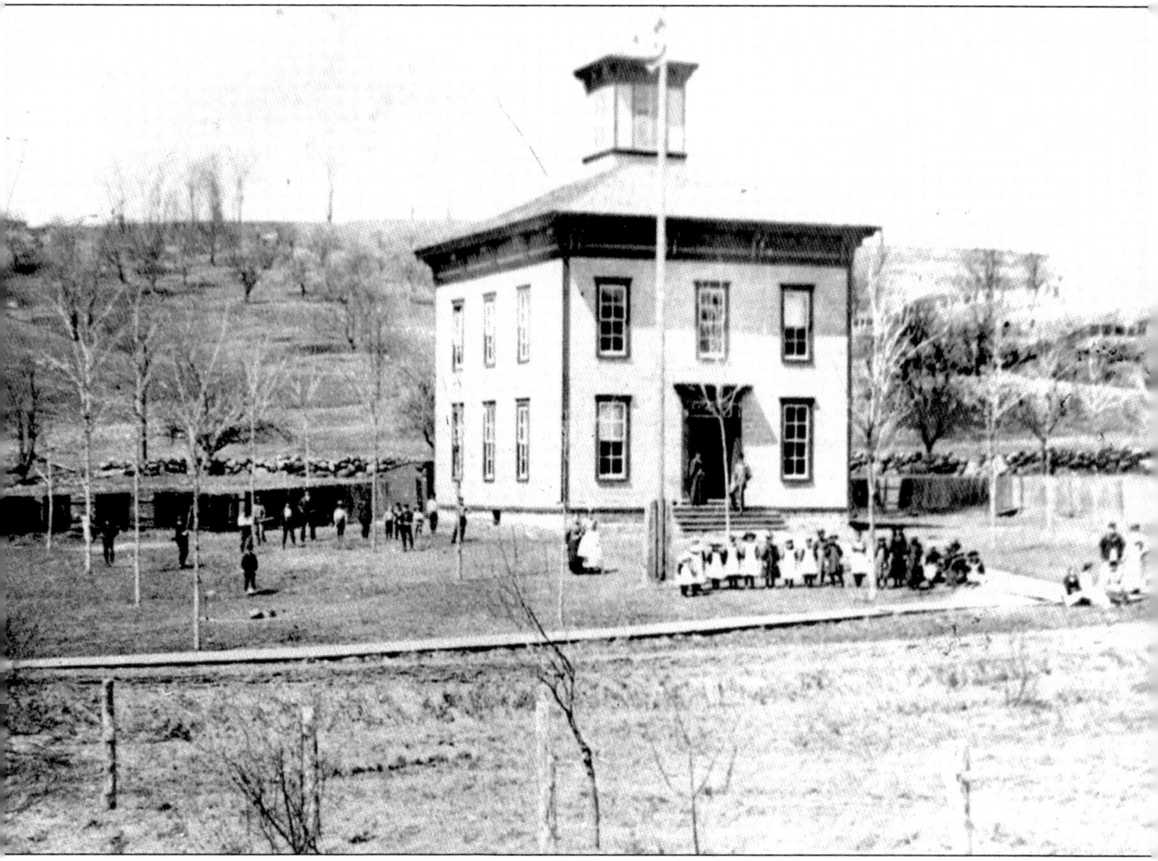

By 1870, the old Cold Brook school had enrolled nearly 80 students. Plans were made to build a new school with separate departments and teachers for the primary and advanced grades. In 1880, this large, square wooden building, complete with a cupola and bell, was erected on Main Street in Cold Brook. This photograph shows an Arbor Day celebration in 1903. After graduating from eighth grade in this school, students wishing to continue their education could attend high school in Poland. The Cold Brook School closed its doors in 1936, after 21 country schools were centralized to form the Poland Central School District for grades 1 through 12.

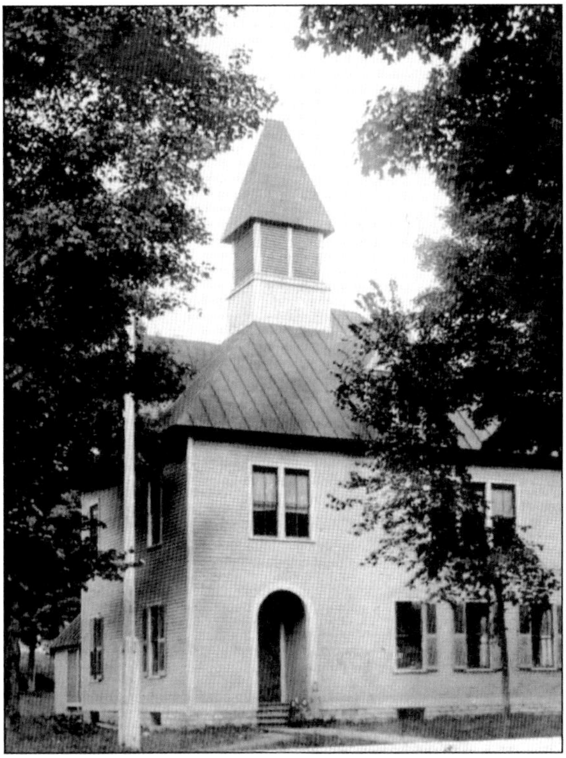

This Poland school was the seventh school building to be located in the village of Poland. Records show that a log building served as the first school in 1793. This building was erected in the 1870s on South Main Street. It provided classes for primary, intermediate, and advanced students. Students from the surrounding areas of Gravesville, Russia, Cold Brook, and Gray who had graduated from eighth grade could continue their education here. To get to school, some students walked several miles, some hitched rides on milk wagons or sleighs, and others drove a horse and buggy.

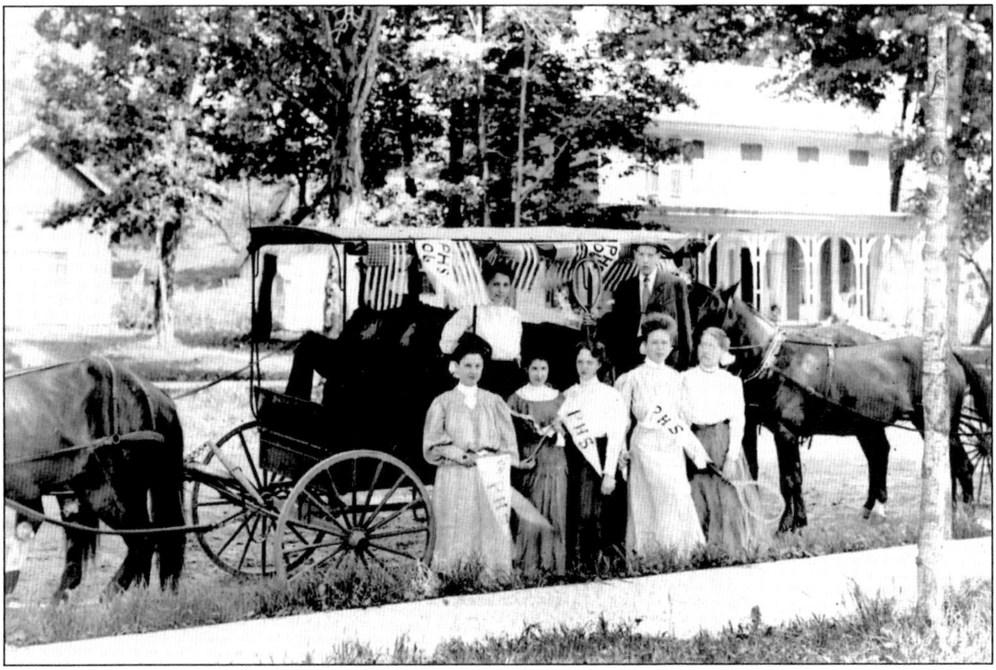

Members of the Class of 1906 pose by a horse-drawn carriage for a graduation photograph. Note the banners, both in hand and on the carriage, that read "PHS '06." The graduates are Lulu Brenning, Maude Countryman, Gertrude Cox, Sydney Cox, Henrietta Fitch, Frances Stillman, and Carrie Fralick.

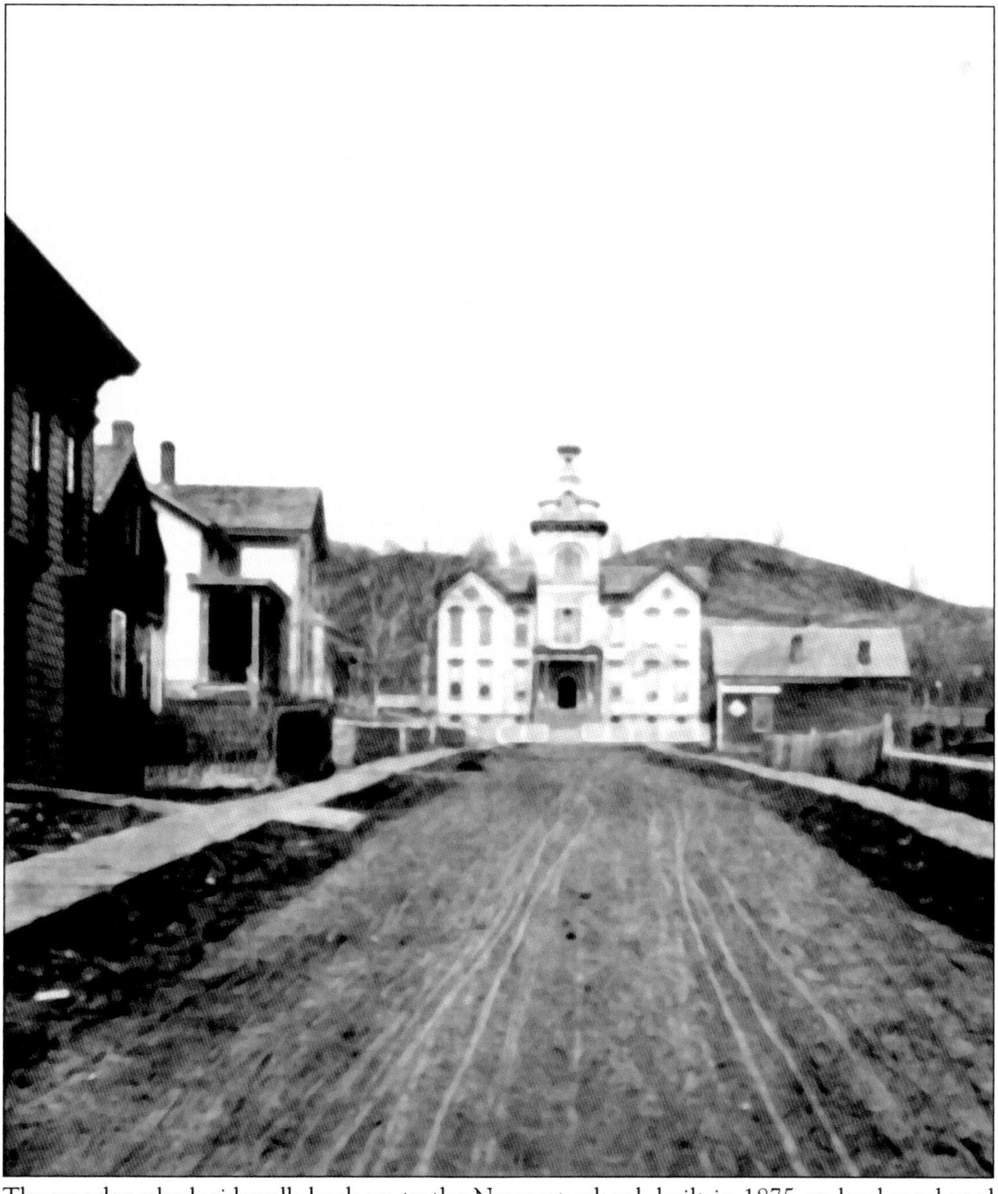

The wooden plank sidewalk leads up to the Newport school, built in 1875 on land purchased from Olive M. Hall. The school stood on East Street at the head of School Street and took the place of two village schools, one on each side of the West Canada Creek. The school was granted an academic department in 1896 and was converted into a high school in 1901. The library was considered to be the best among schools of its size. A fire of mysterious origin destroyed the building in 1928, one day after a contract to build a new school on the same site was signed.

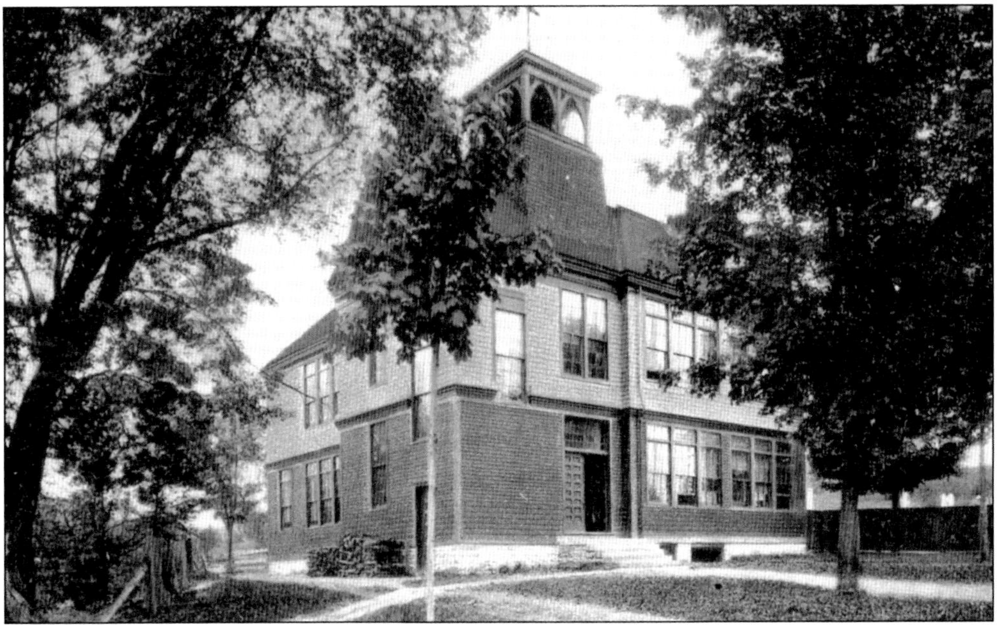

The consolidation of Fairfield's District No. 5 and Newport's District No. 9 resulted in the establishment of a union free school in 1874. The school was erected next to the Methodist church on Fairfield Street in Middleville. The first building on this site burned during the late 1800s. The building in this picture replaced it. Nonresident students could attend by paying tuition. The tuition for a 10-week period ranged from $1.50 in the primary department to $3 in the grammar and academic department. By the 1920s, the building was too small for the number of students it served and a proposition to build a new school was passed by the voters.

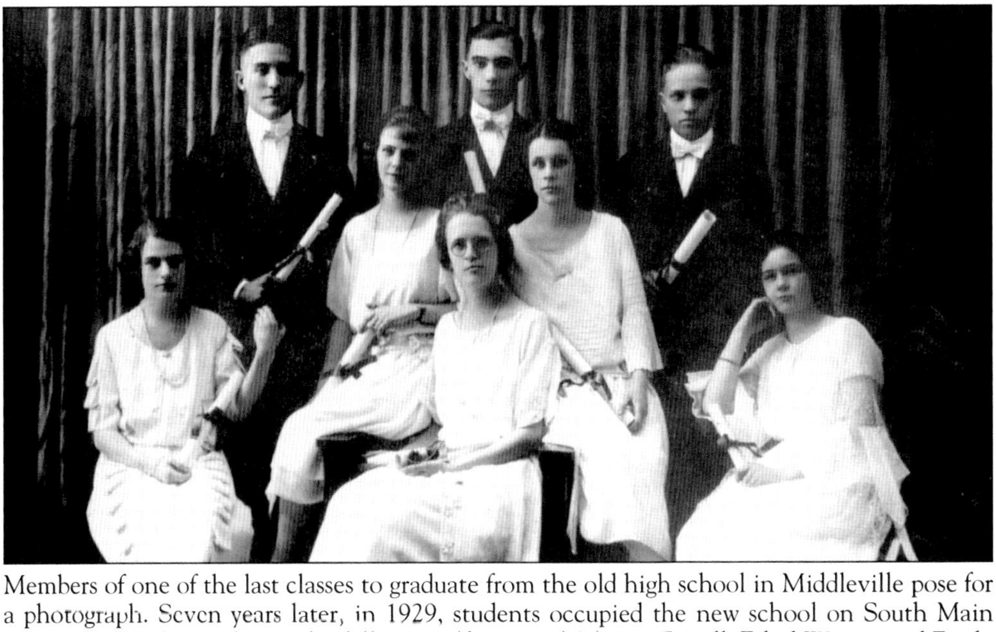

Members of one of the last classes to graduate from the old high school in Middleville pose for a photograph. Seven years later, in 1929, students occupied the new school on South Main Street. From left to right are the following: (front row) Marian Farrell, Ethel Wager, and Emily Wood; (middle row) Irene Higby and Marion Dickens; (back row) Floyd Rasbach, William VanVechten, and Walter Rantanen.

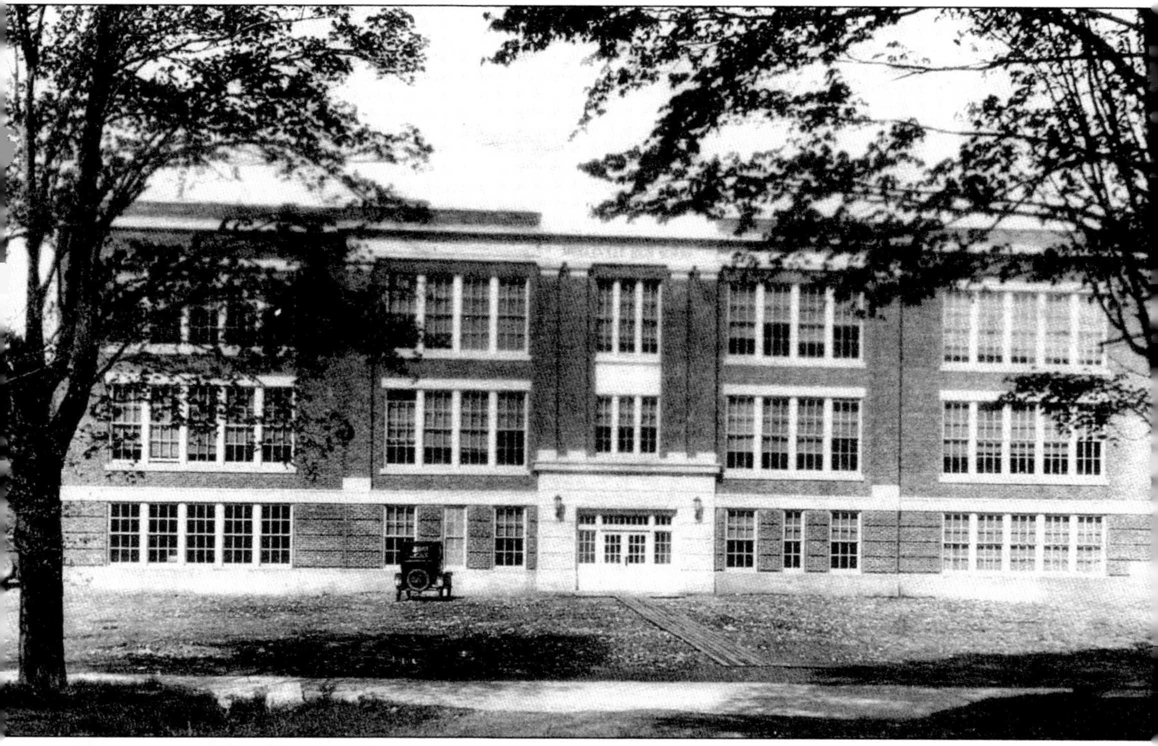

The new Middleville school opened to grades 1 through 12 in 1929. The walls were tapestry brick, ornamented with Onondaga litholite. The floors were maple wood, and the rooms were trimmed with Arkansas pine. In June 1938, a vote to centralize was carried, and the West Canada Valley Central School District was created, joining the various schools in the Fairfield, Newport, and Middleville area. The last class graduated from the old high school in 1938. Newport was chosen to have the high school in 1938, but the following year, Middleville was selected because of its school's excellent playing field. In 1963, a new high school was built between Newport and Middleville. Elementary classes left Middleville in 1990, when an elementary wing was added to the high school.

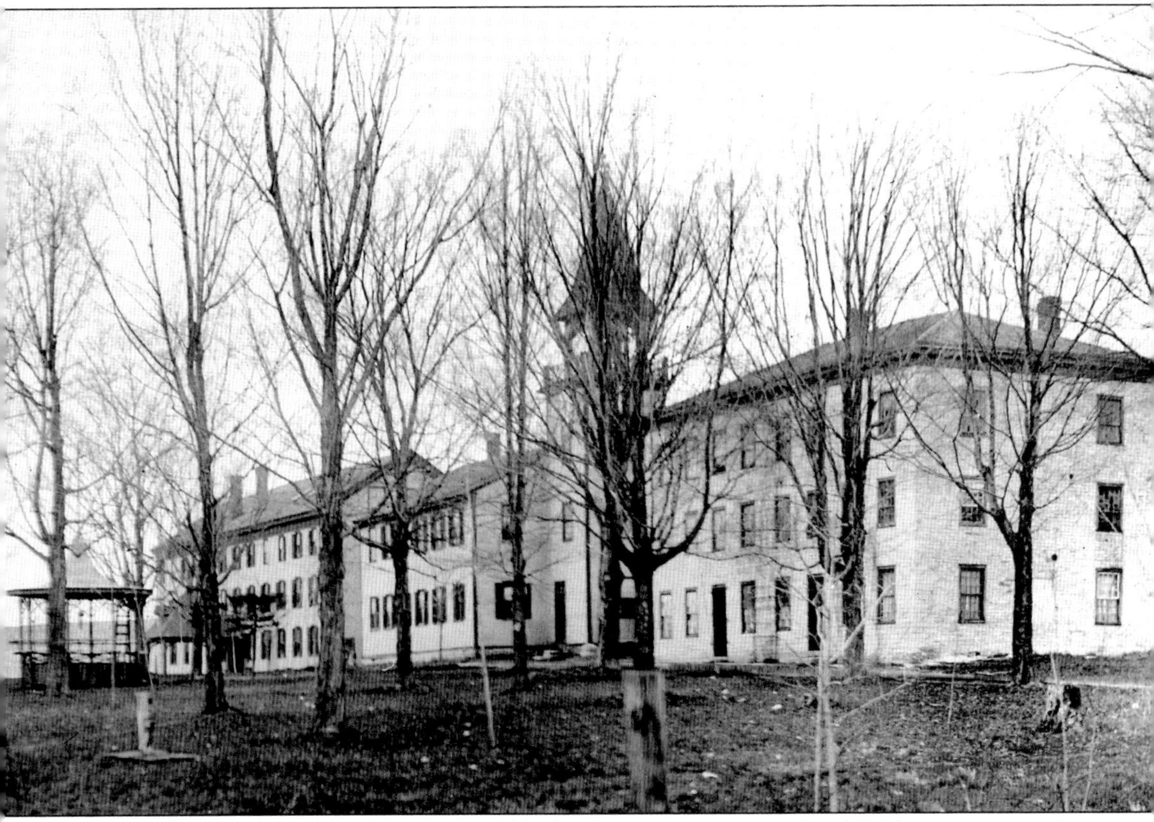

The Fairfield Academy, an institution of higher learning, was started in 1802 by circuit preacher Caleb Alexander. From 1854 to 1891, it was known as the Fairfield Seminary, and from 1891 to 1901, it was the Fairfield Seminary and Military Academy. Also located on the campus, from 1812 to 1841, was the College of Physicians and Surgeons of the Western District of New York, the third such medical college in New York State. From left to right in this view of the Fairfield campus are the Ladies Seminary, Old Chapel, and Worden Laboratory. The Ladies Seminary was built of wood in 1854 and was connected to the Old Chapel, where the dining hall was located. The female department of the seminary was established in 1840, greatly increasing the number of girls in attendance. Music and art were taught, as well as teacher training and, later, commercial subjects. The Ladies Seminary building was dismantled in 1907, and the wood from the structure was used to erect a barn on Route 170. The Worden Laboratory, where more than 600 medical students lived and studied, was dynamited in 1919, along with the Old South dormitory. The stone from these buildings was crushed and used on local roads.

The gazebo on the Fairfield Seminary campus was the site of many concerts and outdoor entertainments. The school was closed permanently in 1901. Efforts to generate funds sufficient to repair and maintain the last remaining structure were unsuccessful. A schoolhouse for District No. 6 was erected on the campus and used until 1960. Purchased by the town of Fairfield in 1961, the building remains in use as the Fairfield Community Hall.

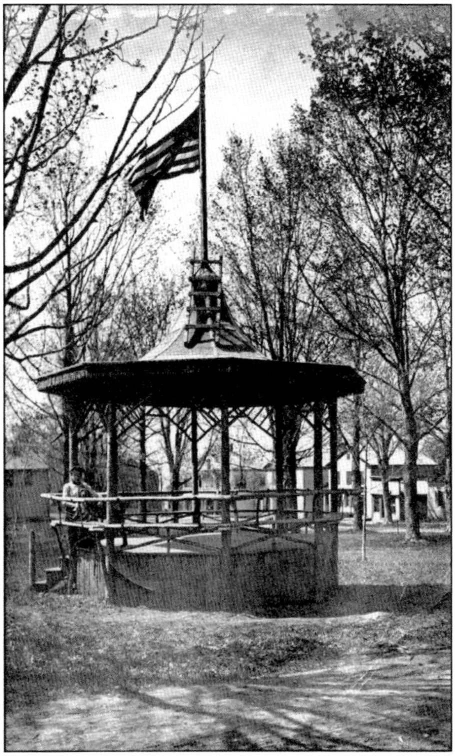

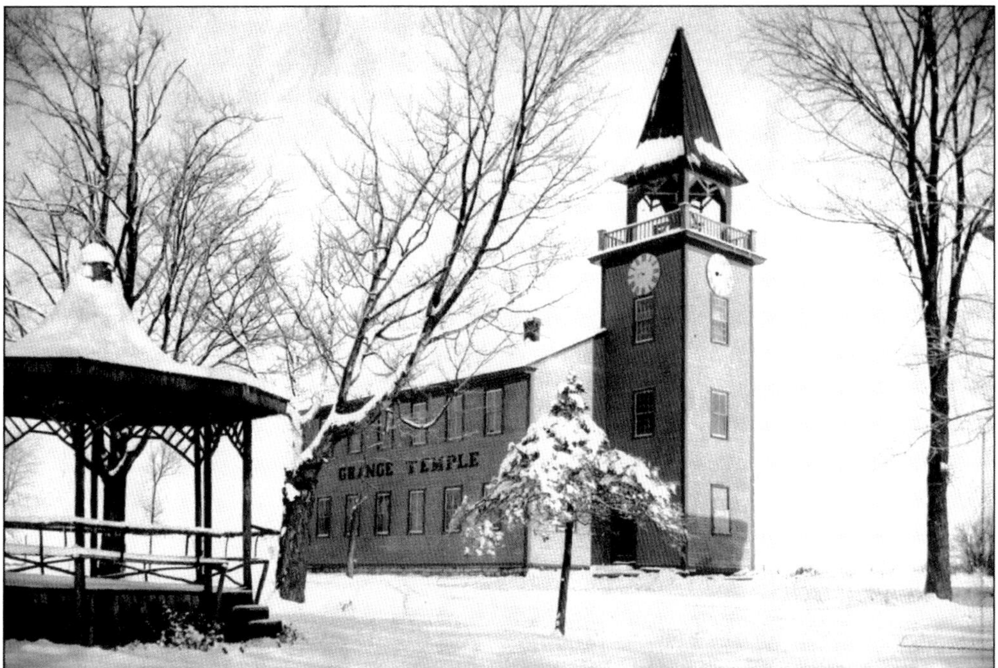

The Old Chapel of the Fairfield Academy is shown here before its demise in 1979, when the steeple crashed to the ground. Built in 1802, the chapel was the first building on the campus and the last to be demolished. From 1906 until 1962, the Grange used it for a meeting hall.

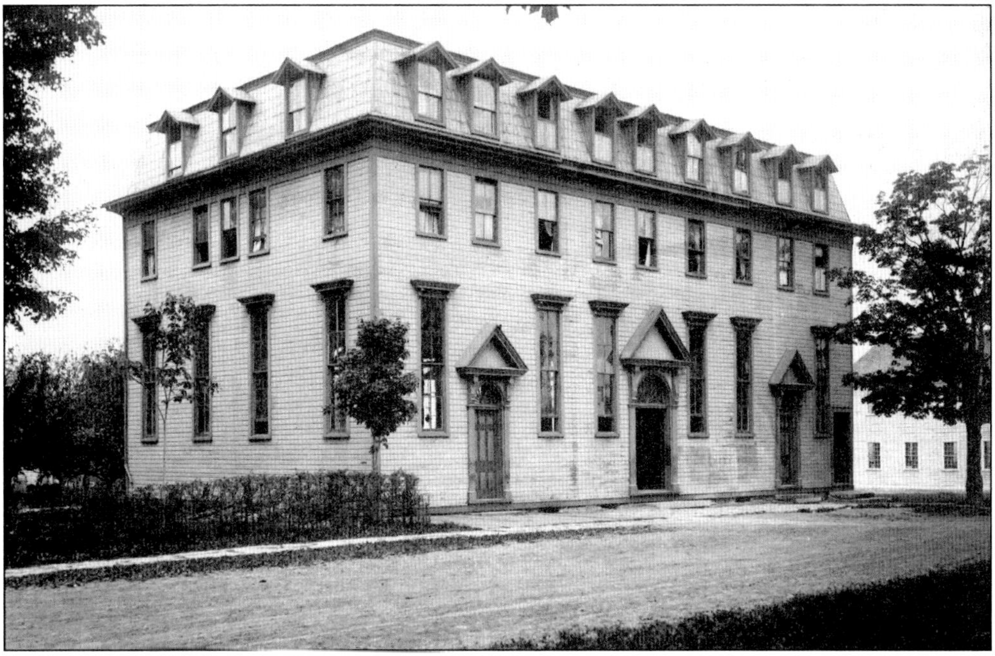

Constructed from the Wood Hotel in 1891, the armory of the Fairfield Military Academy was across the road from the campus. With the advent of free high schools, the student body of a school that charged tuition dwindled. A new drawing card was needed at Fairfield, and this was provided in the form of military training, offered by school administrators Dwight D. Warne and Frank L. Warne. The armory was razed when the school closed in 1901.

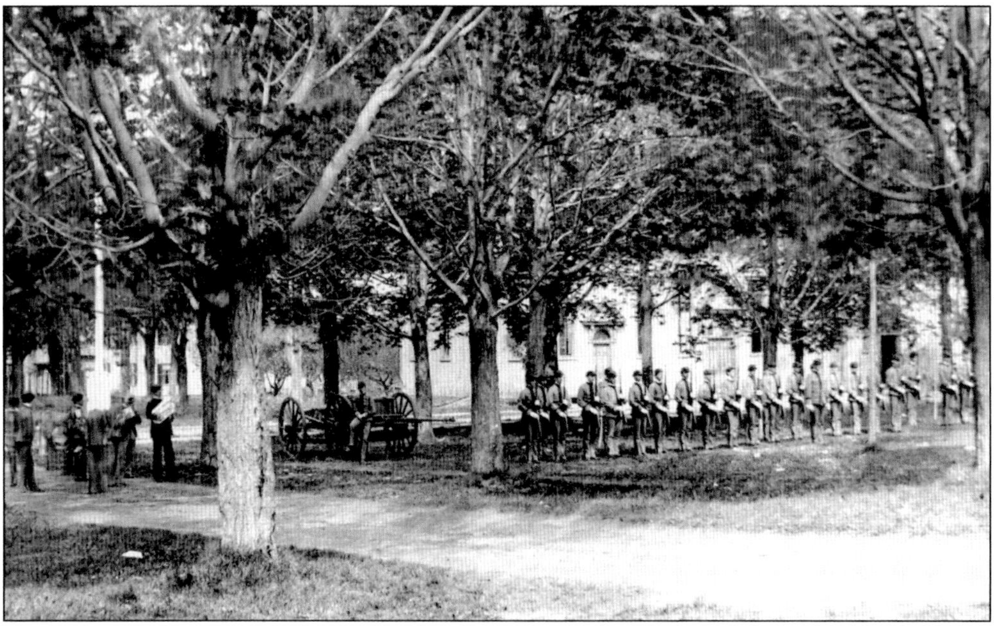

The cadets are seen here during a drill practice. Their uniforms were similar to the cadet uniform at West Point. Each cadet was required to have a full dress uniform, costing $22.53, and a fatigue uniform, costing $17.60. Female cadet uniforms were gray, trimmed with black braid, and cost $13.

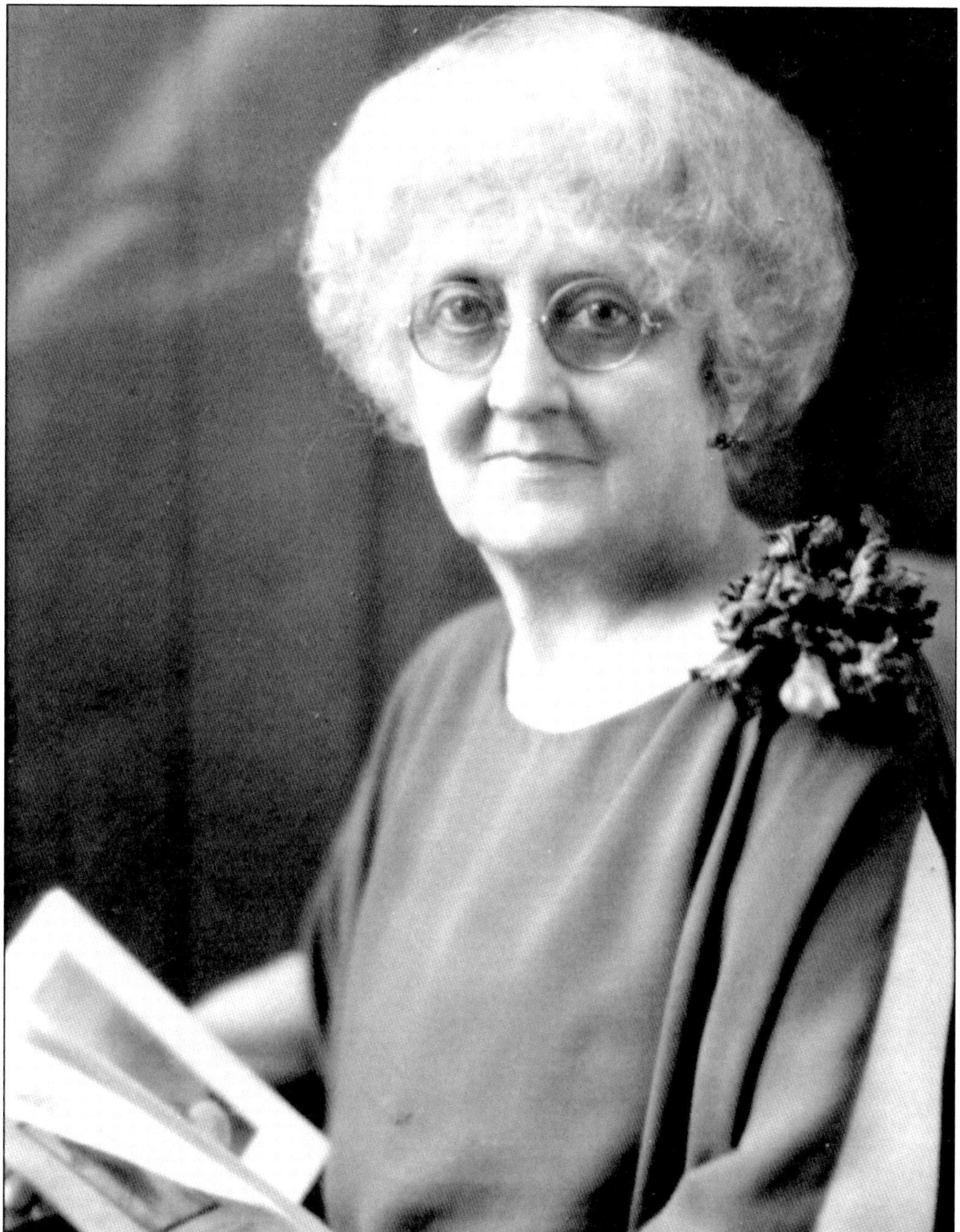

Ella M. Edsall, wife of Dr. Irving A. Edsall, proposed the organization of a public library for the village of Middleville in 1914. After a public meeting was held, citizens rallied to support the effort. The Middleville Free Library Association was organized, and the library was opened in 1915 with 325 "traveling library books" supplied by the state. Ella Edsall also organized the Middleville Literary Union in 1898. This group continued until 1946, bringing culture, scholarship, and intellectual expression to the village. The library, chartered by the Regents of the State of New York, is currently quartered in Corey Hall and continues to serve the area as a member of the Mid-York Library System.

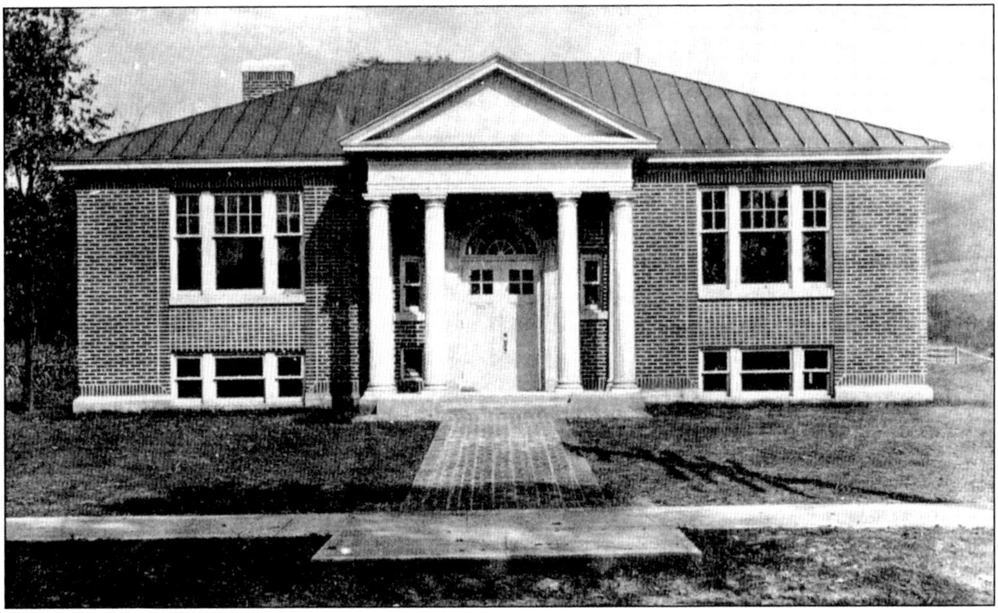

George Bradford made a gift of this building in 1922 as a library for the village of Newport. The building, valued at that time at $20,000, was given in memory of his parents. The Bradford Memorial Library opened in 1923 with more than 2,300 books. An early member of the Mid-York Library System, the library has introduced computers for public as well as library personnel use. The downstairs room is available for use by community groups. George Bradford's daughter deeded the adjacent vacant lot to the library for future expansion purposes.

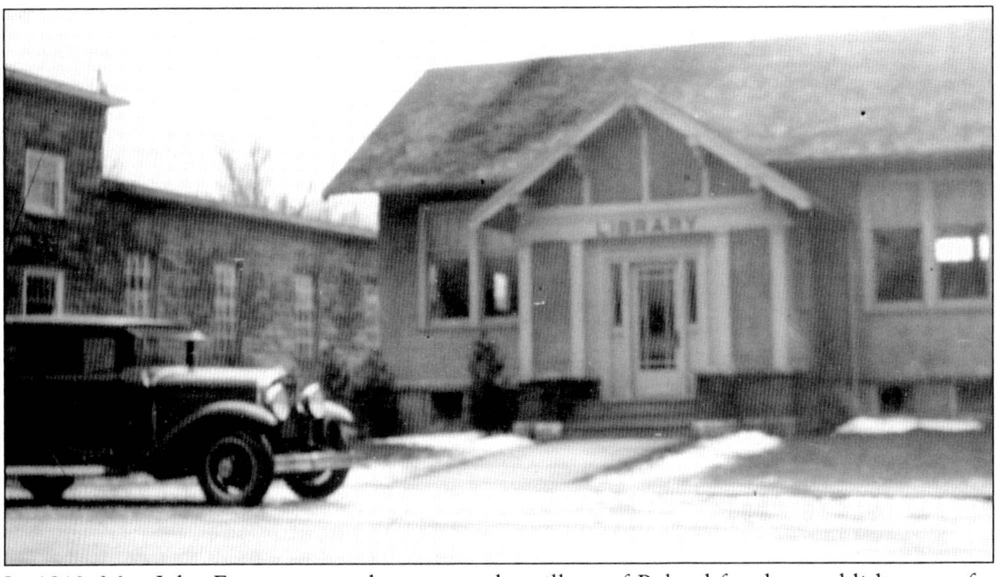

In 1919, Mrs. John Forrest gave a bequest to the village of Poland for the establishment of a library. A one-story library was constructed on the site of the Wooster House, Poland's earliest hotel. Designed in the Arts and Crafts style popular in the early 1900s, the library has stained oak interior doors, windows, and bookshelves. The basement space has a meeting room for community groups and storage space for books not in active circulation.

Five

GIVING THANKS AND PRAISE

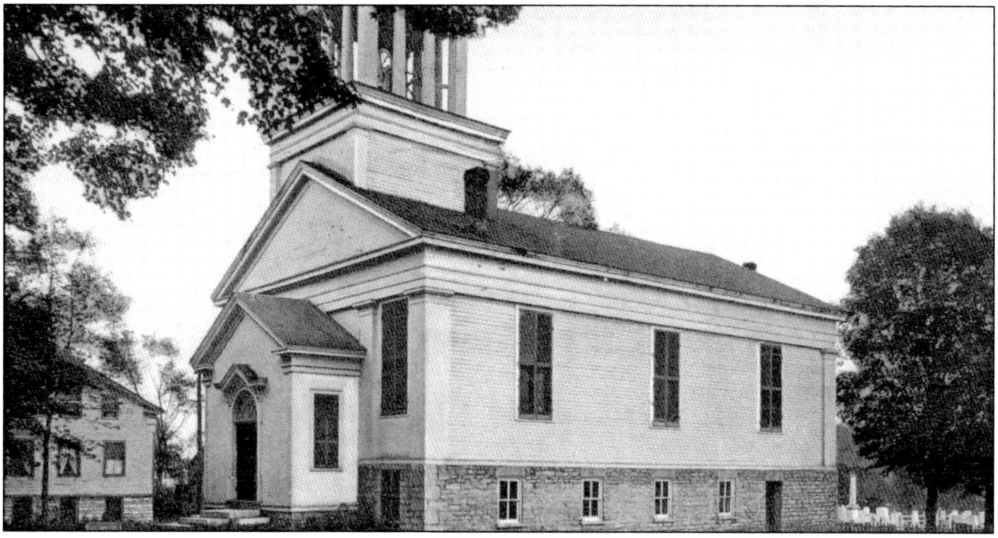

The early settlers of the Kuyahoora towns came to their new home on the frontier primarily from Rhode Island, Massachusetts, Connecticut, and Vermont. They brought with them their religious faiths: Baptist, Methodist, Presbyterian, Episcopalian, and Congregational. Over the years, other pioneers brought the Roman Catholic religion to the area. In the late 1700s and early 1800s, circuit rider preachers visited the settlements and held services in homes. By 1810, villages in the area sold shares to raise money to erect meetinghouses for religious purposes. The denominations received the use of the building in proportion to the number of shares held by their members. These churches were often called Union churches. One of the earliest churches in the Kuyahoora Valley area was the First Baptist Church of Newport. In 1794, a small group of Baptists settled near Fairfield and organized a church. In 1799, a group of Baptists living along the West Canada Creek formed a church group and met at the home of Fisher Potter, in the town of Norway. After a portion of the town of Norway became the town of Newport in 1806, the group became the First Baptist Church of Newport. In 1811, the group acquired a parcel of land and erected a stone meetinghouse. By 1846, the walls of the church were beginning to cave in. The building was razed and the one pictured here was erected on the same foundation. In 1873, member John Fortune gave the church a rare and beautiful Marklove organ. A different set of pipes was installed in 1973, and James Autenrith was the organist for the 200th anniversary celebration in 1999.

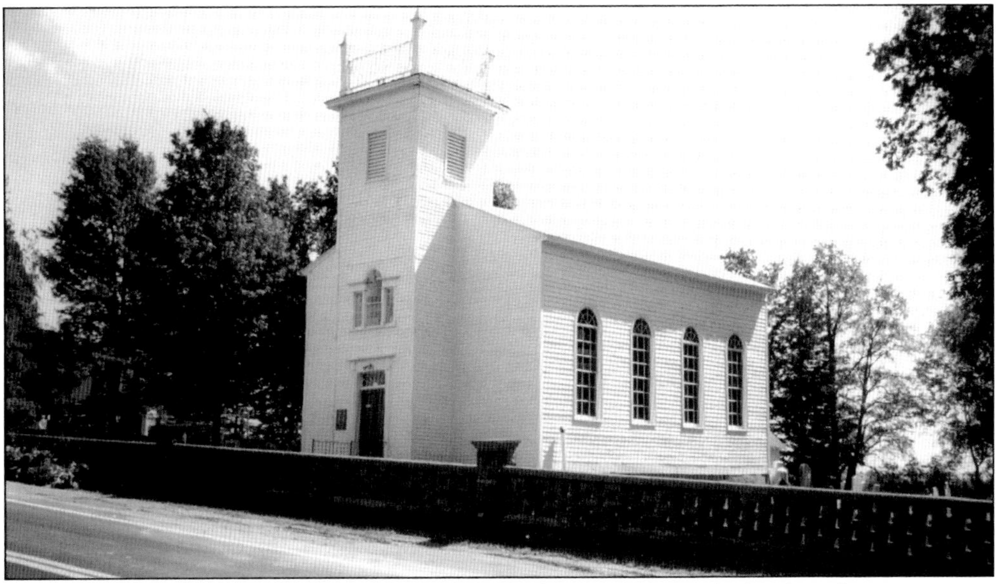

Trinity Episcopal Church at Fairfield was organized in January 1807. A white frame structure with a four-spire belfry was built to serve residents and students and faculty of the Fairfield Academy. Trinity Church of New York City contributed financially to the building as part of a program to establish small Episcopal mission churches in upstate areas. Trinity's clergy helped organize churches in Norway, Middleville, Herkimer, and Little Falls. The gallery and some of the original furnishings remain. Services are held at Trinity during the summer months.

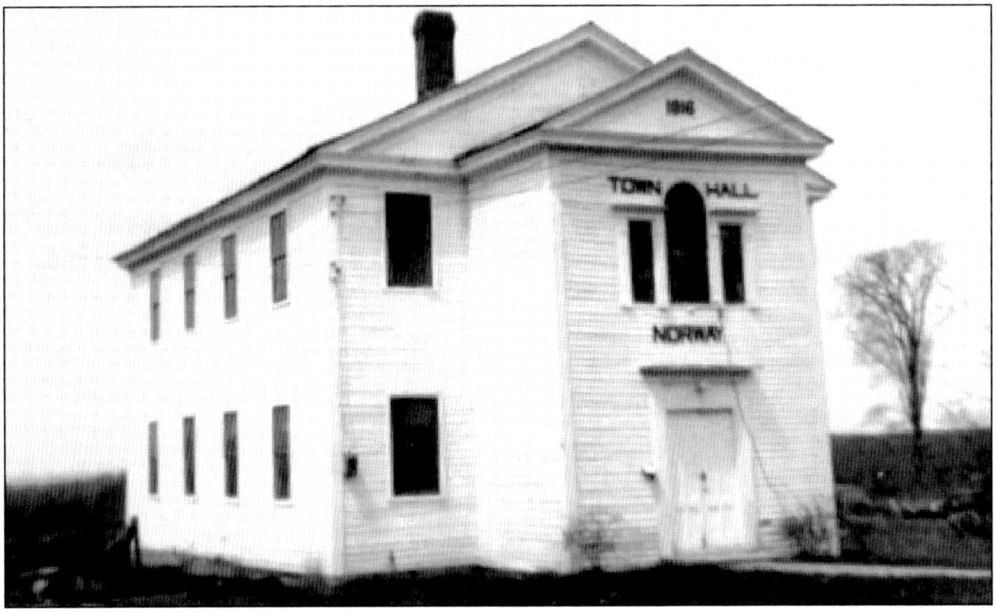

The Norway Union Church was built in 1814. Organized in 1798, the Presbyterians were the leading religious society in Norway for more than 30 years. The Calvary Society sold shares to earn money to build this meetinghouse. According to the number of shares their members had contributed, the Methodists, Baptists, and Episcopalians shared the use of the building with the Presbyterians. The town of Norway used the building for a town hall for several years after the church closed. The building was later razed.

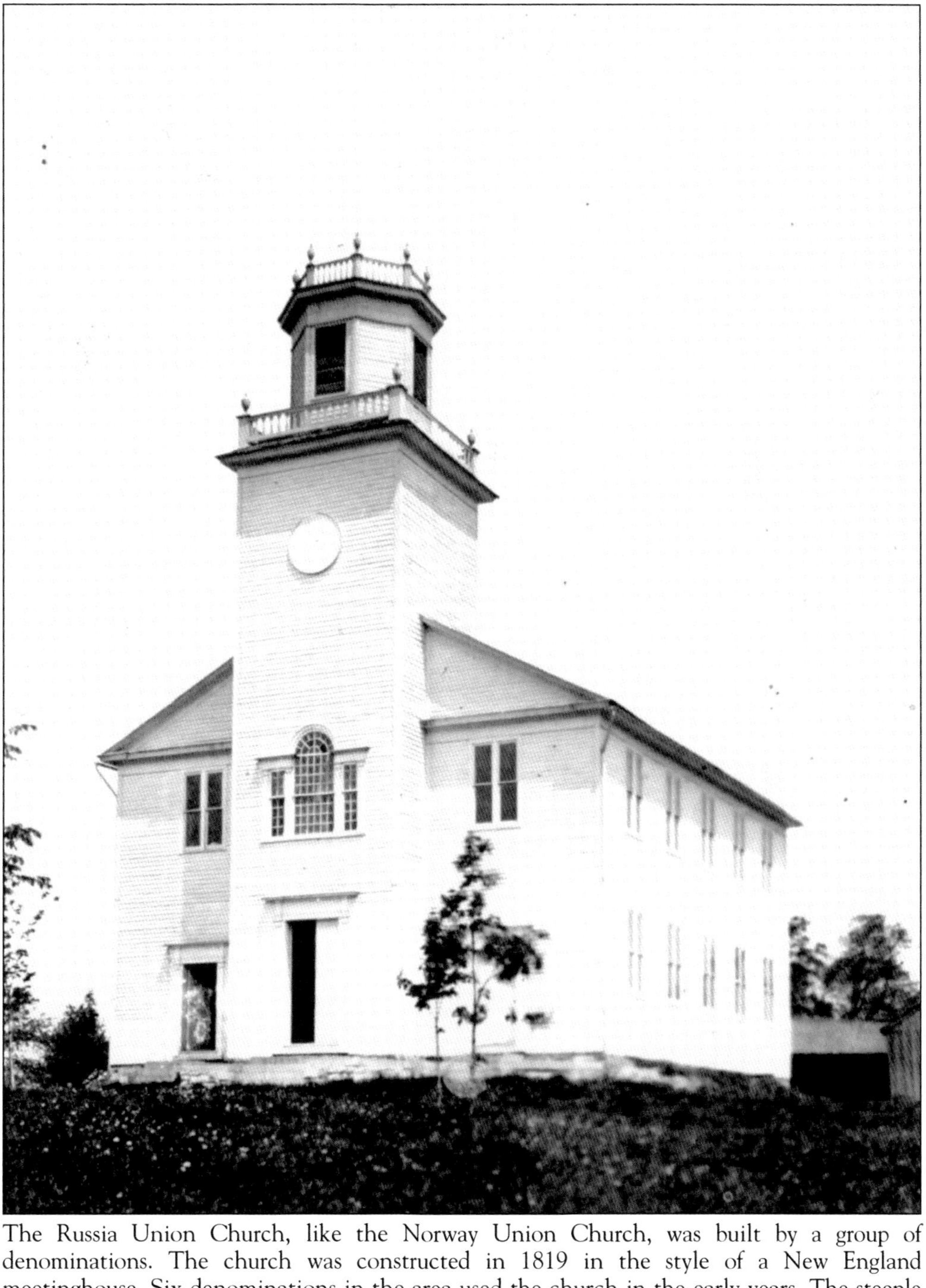

The Russia Union Church, like the Norway Union Church, was built by a group of denominations. The church was constructed in 1819 in the style of a New England meetinghouse. Six denominations in the area used the church in the early years. The steeple was wrecked by a hurricane in 1850 and rebuilt. In 1996, Russia Corners was placed on the National Register of Historic Districts. A new belfry and bell were placed atop the church in 2002. Nondenominational services are held in the church during the summer.

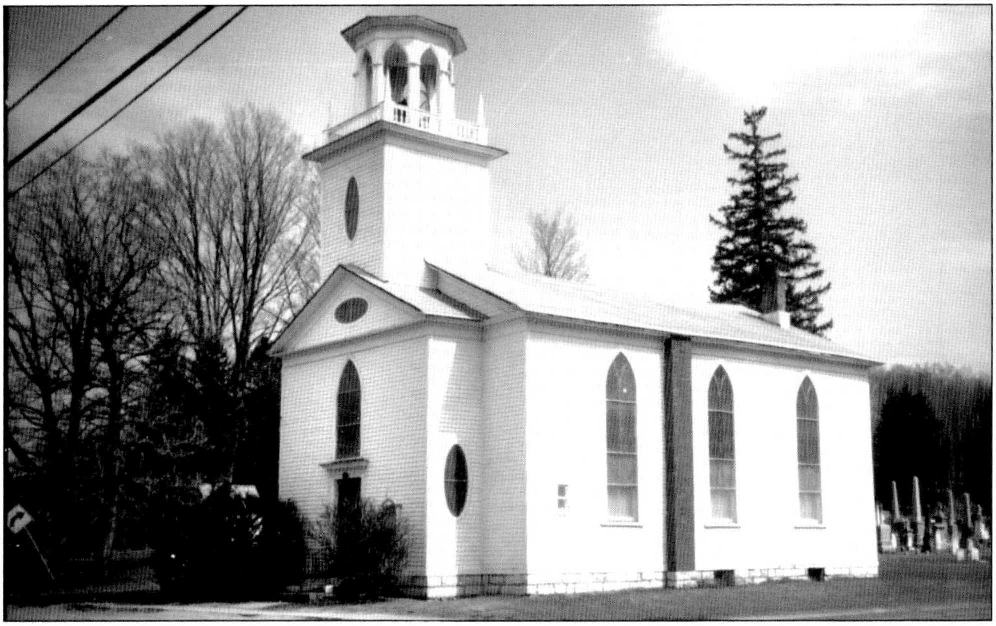

Prior to 1881, the Methodist church in Middleville was known as the Middleville Union Church. George Buell, who had built the Russia Union Church, built this church in 1825–1826. The present bell, purchased on December 24, 1889, bears the inscription "Christmas 1889. When you hear me, please come." The steeple was lost in 1950 and replaced by a shorter one. The church is now known as the United Methodist Church.

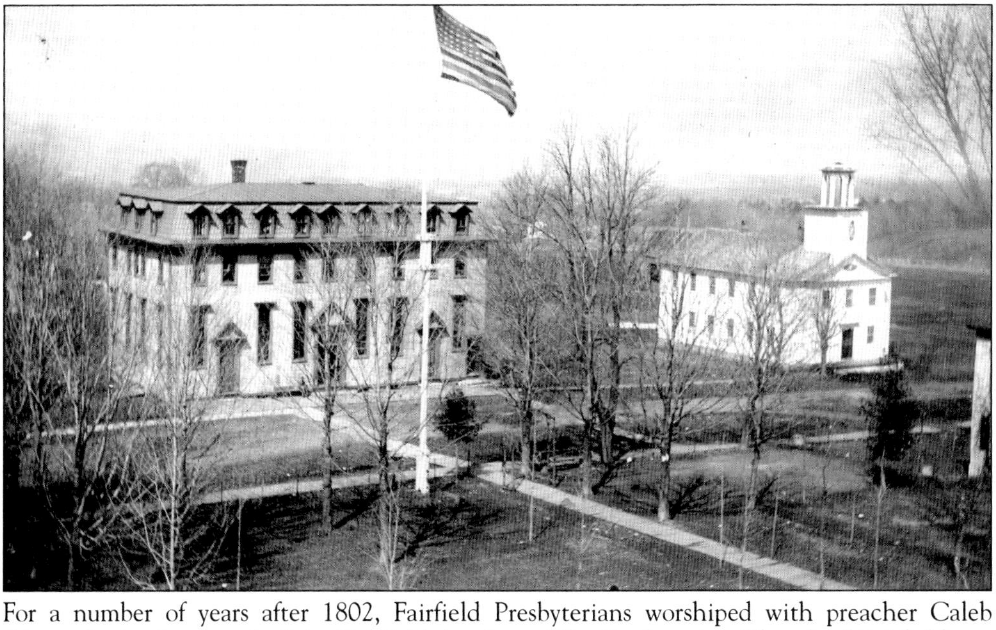

For a number of years after 1802, Fairfield Presbyterians worshiped with preacher Caleb Alexander in the chapel of the Fairfield Academy. The Presbyterian Church of Fairfield was built and dedicated in 1829 on the corner of Platform Road and Old Route 29. In the late 1800s, the congregation dwindled and the academy used the church for programs and exercises. In 1892, the Fairfield Academy acquired the church and moved it next to the armory, as shown in this picture. The building was razed *c.* 1905.

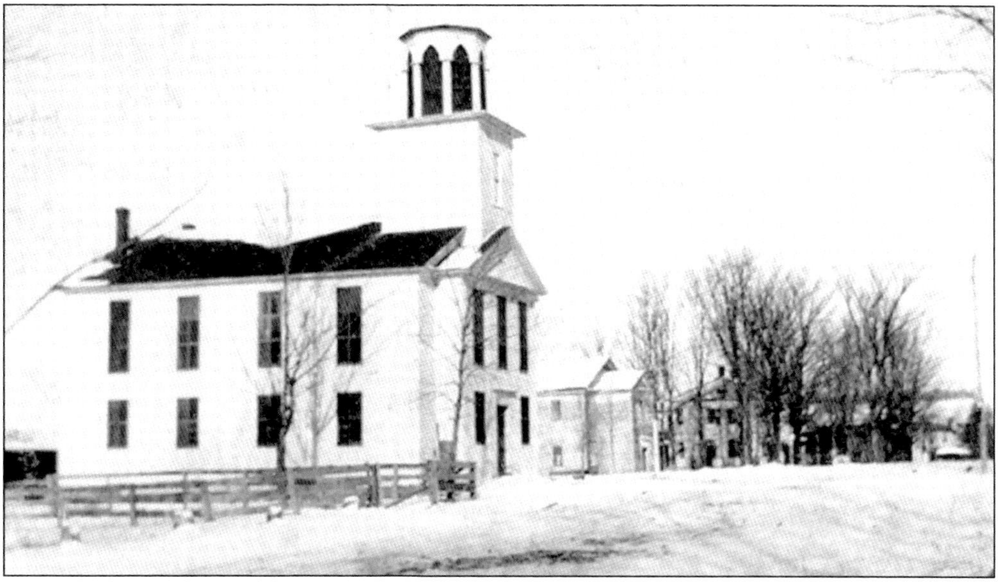

In 1831, Robert Crandall built the Norway Baptist Church on land deeded by Dudley Smith. Previously, the Baptists had traveled to Newport or occasionally used the Union church for their services. Both this church and the adjacent Union church lost their steeples in a severe storm in 1856. Neither steeple was replaced. The Norway Baptist Church discontinued services in 1998. In 2001, the building was turned over to the town of Norway, and in November 2002, it was dedicated as the Norway History Center.

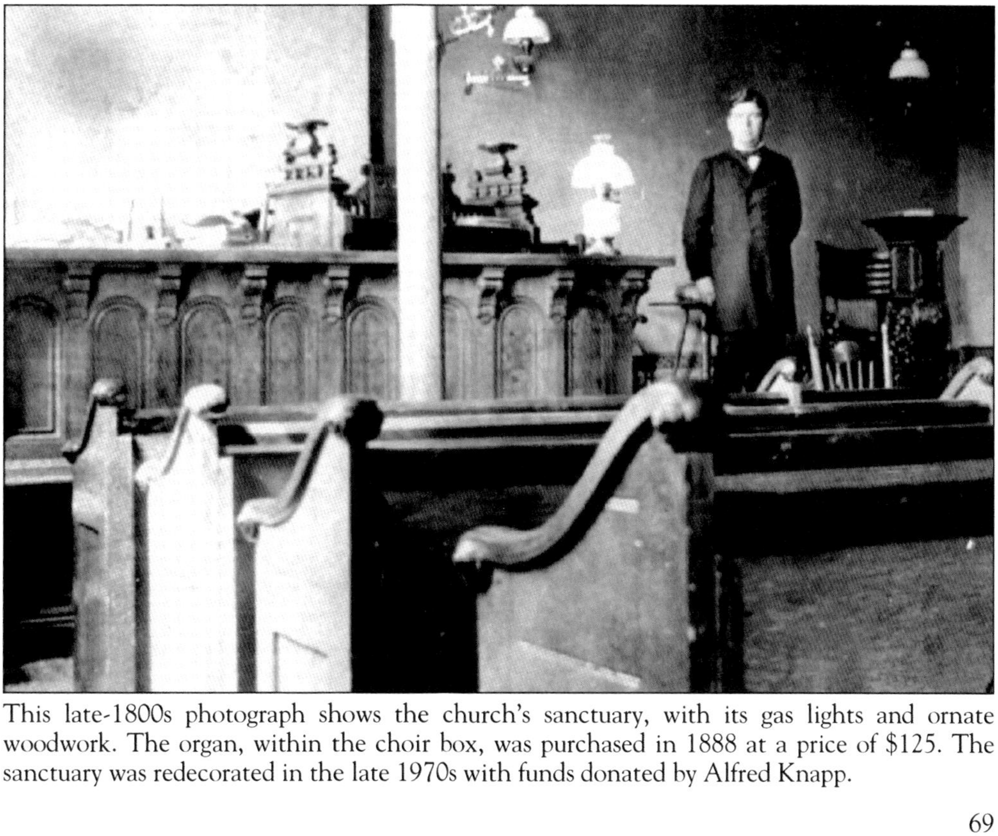

This late-1800s photograph shows the church's sanctuary, with its gas lights and ornate woodwork. The organ, within the choir box, was purchased in 1888 at a price of $125. The sanctuary was redecorated in the late 1970s with funds donated by Alfred Knapp.

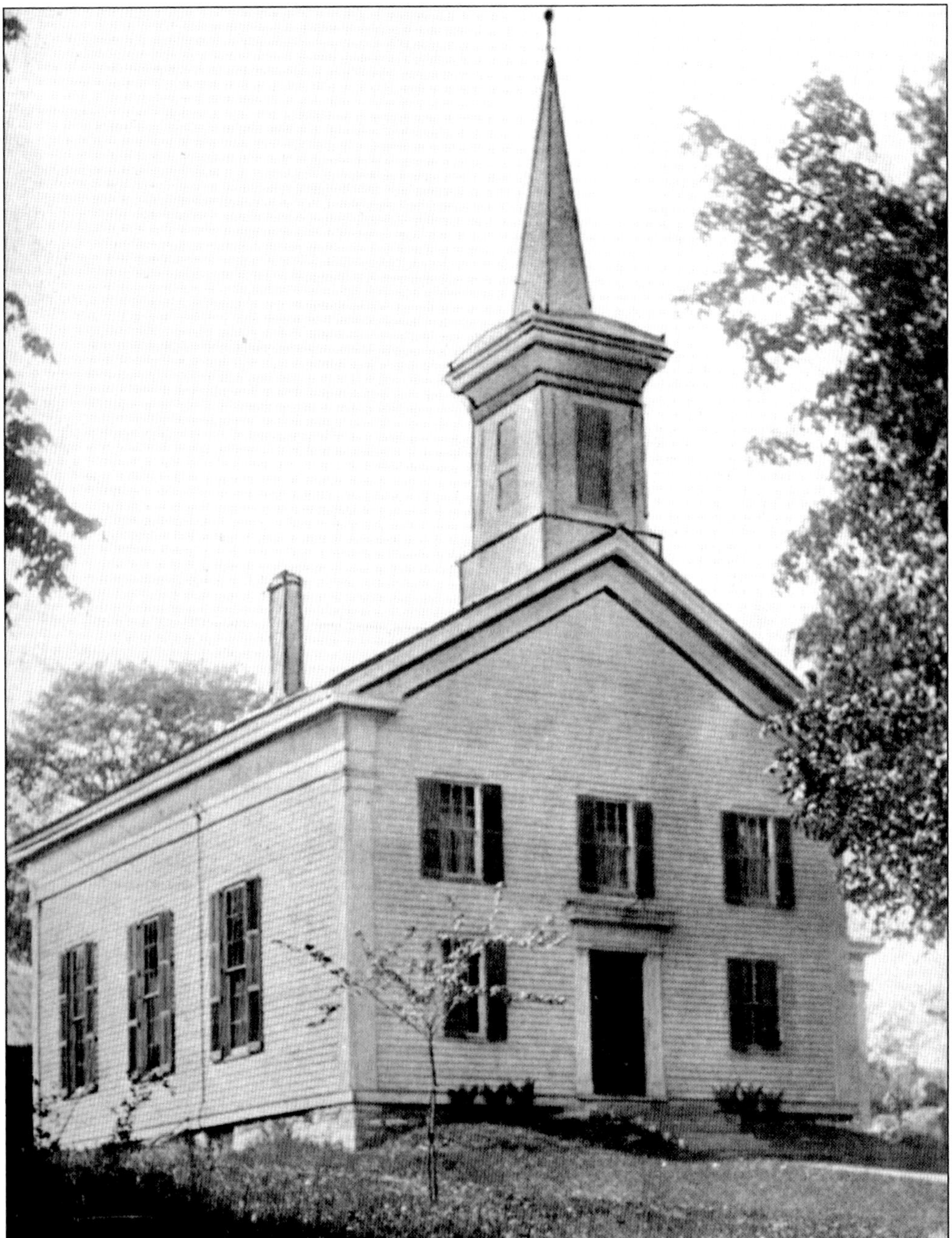

The Cold Brook Methodist Episcopal Church was built in 1829 in the Colonial meetinghouse style. The church stood on property leased from Reuben Robens until 1881, when Robens issued the Methodists a deed to the property. This deed contains provisions set up by the church trustees that "only the Methodist Church can ever hold the property." At one time there were large horse sheds behind the church that were owned by individual members of the congregation. The church parlors were added in 1889. In 1978, the old steel ball atop the steeple was replaced with a cap and a three-foot reflective gold cross. The Cold Brook United Methodist Church remains active today.

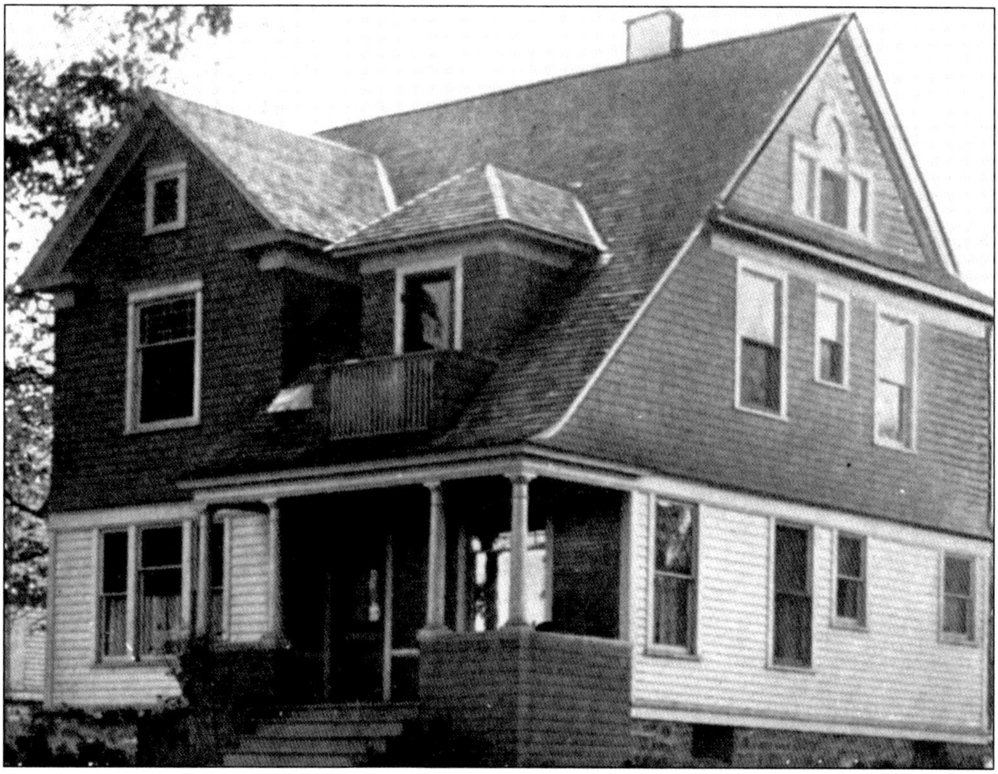

In the early days of the Methodist Episcopal church, several local businessmen formed the Cold Brook House Association and provided a parsonage for the pastor. In 1905, the efforts of the Ladies' Aid Association helped make it possible to build the parsonage shown above at a cost of $2,906. The ladies raised $1,400 by conducting "Ten-Cent Teas." Since recent pastors of the church have lived elsewhere, the parsonage has been rented.

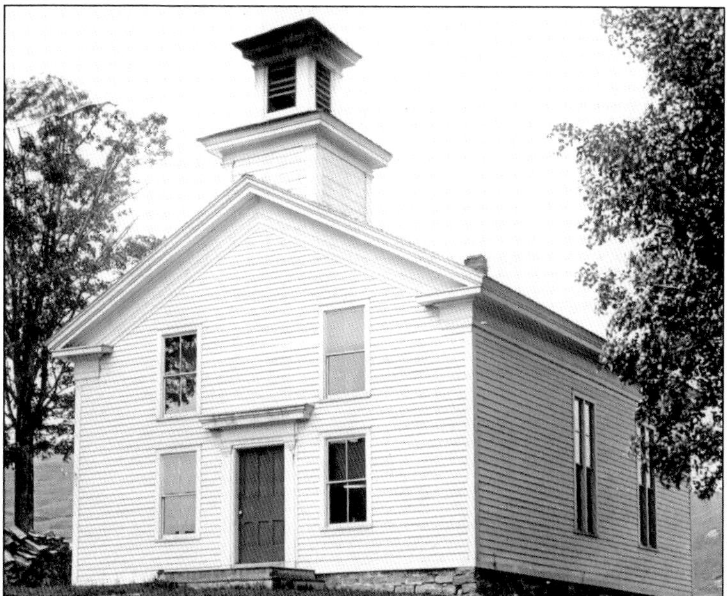

Pictured here is the Grant Methodist Episcopal Church, organized in 1860. The wooden structure, 26 feet by 36 feet, cost $800. Through the years the church has also been known as the Grant Union Church. Services have not been held here since the 1960s. In the late 1970s, the Black Creek Conservation Club took over the church for its meetings. The building is now privately owned.

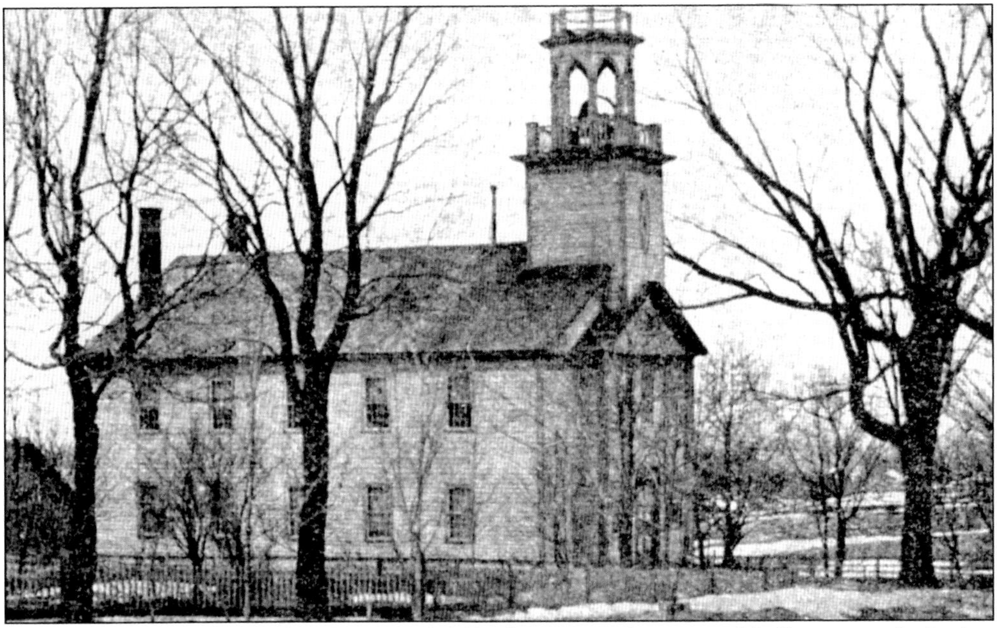

The Methodist Episcopal church in Fairfield had an unusual octagonal bell tower with Gothic arches and decorative carvings of four pillars in low relief on the front facade, which mark it as a Classical Revival design. Erected in 1837, the church served the students of Fairfield Seminary, as well as the community. The church consolidated with the Newport and Middleville Methodists in 1965 under the pastorate of Rev. Russell Little. Donald Webb, director of a nearby Christian camp, purchased the building in 1973, and it became the Fairfield Bible Church in 1976. The congregation moved to Dolgeville in 1994. Today, the building is a private home.

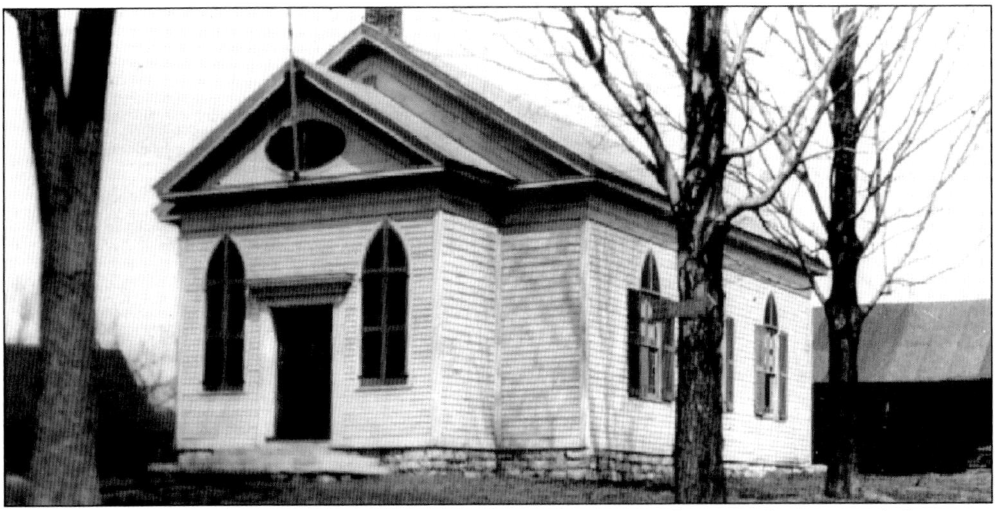

Methodism in Norway began as early as 1794, when circuit rider preachers visited the town and preached in the log homes of the pioneers. The first church building was erected in 1809 in the Dairy Hill area. After it closed, another Methodist church was built in 1838 in the Black Creek area. The church pictured here, across the street from the Union church and the Baptist church, was built in 1837 at a cost of $1,000. Although still standing, the building has not been used in many years. Its pews were exchanged with those of the Baptist church in the 1930s.

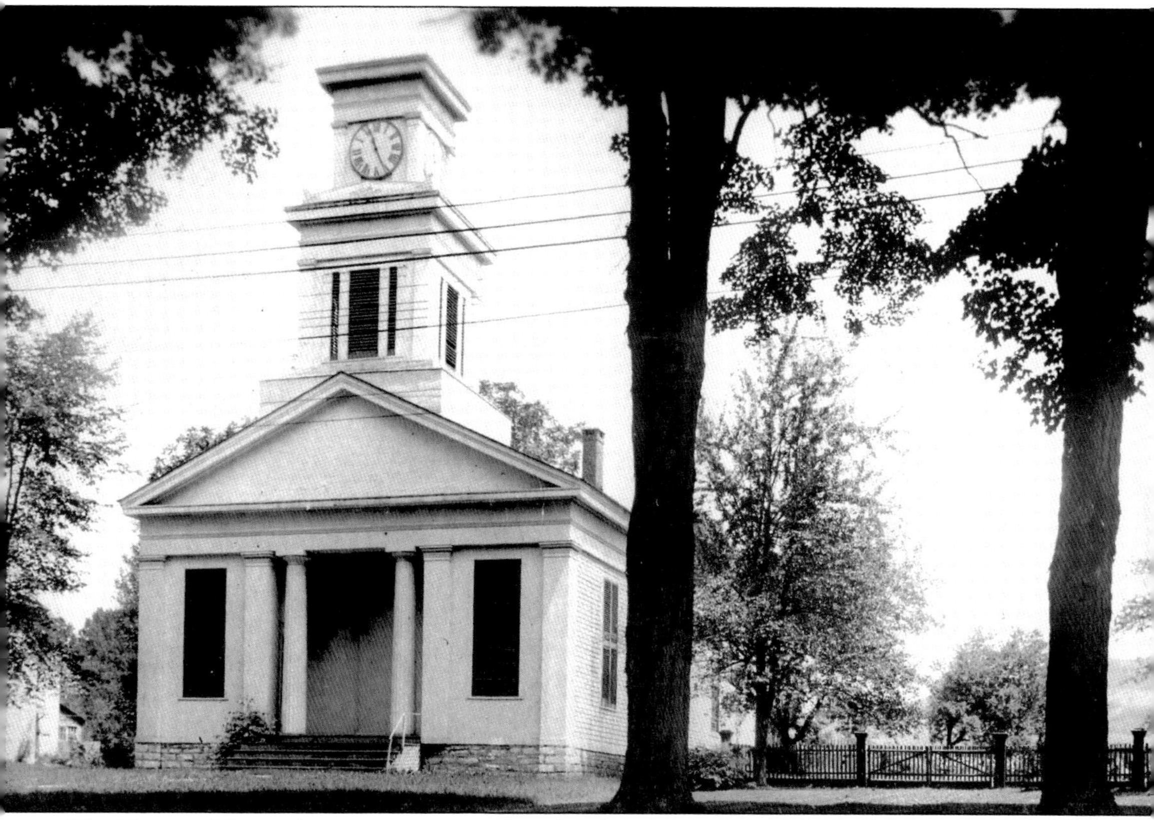

The Newport Union Association was organized in 1842 as a union of Universalists, Unitarians, and Episcopalians. This Greek Revival–style structure was erected in 1843 at a cost of approximately $4,000. As was common in many churches of the early years, the pulpit stood between the two front doors, and a gallery overlooked the auditorium on the other three sides. Some years later, the gallery was removed and the pulpit placed at the back of the room. The bell tower was topped by a unique clock, which had four faces and required daily hand winding. Purchased by public subscription, the clock faithfully struck on the hour for almost 100 years. Since the Unitarians and Episcopalians failed to make use of the building, it passed exclusively into the hands of the Universalists in 1844. During the early 1930s, the congregation dwindled. The failure of the Newport Bank, where the church funds were on deposit, forced the closure of the church. In 1941, a nearby grass fire ignited the church building, which was not covered by insurance.

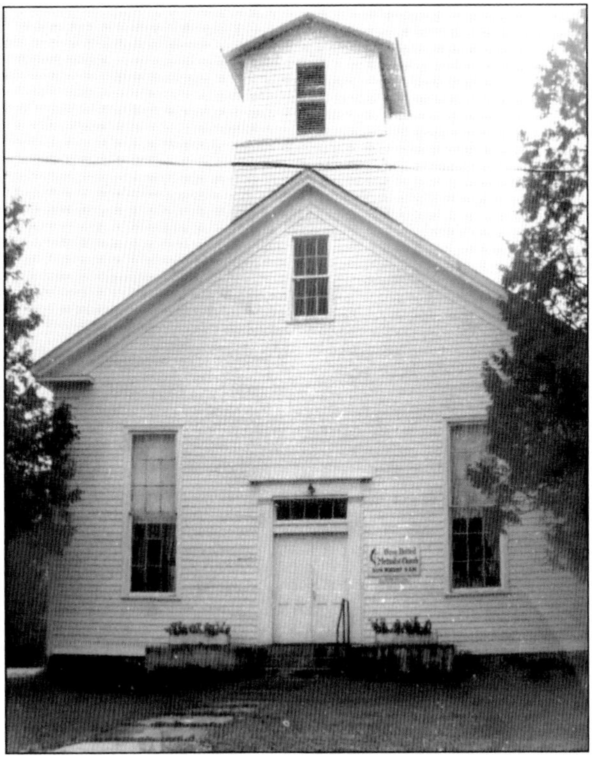

The First Methodist Episcopal Church of Gray was built in 1870. It was a white frame church with a square cupola, surmounted by a weather-beaten weathervane. A 1933 newspaper article described the church's interior as a square, high-ceiling auditorium and vestibule, with kerosene lamps on the side walls, old-fashioned kerosene chandeliers in the center of the room, near the piano at the front of the room, and beside the raised pulpit. A dwindling congregation forced the church to close in the mid-1990s. The building is now a private home.

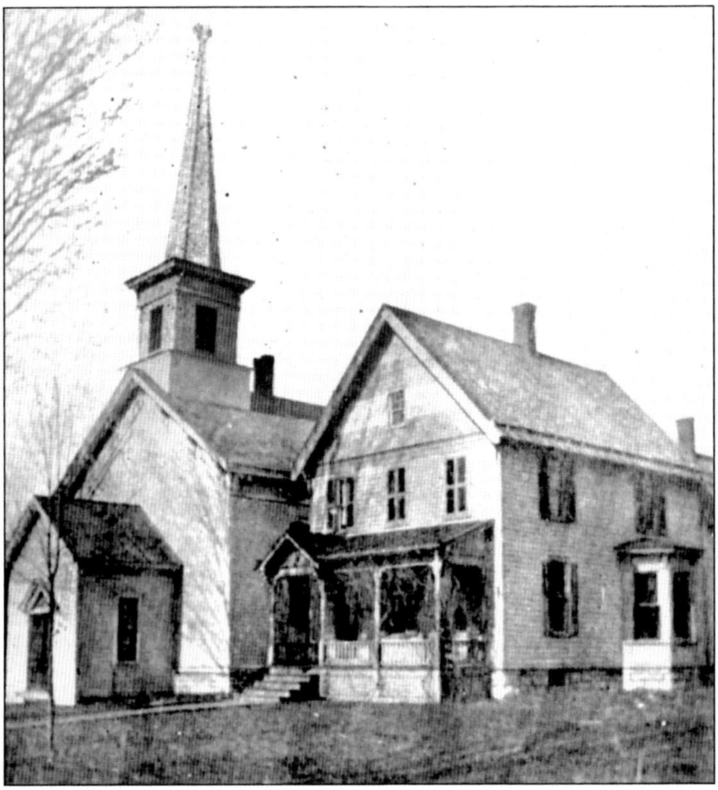

The Newport Methodist Church was built in 1870. The white frame structure of simple design has brackets under the roofline of the entrance and a small belfry. In 1954, it was extensively damaged by fire. An alliance between this congregation and the Poland Methodist Church continued until the early 1920s, when the Poland church closed. The Newport United Methodist Church is active to this day.

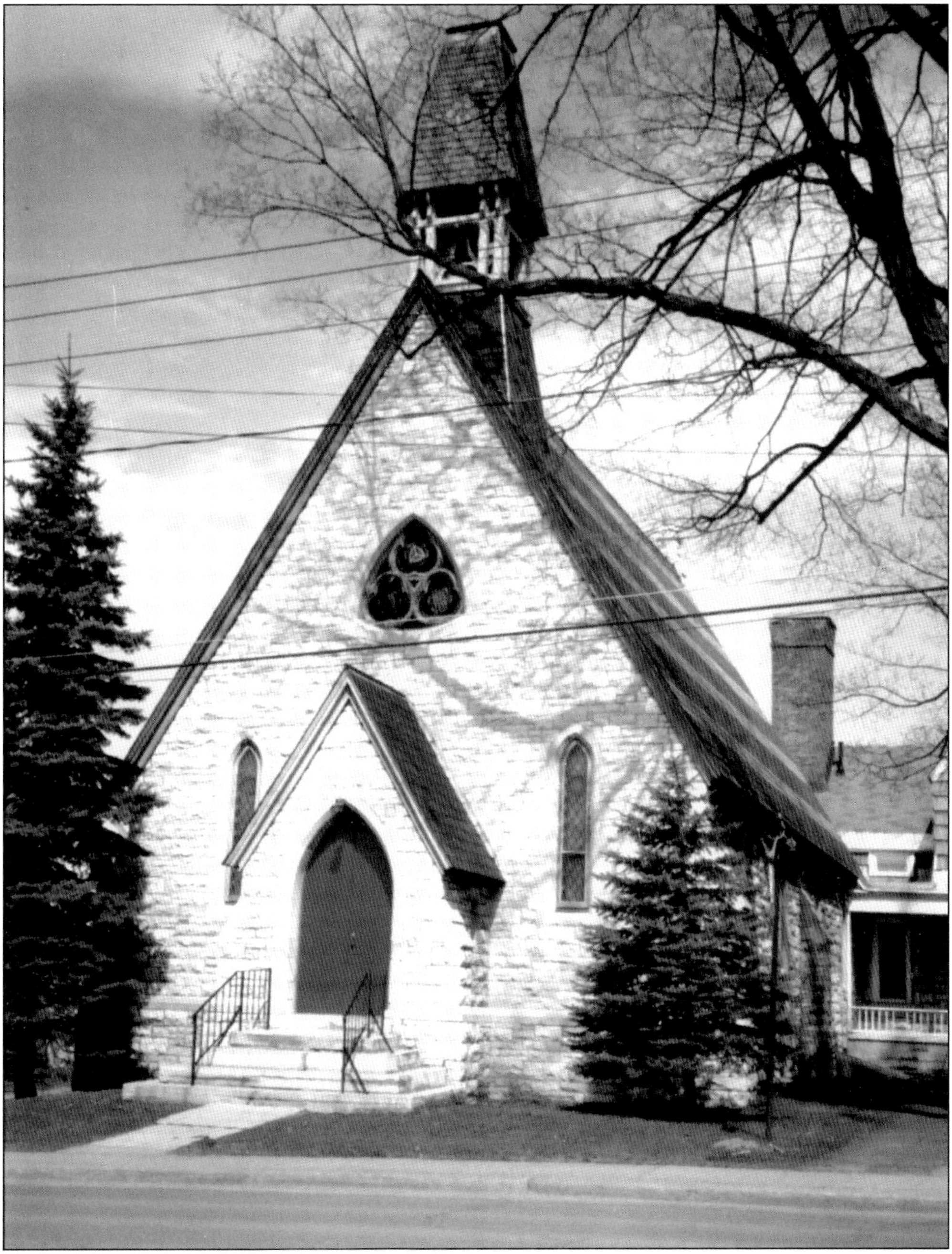

St. Michael's Episcopal Church in Middleville started as a mission of the Fairfield Episcopal Church in 1871–1872. Prior to that time, Episcopal services were held in the Union Church, which was shared with the Methodists and Universalists. The land on which St. Michael's was built was purchased from Varnum Kenyon for $600. The Kenyons maintained the right to "own, possess and enjoy two pews to be selected by them out of all pews" in the new church. The church and the rectory were constructed of limestone at a cost of $11,000. In 1959, St. Michael's and Trinity Church in Fairfield were consolidated. Worship services are held at Trinity Church during July and August and at St. Michael's during the rest of the year.

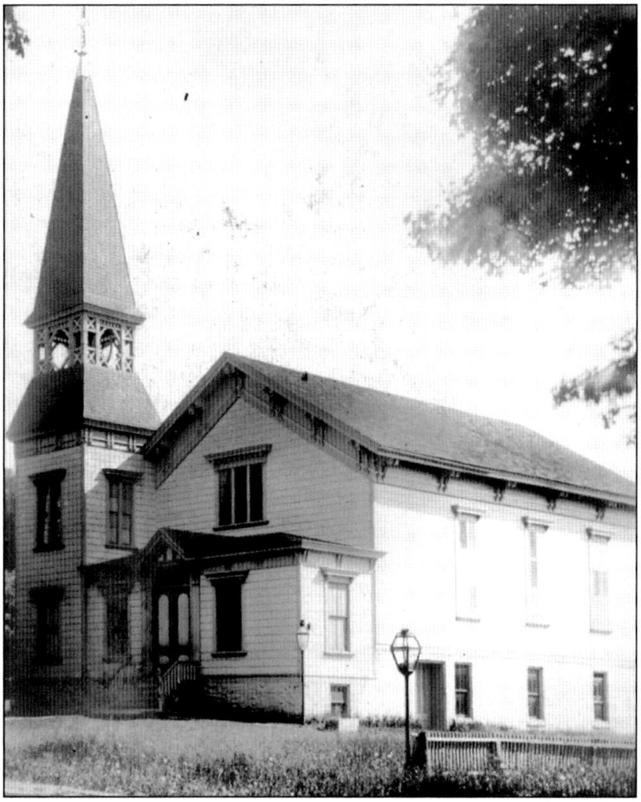

The Poland Baptists organized in 1840 in a schoolhouse at Brayton's Corners as a branch of the Norway Free Will Baptists. In 1844, a church was erected across the road from the present Baptist church. The Baptist church shown in this picture was constructed in 1872. The roof brackets, the elaborate design at the base of the belfry, and the high stone foundation are typical of that era. In 1912, the congregation was received into the Mohawk River Baptist Association. In 1937, it became known as the Community Baptist Church of Poland. From 1960 to 1994, the Poland and Newport Baptist churches formed a parish council and shared a minister and finances. Each church now functions independently.

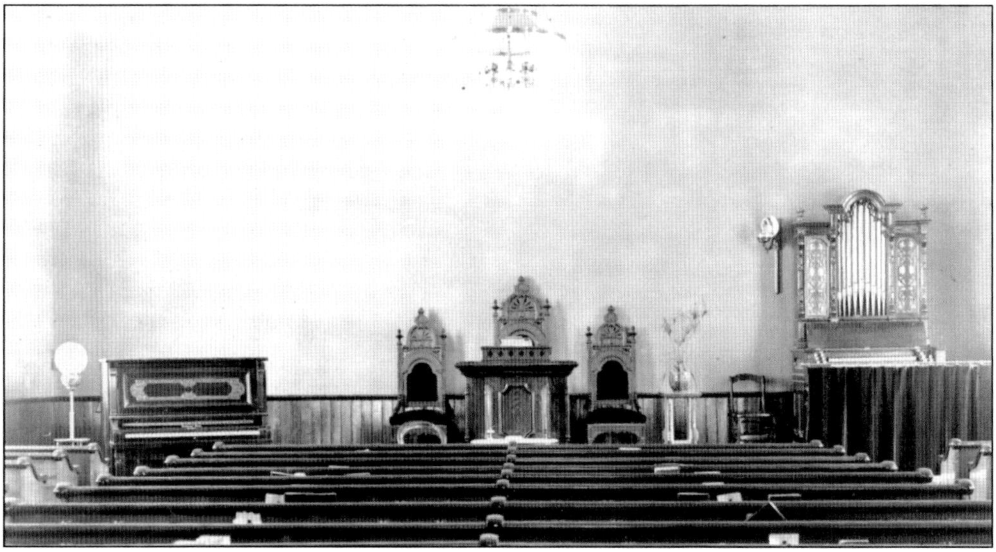

This interior view of the Poland Baptist church shows no center aisle between the pews. The choir sang from the back of the church. In the early 1900s, five rooms were added, a pipe organ was given to the church, stained-glass windows were installed, and a baptistery was built. Many other renovations have been made over the years, including the installation of an elevator in 1989 to make the sanctuary wheelchair accessible. The 100th anniversary was celebrated in 1972 with a dedication of the redecorated sanctuary.

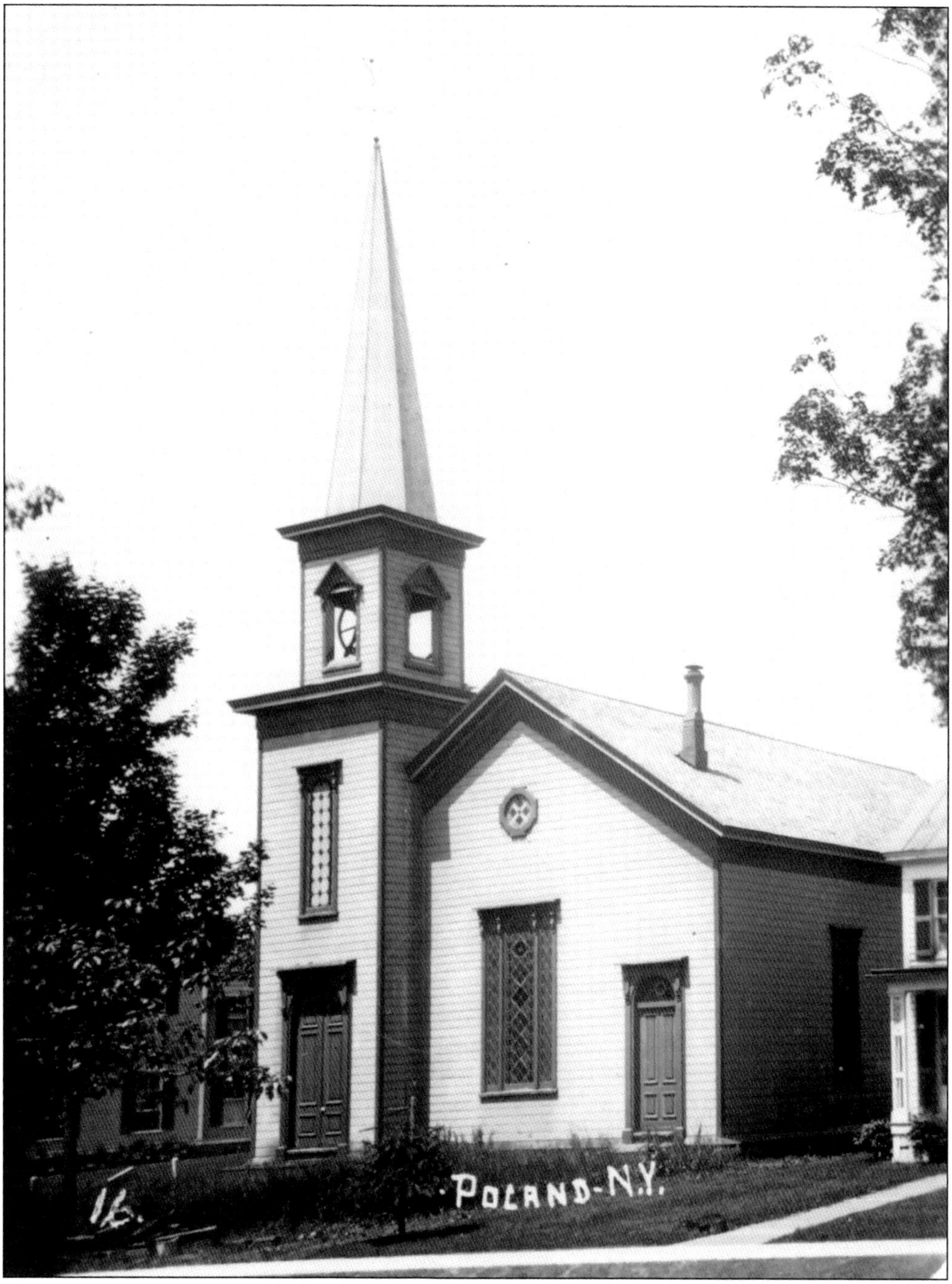

The Poland Methodists worshiped in various places before their church was built in 1875–1876 on Cold Brook Street in Poland. For a time the parishioners met in a hall owned by Peter Countryman, who ran a large tannery nearby. One of the tannery hands acted as sexton and called the people to church meetings by ringing the tannery bell. The new church was debt free by 1880, just four years after its dedication. Services were discontinued in 1932 due to a lack of financial support and a decline in membership. The church building was demolished in 1940 for salvage lumber.

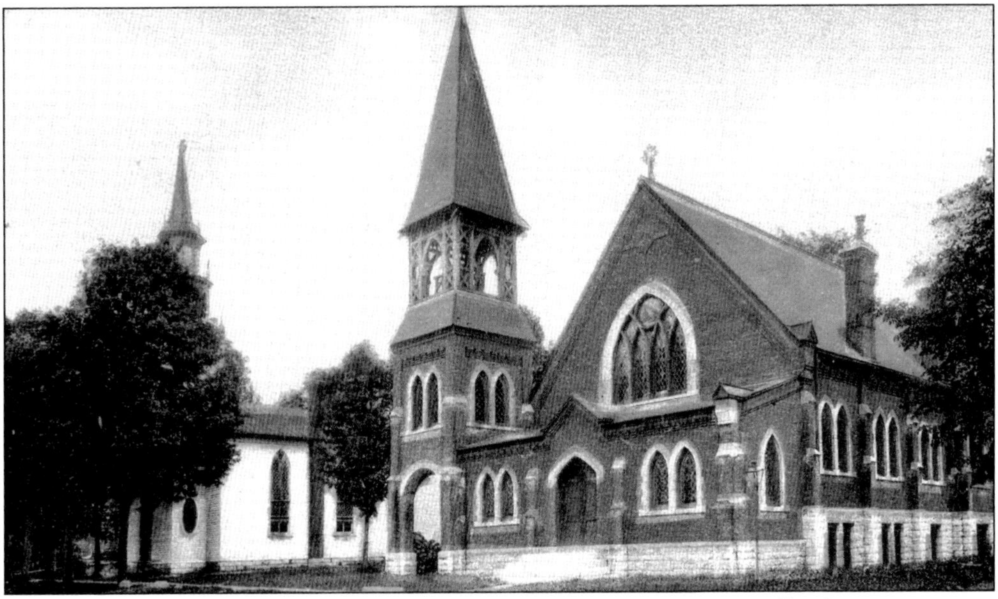

The First Universalist Society of Middleville was organized in 1835. Initially, the congregation shared the Union church with the Methodists and Episcopalians. In 1881, the Universalists' church, known as the Church of the Messiah, was built on land next to the Union church. Services were discontinued in the 1930s. Since then, the building has been used for many purposes. It has housed a machine shop, the Mank Manufacturing Company, a plastic molding workshop, and an apartment.

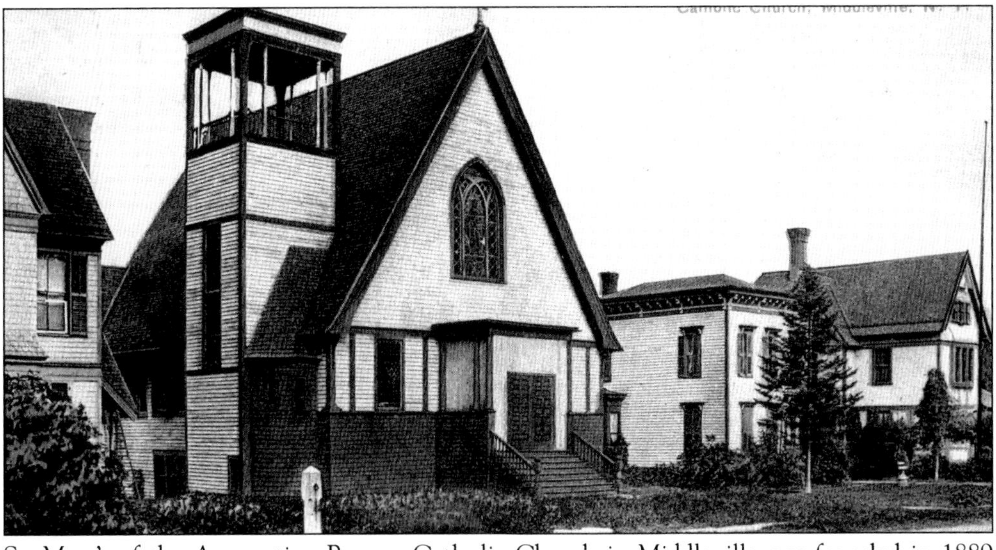

St. Mary's of the Assumption Roman Catholic Church in Middleville was founded in 1889 upon the encouragement of Rev. Herfkins, pastor of Old St. John's in Newport. The church was of wood frame construction and siding. In 1960, it was re-sided with aluminum. In the early 1900s, side altars (probably from St. John's) were added in the alcoves, and the windows were replaced with new ones, including a beautiful stained-glass one depicting the Assumption of the Virgin Mary. In 1891, Emma Seavey became the first baby to be baptized in the new church. In the early years, the church had chairs, not pews, and a pump organ in the front of the church. A Hammond electric organ replaced the pump organ in 1950. St. Mary's remains active today.

Rev. Joseph Herbst, a missionary from St. John's in Utica, became a resident of Newport in 1858 and held services in his home for worshipers from Newport, Norway, Fairfield, and Middleville. In the 1860s, the Irish Settlement church was abandoned. A church that had formerly served the Methodists and Presbyterians in the village of Newport was purchased and used until St. John the Baptist Church was built. Land was acquired in 1894, and a rectory was completed first. On June 22, 1902, a cornerstone was laid for the new church. Constructed of native limestone, it was built in the Gothic style that stresses simple lines and pointed arches. The stonework was completed in one season, and the first mass was celebrated in June 1903. In 1956, the original slate roof was replaced with shingles, and it was again reshingled in 1986. The roof of the 100-foot steeple was replaced in 1986. The church celebrated its 100th anniversary in 2002.

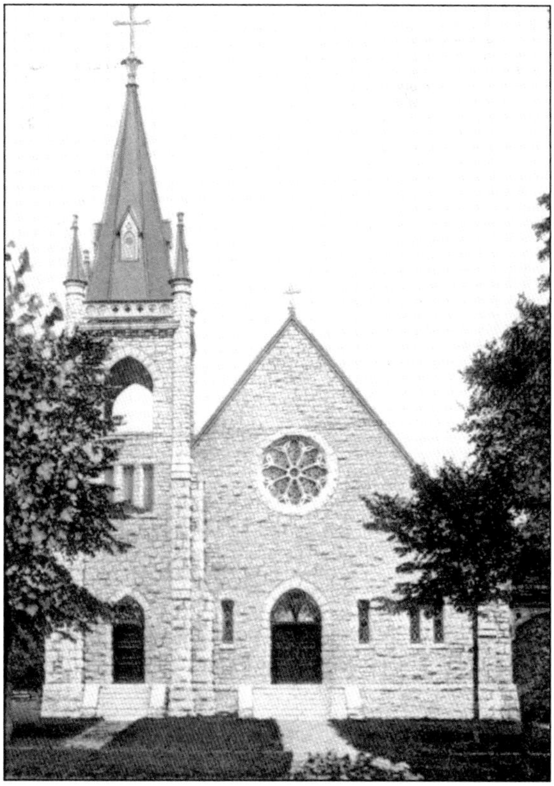

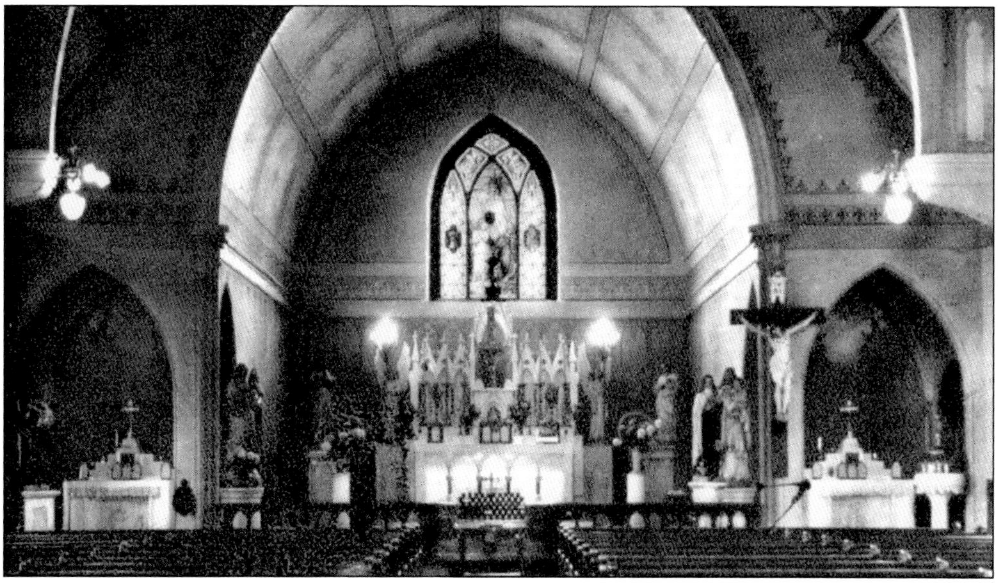

This interior view of St. John's shows the beautiful stained-glass window over the main altar, depicting John the Baptist baptizing Jesus Christ. Several changes were made in Roman Catholic churches following the 1963 Vatican Council. The most noticeable was the placement of a new altar in the sanctuary, enabling the priest to conduct the Mass facing the congregation. An Estey manual organ was replaced in 1977 with a new Moeller organ, at a cost of $25,000. The organ was dedicated in 1982 with a recital by James P. Autenrith.

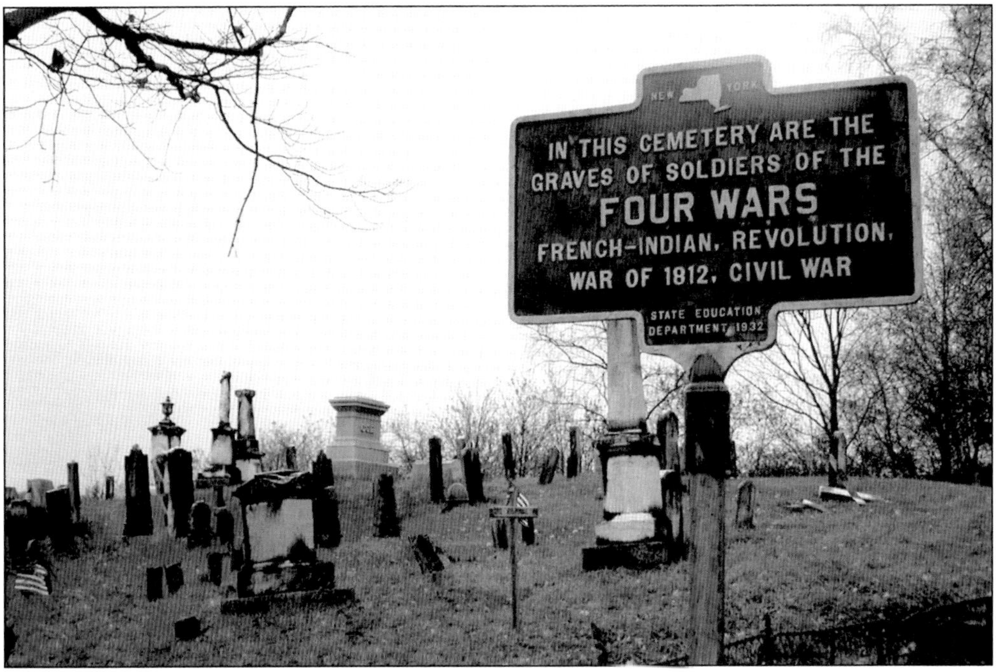

The Old Burying Ground in Norway was organized in 1803 on land deeded by early settler Dudley Smith. It had been used as a burying ground for at least 10 years. As the New York State historical marker indicates, veterans of four wars (French and Indian, American Revolution, War of 1812, and the Civil War) are buried in this cemetery. Since the placement of the marker, World War I and World War II veterans have also been buried here. Today, the cemetery is maintained by a small group of village residents.

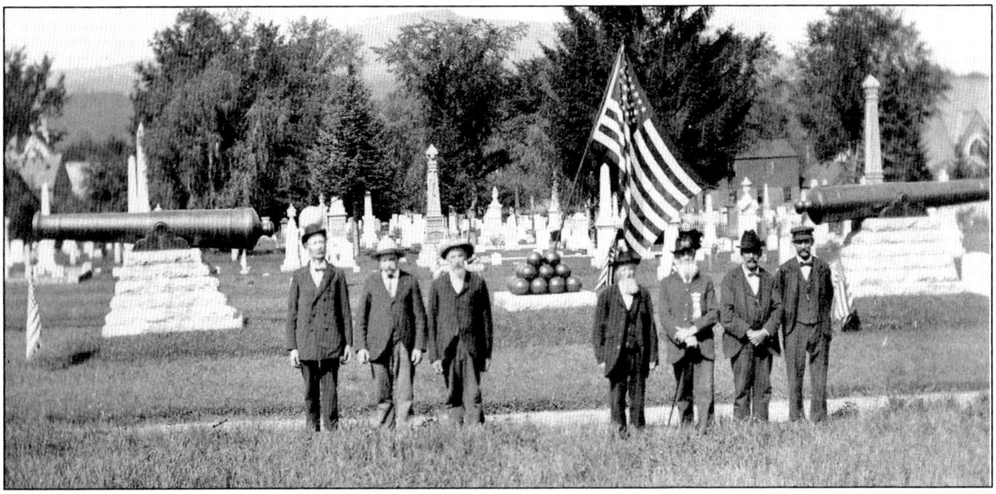

This picture shows the Soldiers' and Sailors' Monument in the Middleville Cemetery. In 1899, the Soldiers' and Sailors' Monument Association requested that the Herkimer County Board of Supervisors provide a plot of land to be used for a monument and a burial plot for veterans in the Middleville Cemetery. The county budgeted $500 for such purposes, to be shared by the Middleville Cemetery and another cemetery in Frankfort. The cannonballs were contributed to a World War II metal drive, to be melted down for the war effort. Identified in this picture are James Whiting (left), William Vincent (fifth from the left), and ? Countryman (sixth from the left).

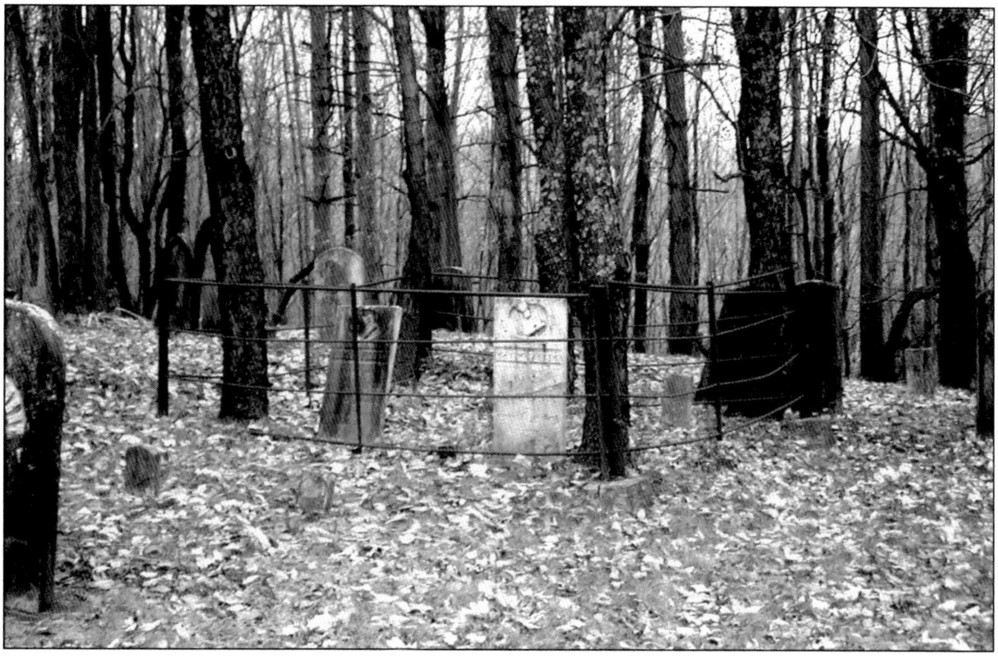

Organized in 1873, the Cold Brook Cemetery Association became the overseer of the burying ground on the knoll in back of the old Cold Brook School. This photograph shows some early monuments enclosed within an iron fence. The cemetery was a gathering place for Cold Brook girls in the early 1900s. Lena Newberry and Belle Condon, who lived on Main Street just below the hilltop cemetery, often enjoyed a summer afternoon in the cemetery with their friends.

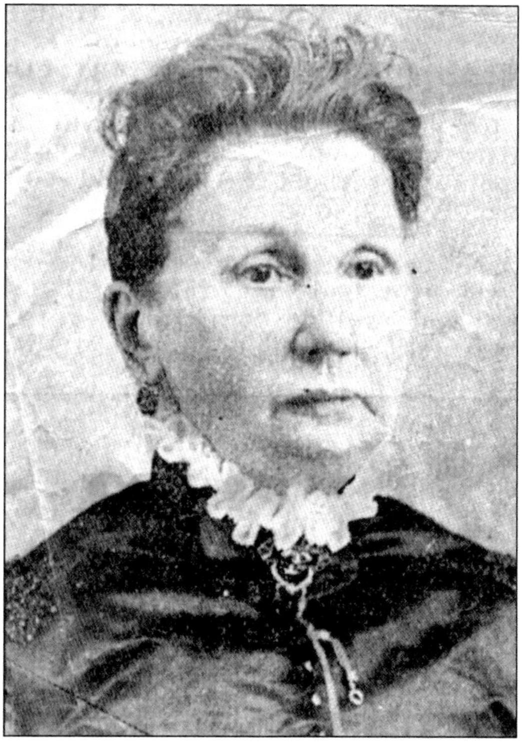

Harriett Moon, a resident of the village of Cold Brook, is said to have visited the cemetery daily in good weather to care for the graves of relatives and friends. Her obituary includes the following account of her death in 1903: "Circumstances of particular pathos attended the passing of Mrs. Harriet Moon which occurred Monday afternoon. The aged and respected lady had gone to the cemetery and placed flowers upon the grave of her late husband, Cameron Moon, who died in 1891, and had apparently started to retrace her steps to the residence of her daughter Mrs. Hattie Coonradt, when she was overcome by exhaustion as the result of her advanced age and expired in the burial ground. Becoming alarmed as darkness approached and she failed to return, the family made search and there found her dead."

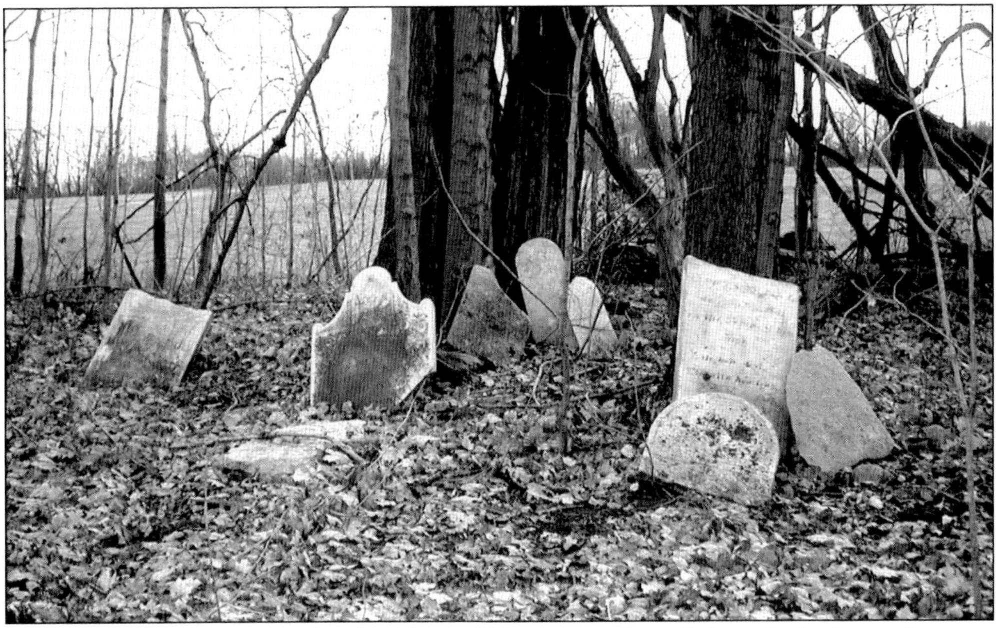

Members of the early pioneer family of Samuel Sherman are buried along the hedgerow between their former farm property and the road from Norway to the Hurricane, now known as the Sulphur Springs Road. Samuel Sherman's stone, with a scalloped top, is the one pictured on the left. It bears the date of his death, June 10, 1822.

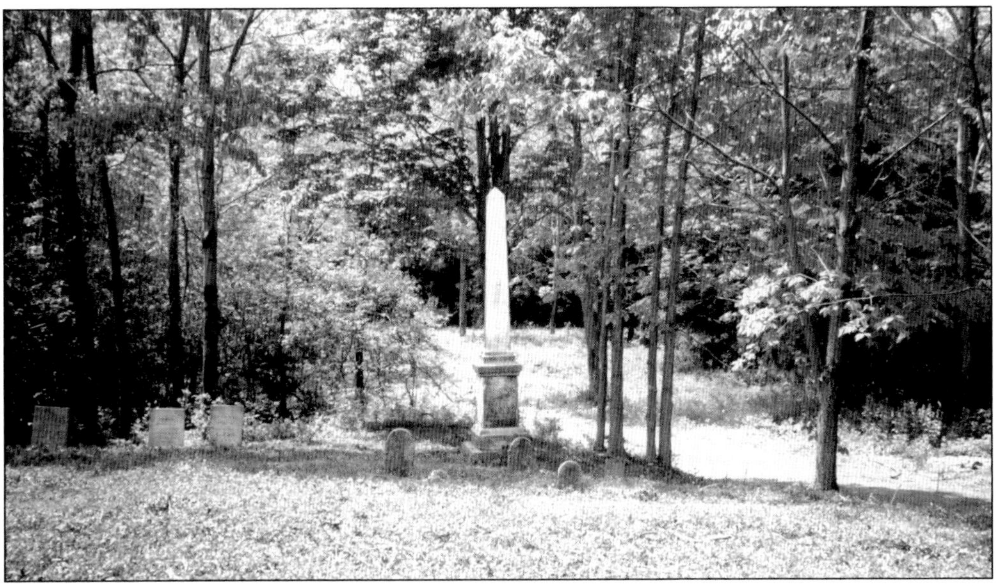

Hardscrabble Cemetery, on Hardscrabble Road in Fairfield, was formerly known as the Bushnell Cemetery. Abandoned as years went by, the cemetery became overgrown with brush and vegetation. In 1993, an effort to restore the cemetery was led by Edward Dedicke. He cleared the area and uncovered many stones. It became a Dedicke family effort to maintain the cemetery. One of the earliest burials in this cemetery was that of Jonathan Sherwood, who died in 1791. Sherwoods, Bushnells, Gages, and other early families were laid to rest in this graveyard.

Six

EARLY ENTREPRENEURS

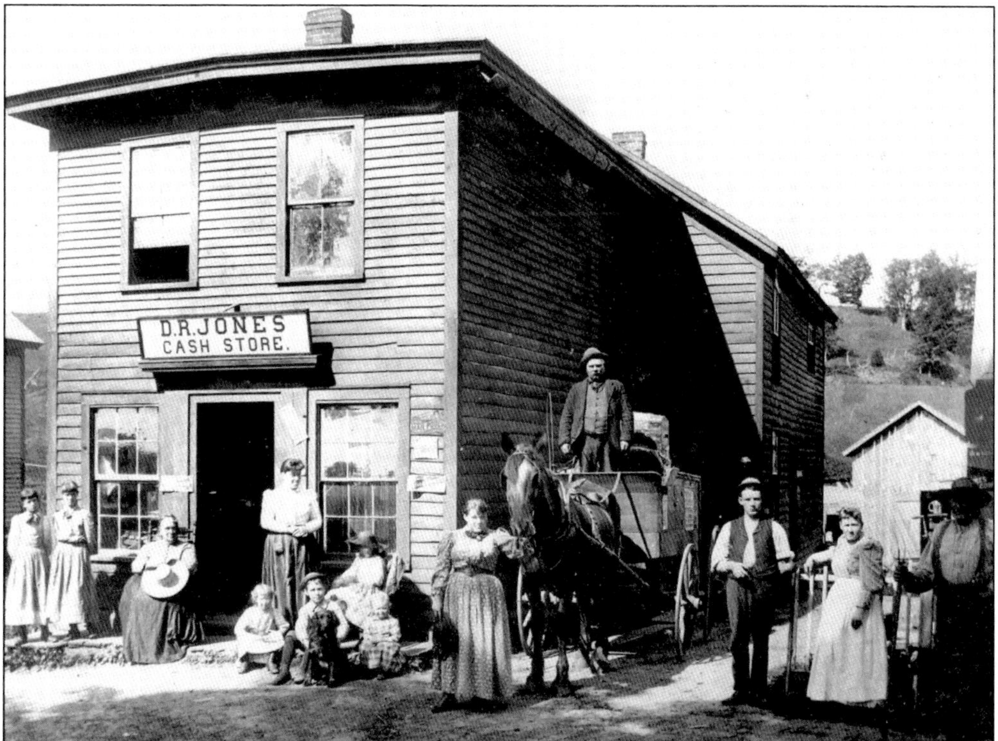

In the second half of the 19th century, the growing population brought demands for goods and services. The early settlers had brought with them trades and talents that served not only the local community but also the steady stream of travelers through the region. Blacksmith shops, wagon shops, general stores, banks, and post offices set up businesses in the villages. This c. 1900 view shows the David R. Jones Cash Store in Grant. Jones dealt in general merchandise and used the horse and cart shown here to go about the countryside selling his products. During the building of the Hinckley Dam, Jones moved one of his buildings to Hinckley, where he supplied the construction workers with food and dry goods.

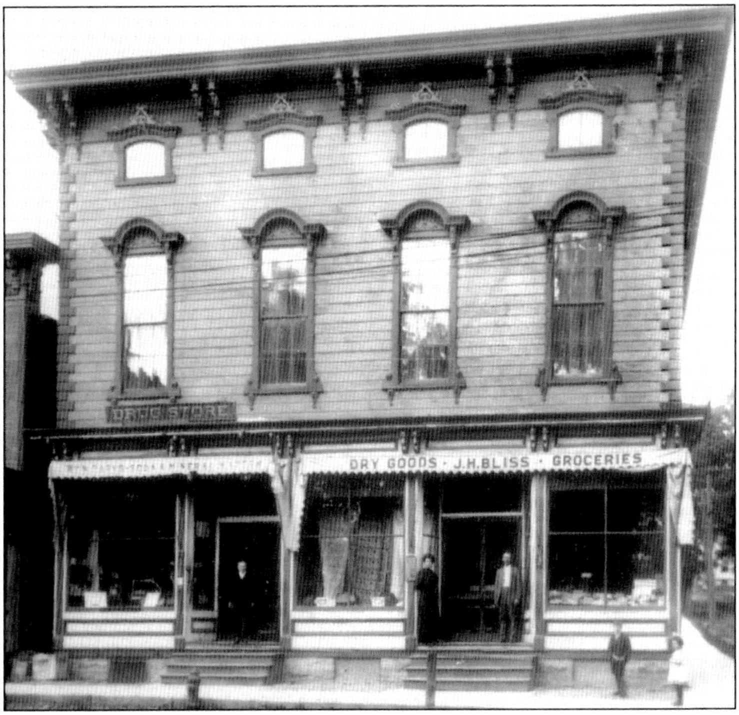

This business, located on the corner of Main and School Streets in Newport, opened as a general merchandise store in 1893. Jacob H. Bliss was its proprietor for 25 years until his retirement in 1918. The building continues to be a mainstay of Newport's businesses, now housing Autenrith's Furniture Store.

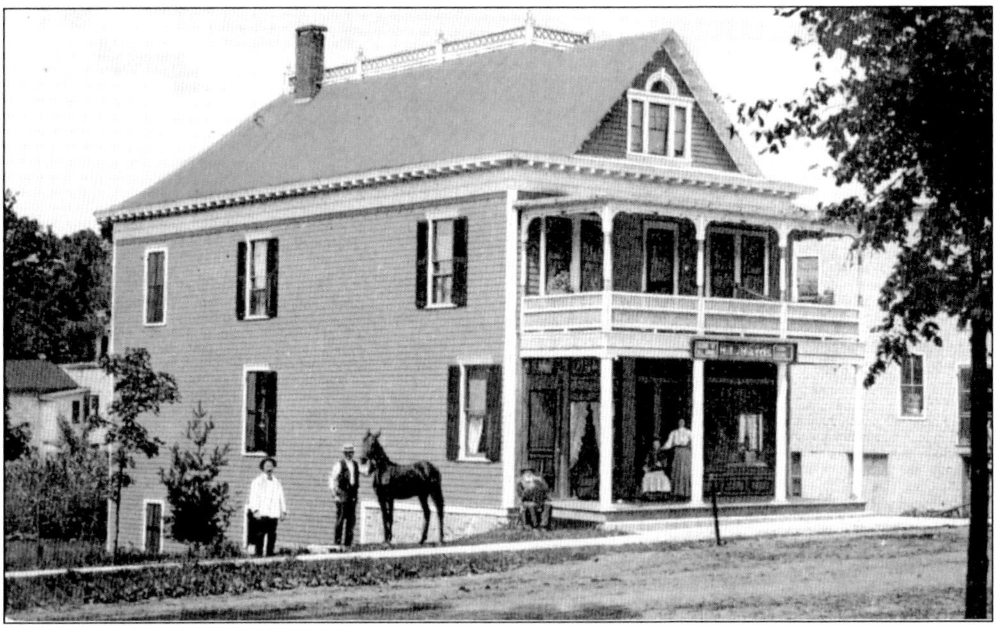

Mortimer Harris built a grocery store in 1905 on the site of an old harness shop in Poland. Harris operated the first ice-cream parlor in Poland and later built a dancing pavilion on the back of the building. A grocery and meat business has remained in the building for nearly 100 years, with Haver and Sons being the most recent owners.

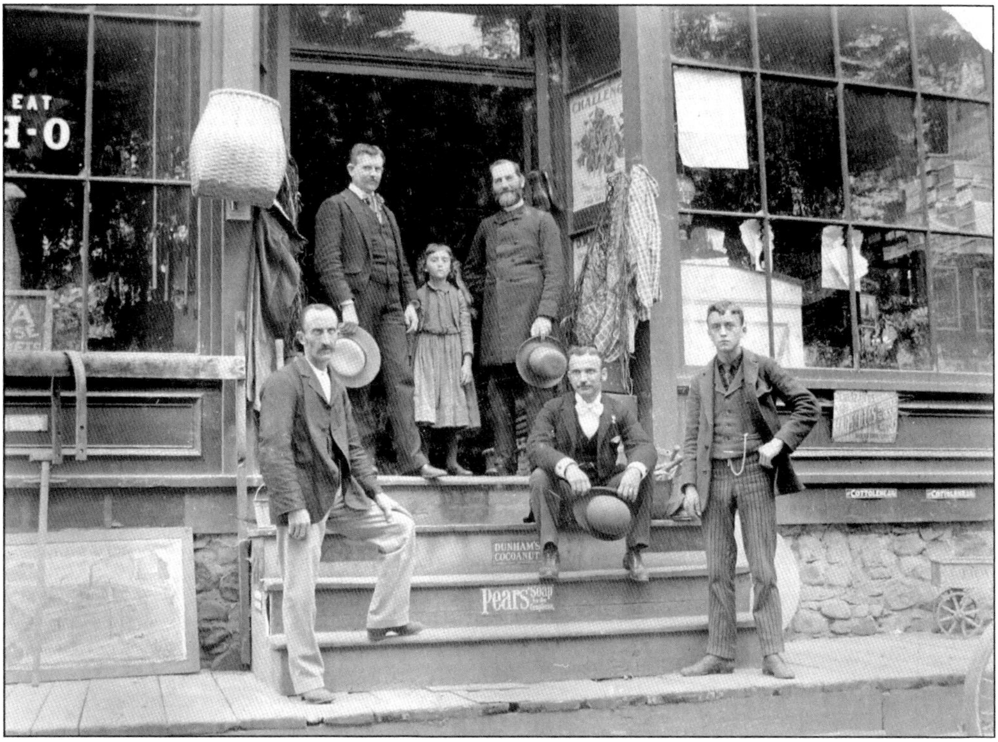

Robbins Read and George Read opened a general store in Poland in 1872. The Read brothers' business was destroyed by fire twice. After rebuilding the second time, the Reads moved the building to the corner of Main and Mill Streets. Over the years, many businesses have begun and ended here. A hardware store continued at the site through several owners. Other enterprises included furniture, undertaking, millinery, movie theater, post office, Victory store, barbershop, and liquor store. The building was razed in the early 1990s. The site is now a parking lot.

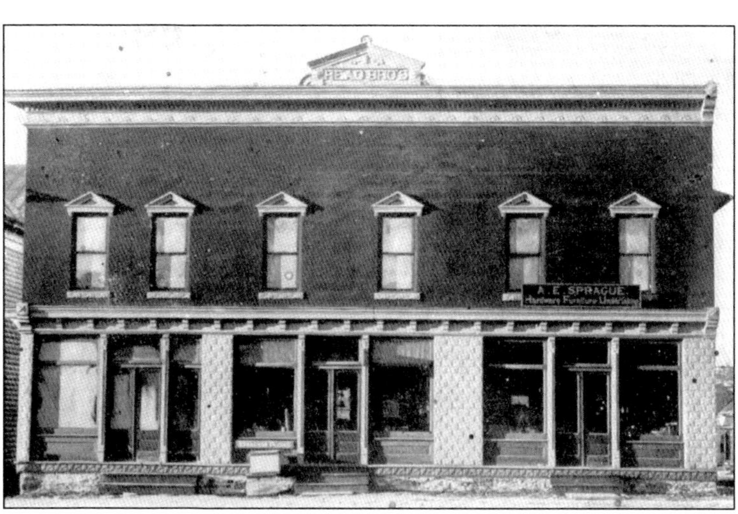

This view shows the Sprague Undertaking and Furniture Business, on Main Street in Poland. The business was sold to W.E. Autenrith and Sons in 1925.

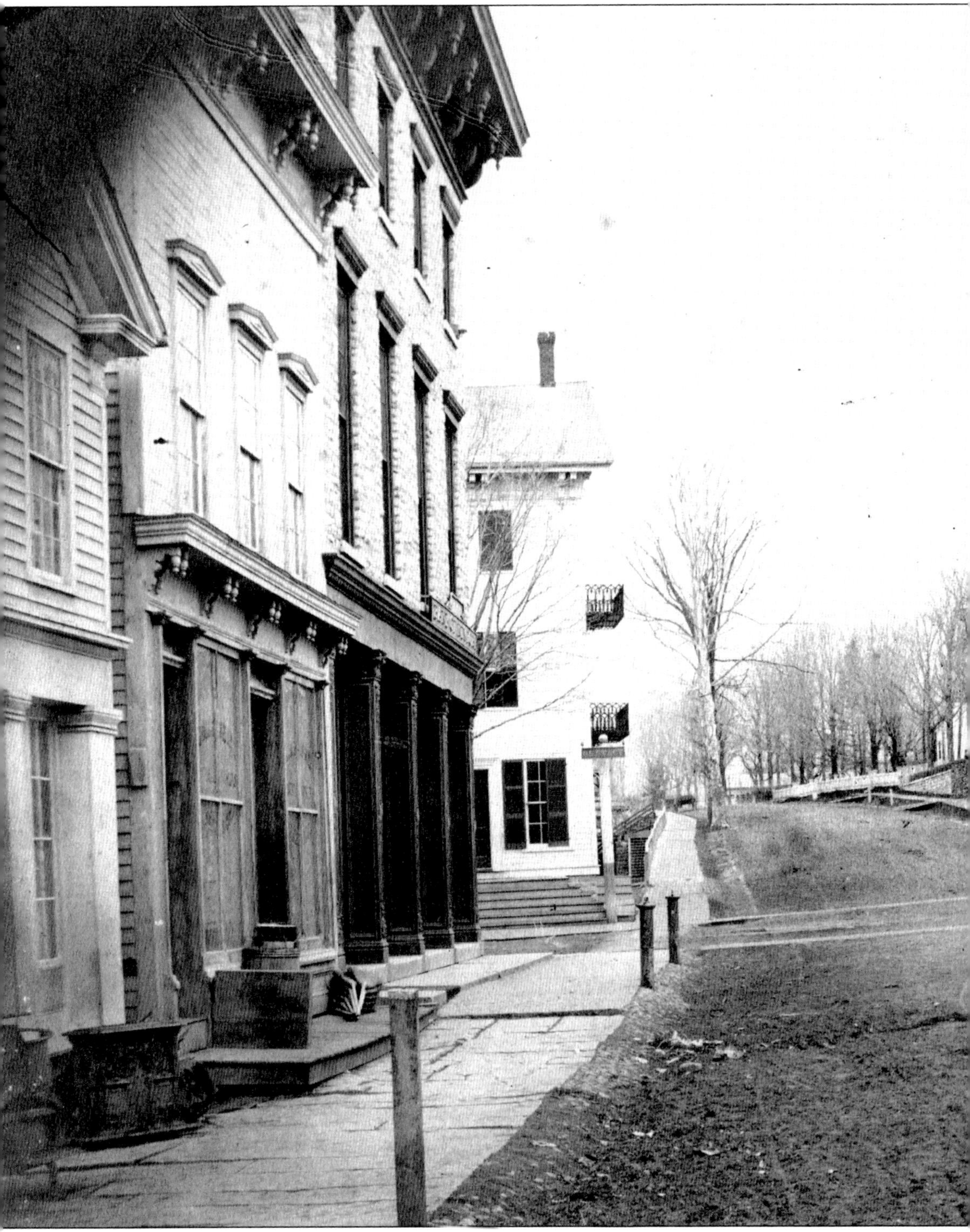

This photograph of a Newport street scene was taken looking north toward the stately homes on Christian Hill. On the right is what was known as the Opera Block, as it originally housed a theater. Orin Spencer opened a harness shop here c. 1840. Elisha Thorton later operated it,

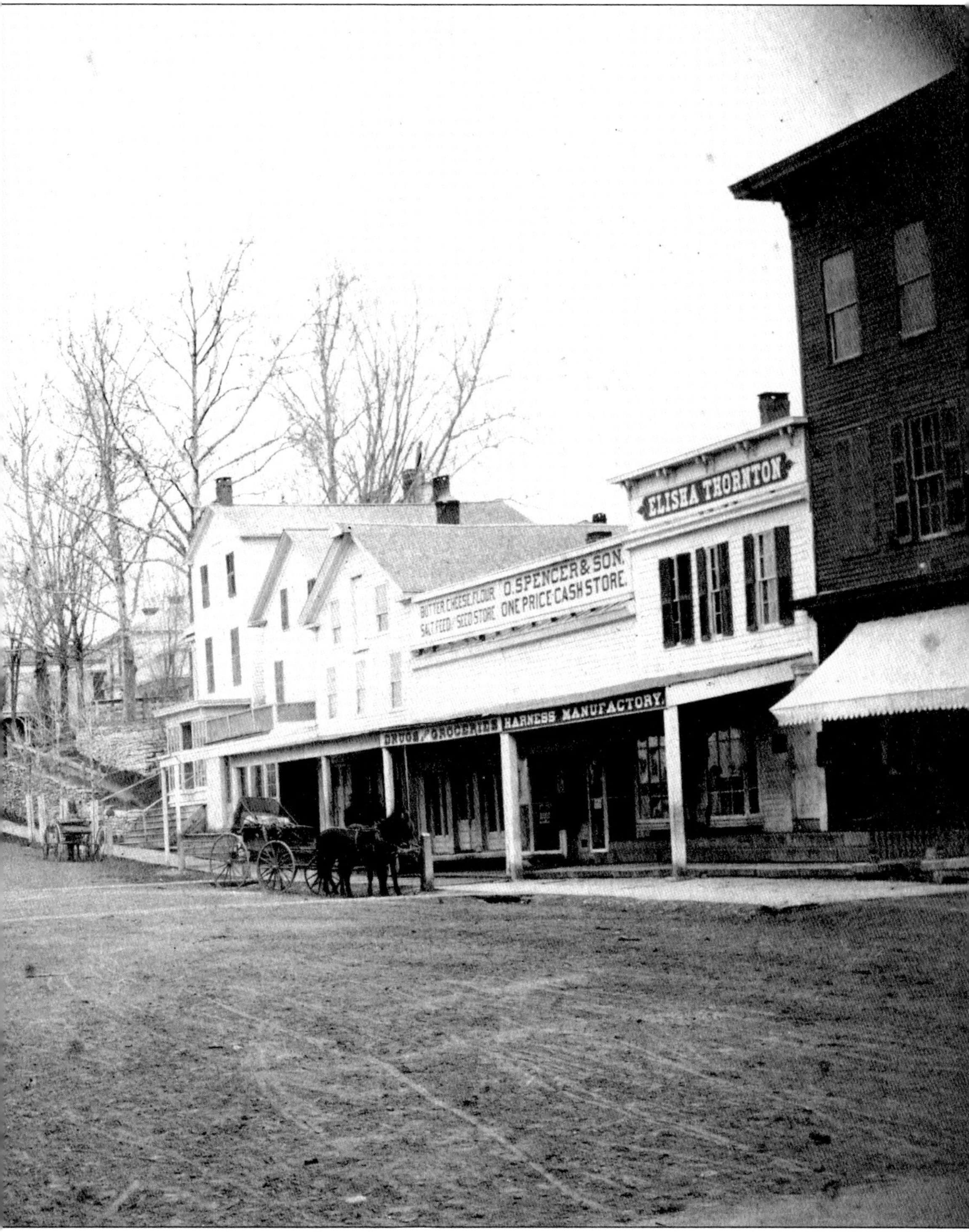

as shown in this picture. Next to the harness shop were a drugstore and a grocery. Bridge Street intersects Main Street between the limestone bank building on the left and the Hotel Post on the opposite corner. Millard Pearce operated a general store in the bank building.

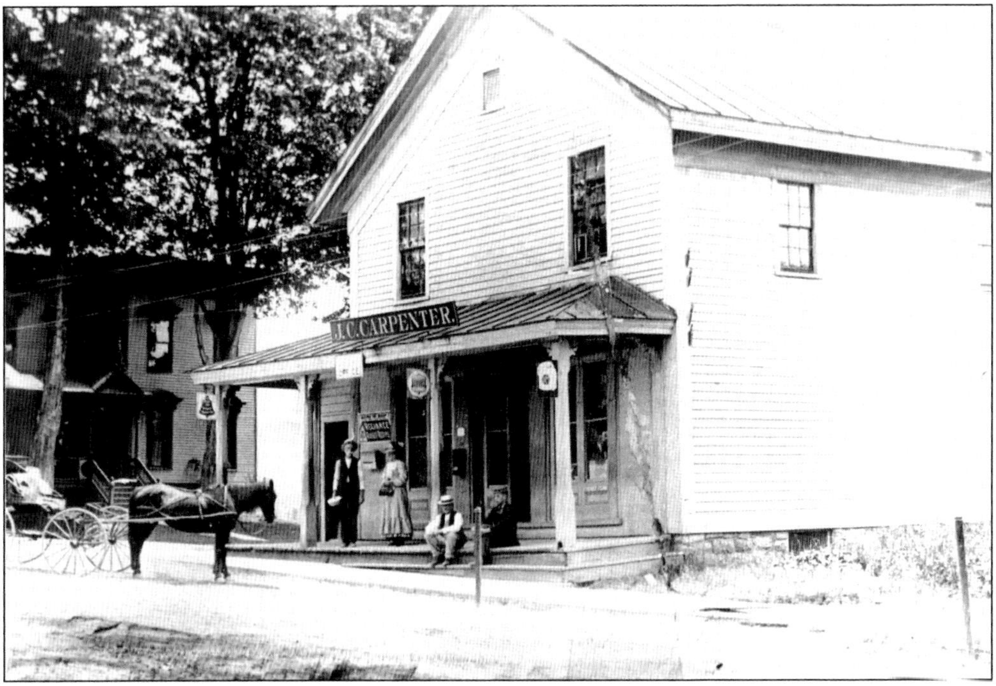

In the mid-1800s, Cameron Moon started a general grocery and dry goods store on the corner of Military Road and Main Street in Cold Brook. At the beginning of the 20th century, A.B. Coonradt and his sons, Frank and Leon Coonradt, operated the store for a number of years. The Carpenter family purchased the store *c.* 1920 and ran the business for many years.

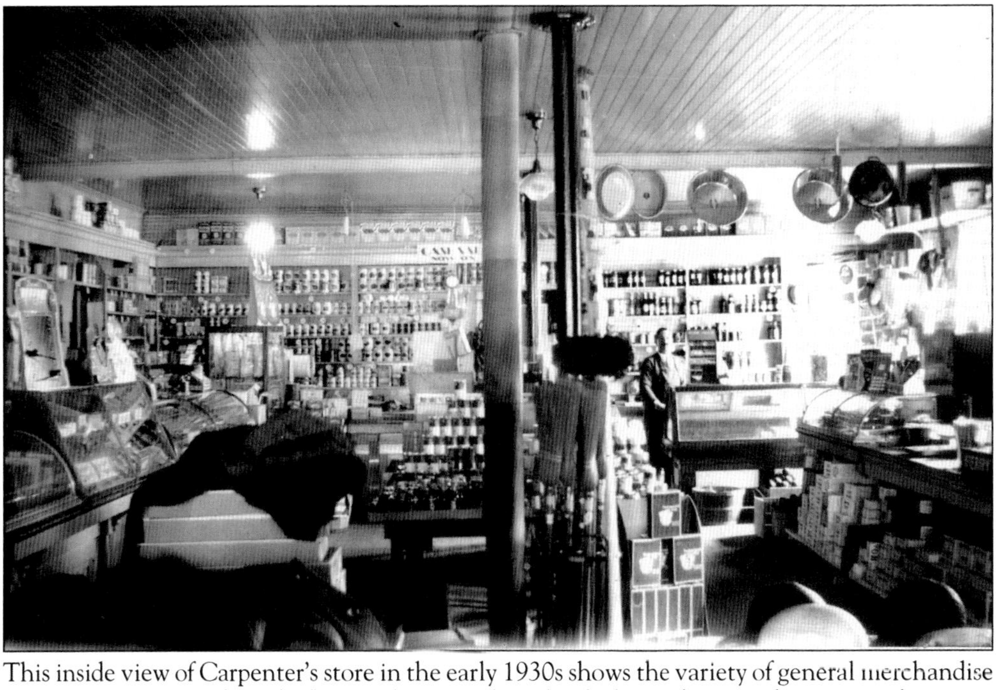

This inside view of Carpenter's store in the early 1930s shows the variety of general merchandise offered—from canned goods, flour and sugar in barrels, clothing, shoes, and patent medicines to pots and pans. A. Stevens stands in back of the counter.

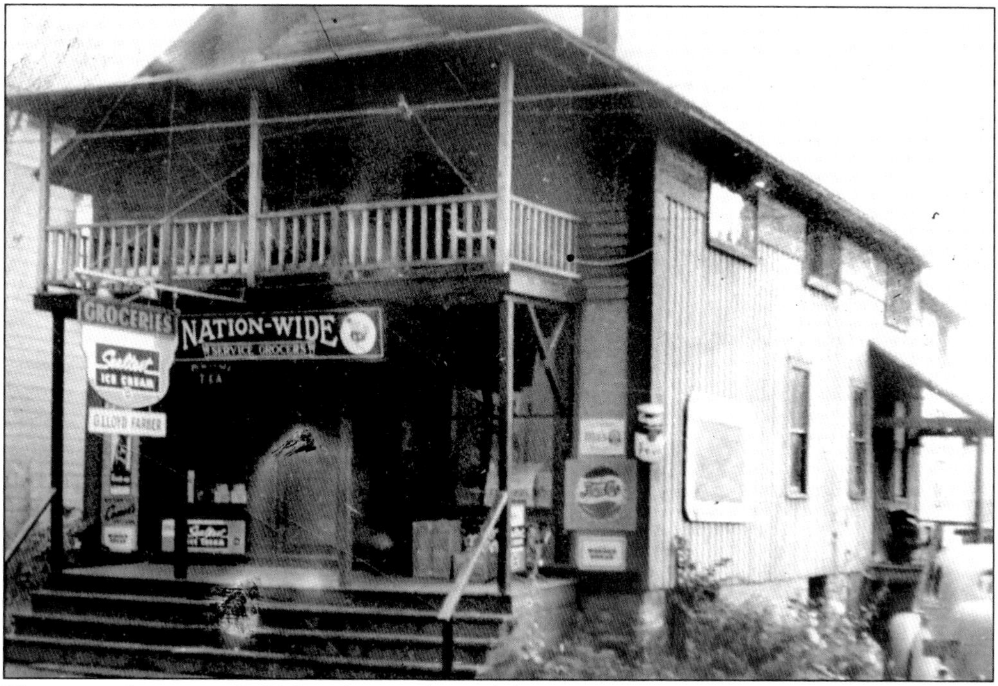

This general store in Cold Brook once housed the post office. Some of its operators over the years were Frank Forrest, David Bennett, Alex Shelp, G. Lloyd Farber, Fred Kelly, and Frank Hiney. The building was razed many years ago for a building lot.

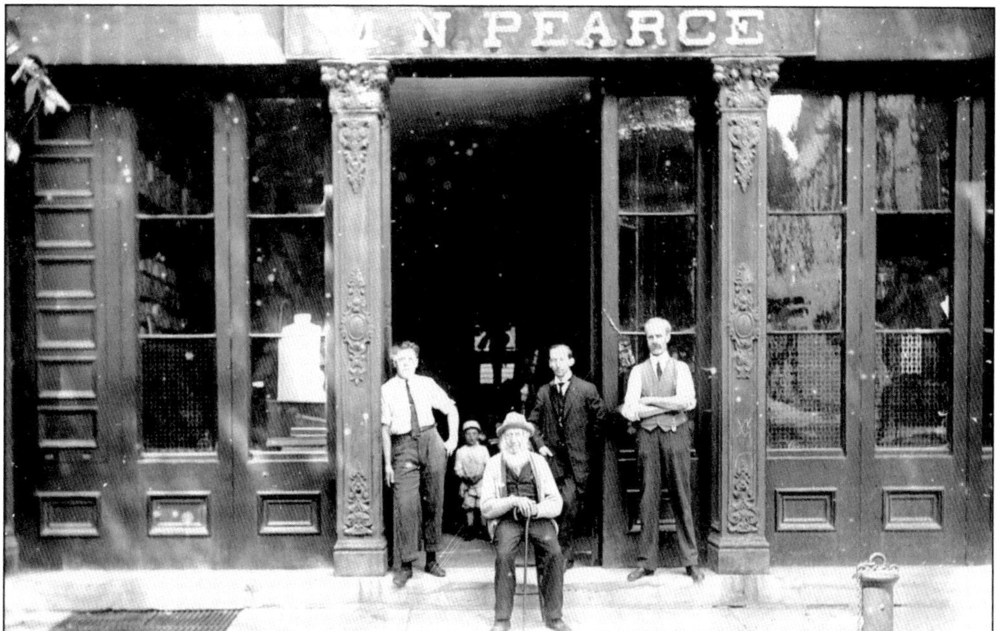

The Newport Union Store was a cooperative business started in the mid-1850s. The store was located on the Main Street side of the limestone bank building. Millard N. Pearce was a salesman for the store from 1864 until 1881, when the cooperative dissolved. Pearce purchased the stock and equipment and continued the store's operation until 1916.

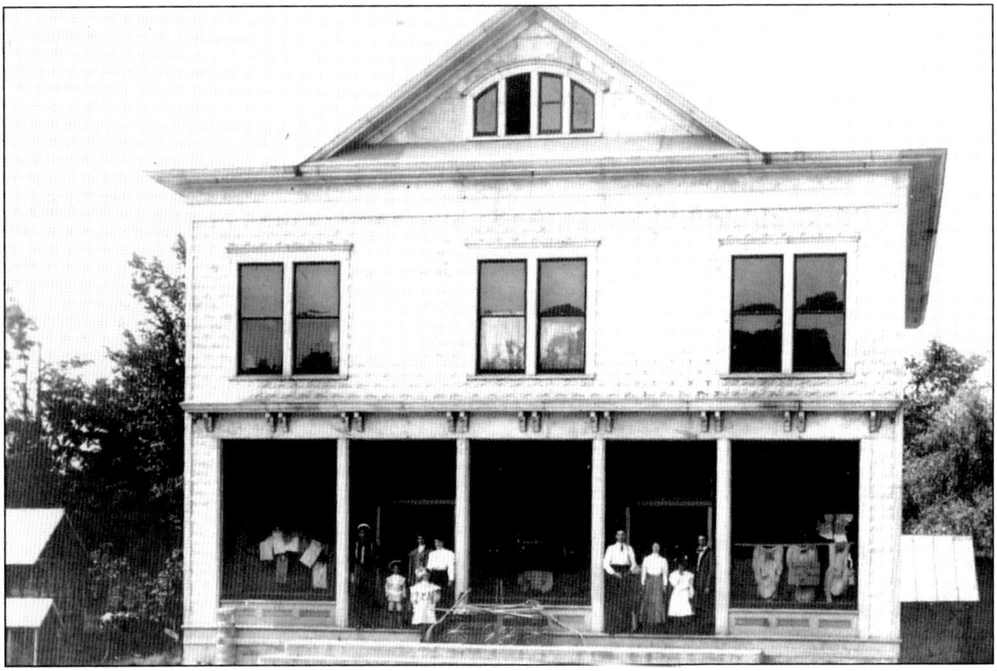

The Poland Union, a cooperative business, was established in 1853. It sold shares at $10 to $20. The goods were sold at two different prices, one for the public and one for the shareholders. The original cooperative operated in several sites in the village. The building that was constructed on this site in 1857 was destroyed by fire in 1904. The Poland Union was rebuilt that same year, with the upper story housing a law office, a tailor, and a dance class studio. J.B. Lamb, general manager of the Poland Union, ran a thriving business for several years. The store was noted for its large and varied stock. The cooperative experienced difficulties during the Depression of the 1930s and closed it doors in 1936.

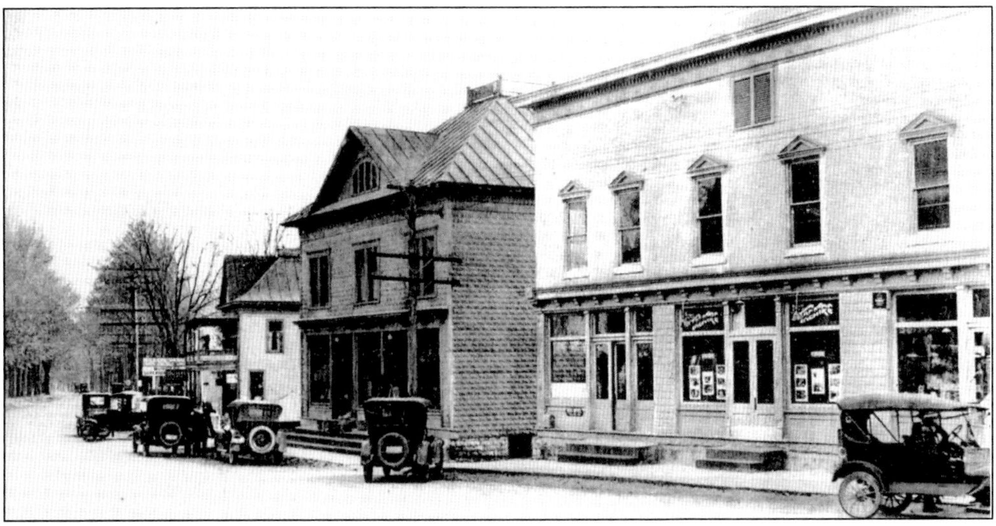

Rudolph Biebow operated a hardware store and tin shop for many years in the Read building, next to the Poland Union. Biebow's fine workmanship produced many high-quality tin utensils. Other hardware operators have included Charles Seavy, Arthur Sprague, J.J. McLoughlin, Willis Gibson, J. Harold "Dutch" Strobel, Harold Goodney, and Tom Christiano.

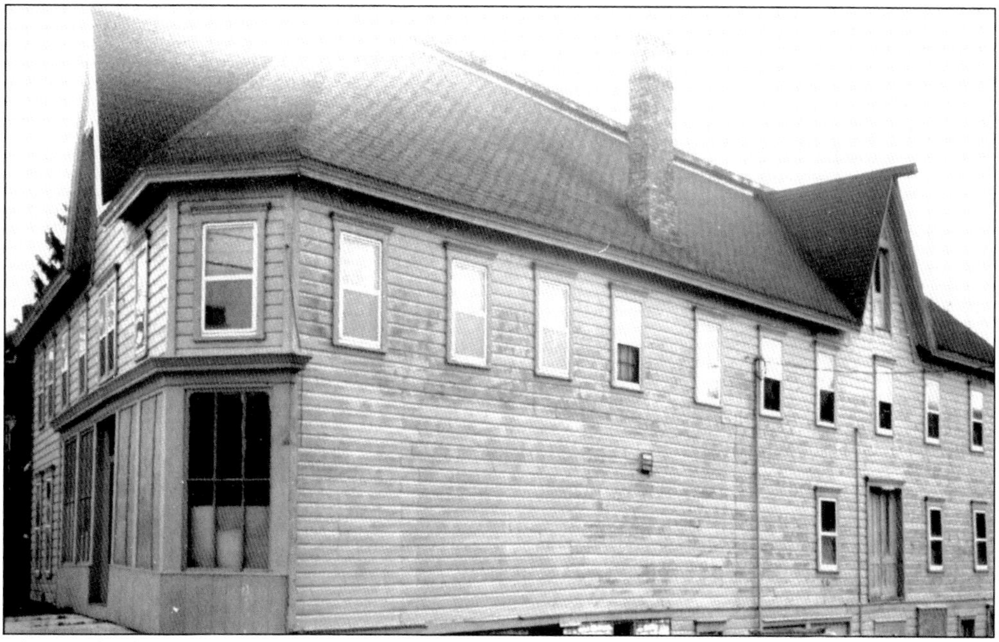

The Casler building, on the south corner of Bridge and South Main Streets in Middleville, housed the store of W.W. Mosher in 1853. The Mosher girls, Emma and Hattie, married Henry E. Jackson and Deville G. Jackson, respectively, and the Jackson brothers later operated the store. Emma and Henry's daughter Mary married George Casler, and the firm became known as Jackson and Casler. The Caslers' son George "Jack" Casler and his wife, Clara (Click), operated the store for a time. They were followed by a series of soda fountain operators. The building was later acquired and demolished by the village, and replaced by Centennial Park.

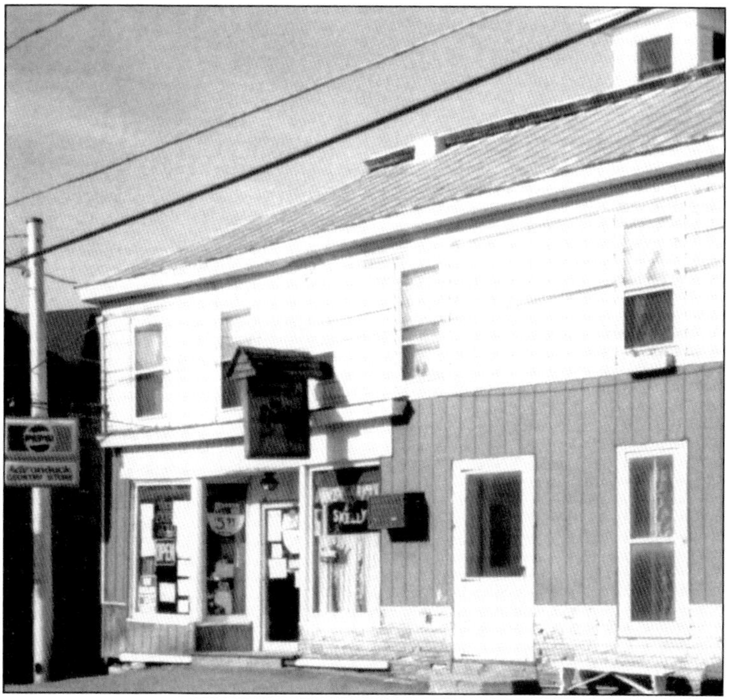

Long the site of grocery stores, this corner building opposite the Casler building in Middleville was demolished in 1993 and replaced by a Stewart's shop. Prior grocers include Kellar, Jubin, Rasbach, and Ivan Louis. Michael O'Hara ran a shoe repair shop in one side of the store during Kellar's ownership.

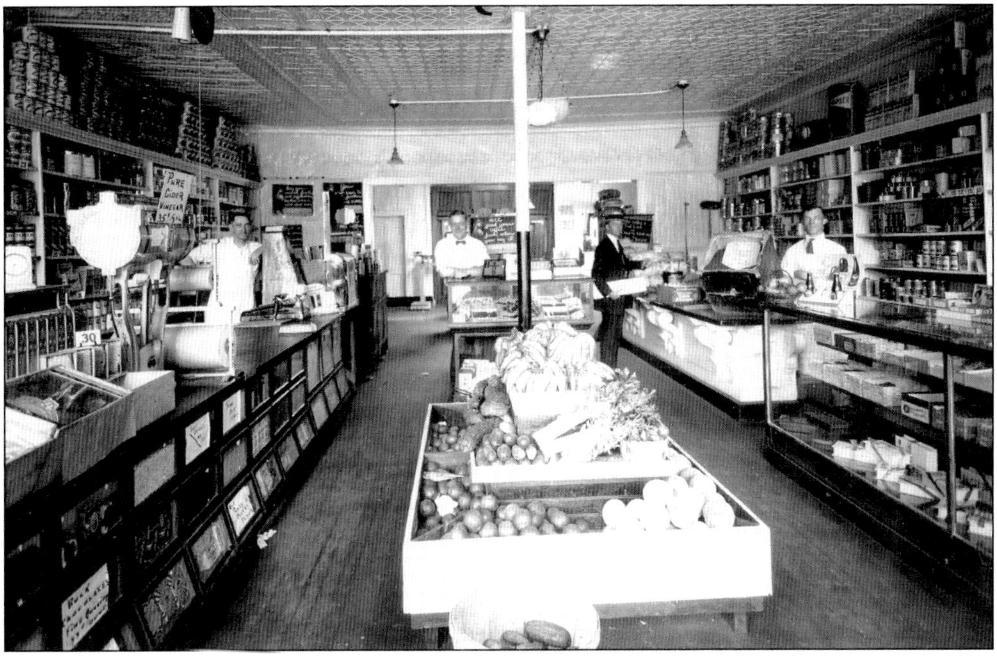

This general store and meat market was located west of the Post Hotel site on Bridge Street in Newport. Leslie Thomas ran the store from 1916 to 1936. From left to right are an unidentified store clerk, Leslie Thomas, a customer, and Harry Fralick. Note the market's tin ceiling.

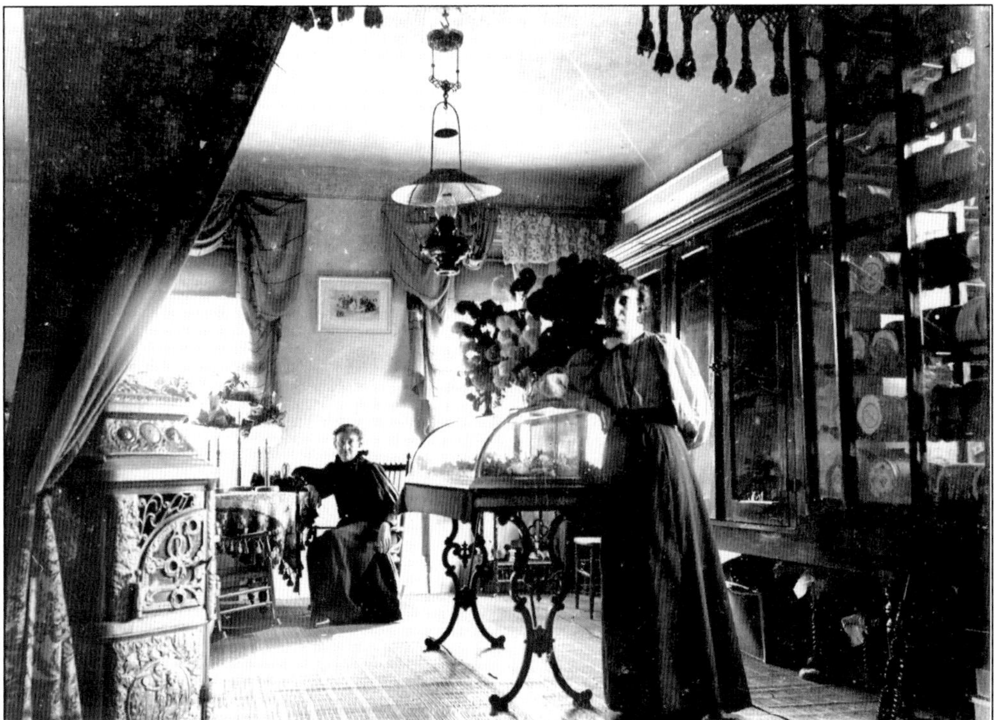

Two women pause for a moment in a specialty shop, with its clocks and figurines in the wall cabinet (right), jewelry in the glass case (center), elaborate draperies, and hanging gas light.

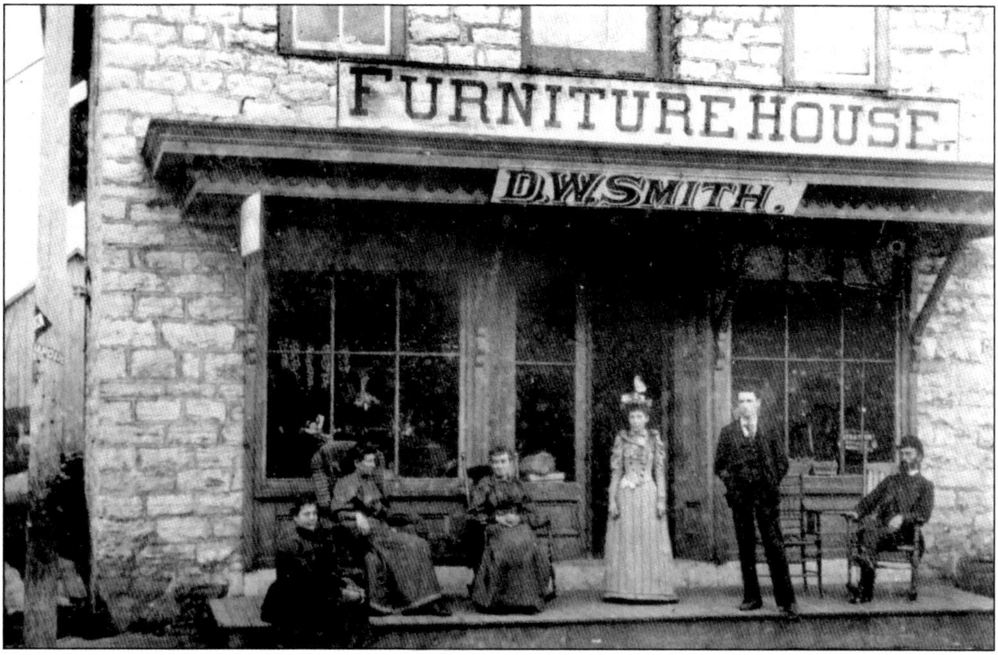

In 1859, Dexter W. Smith built this limestone building on Bridge Street in Newport. For many years it was operated as a furniture and undertaking establishment. Smith was the manufacturer of the Armback bedspring. W.E. Autenrith purchased the business in 1912. At one time it was the Fitch feed store. For the past several years, it has been the home of the Herkimer County Trust bank, recently merged with the Savings Bank of Utica and now known as SBU bank.

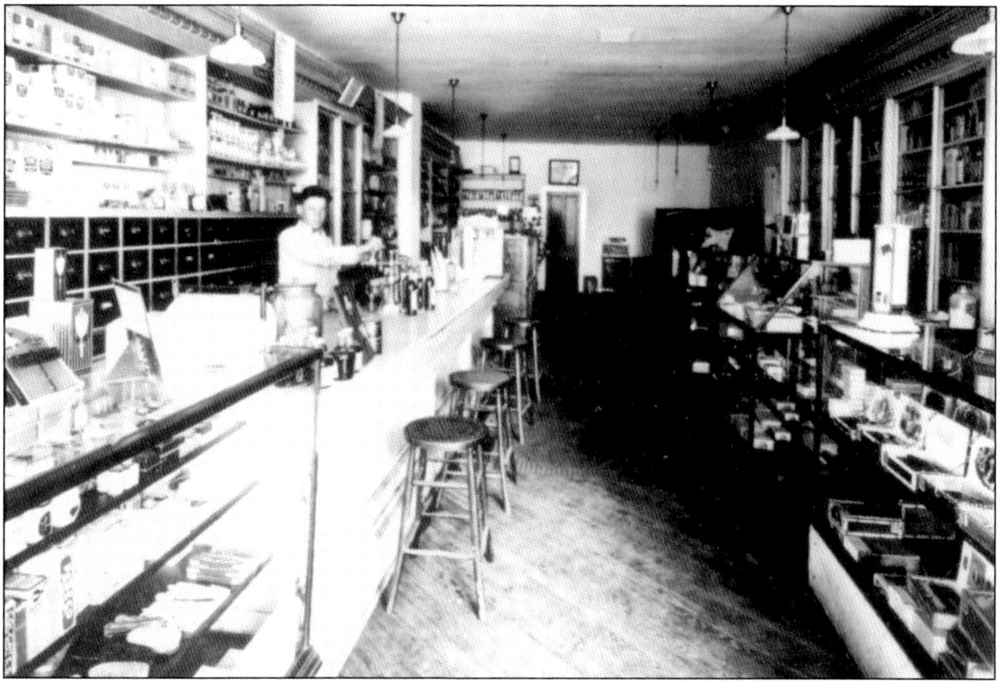

Located in the Opera Block on Main Street in Newport, Park's drugstore operated from 1893 to 1930. The soda fountain offered ice-cream cones for 5¢. John Erwin is at the counter.

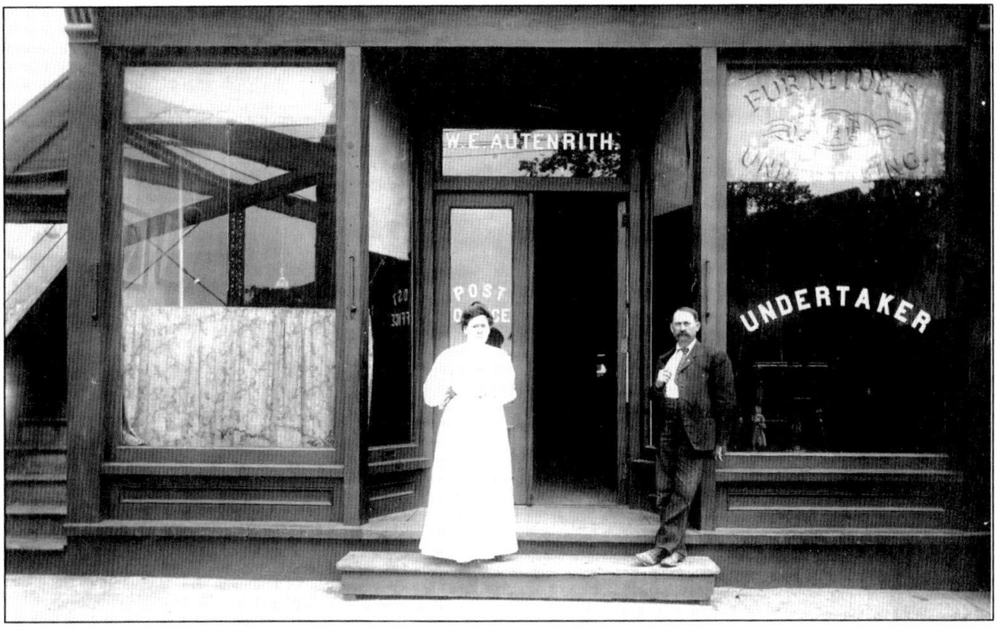

For more than 100 years, the family of W.E. Autenrith has operated a furniture and undertaking business in the Kuyahoora Valley. W.E. Autenrith (right) founded the business in 1894 in Middleville. With him is his sister Amelia. The Autenriths also operated a livery from their home, on Main Street, providing carriages for weddings and funerals. In 1912, they purchased the D.W. Smith business in Newport. W.E. Autenrith's two sons, William and Stanley Autenrith, took over the business in 1924. In 1925, they purchased Arthur Sprague's funeral and furniture business in Poland. W.E. Autenrith's great-grandson Eric Newman now owns and operates both the funeral and furniture businesses in Newport.

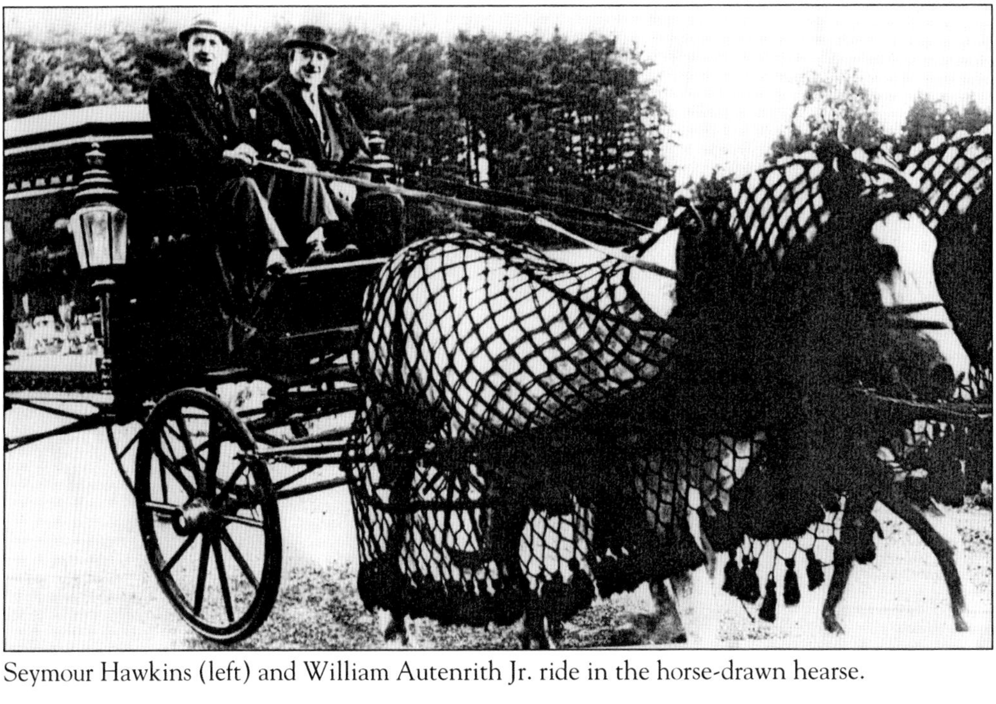

Seymour Hawkins (left) and William Autenrith Jr. ride in the horse-drawn hearse.

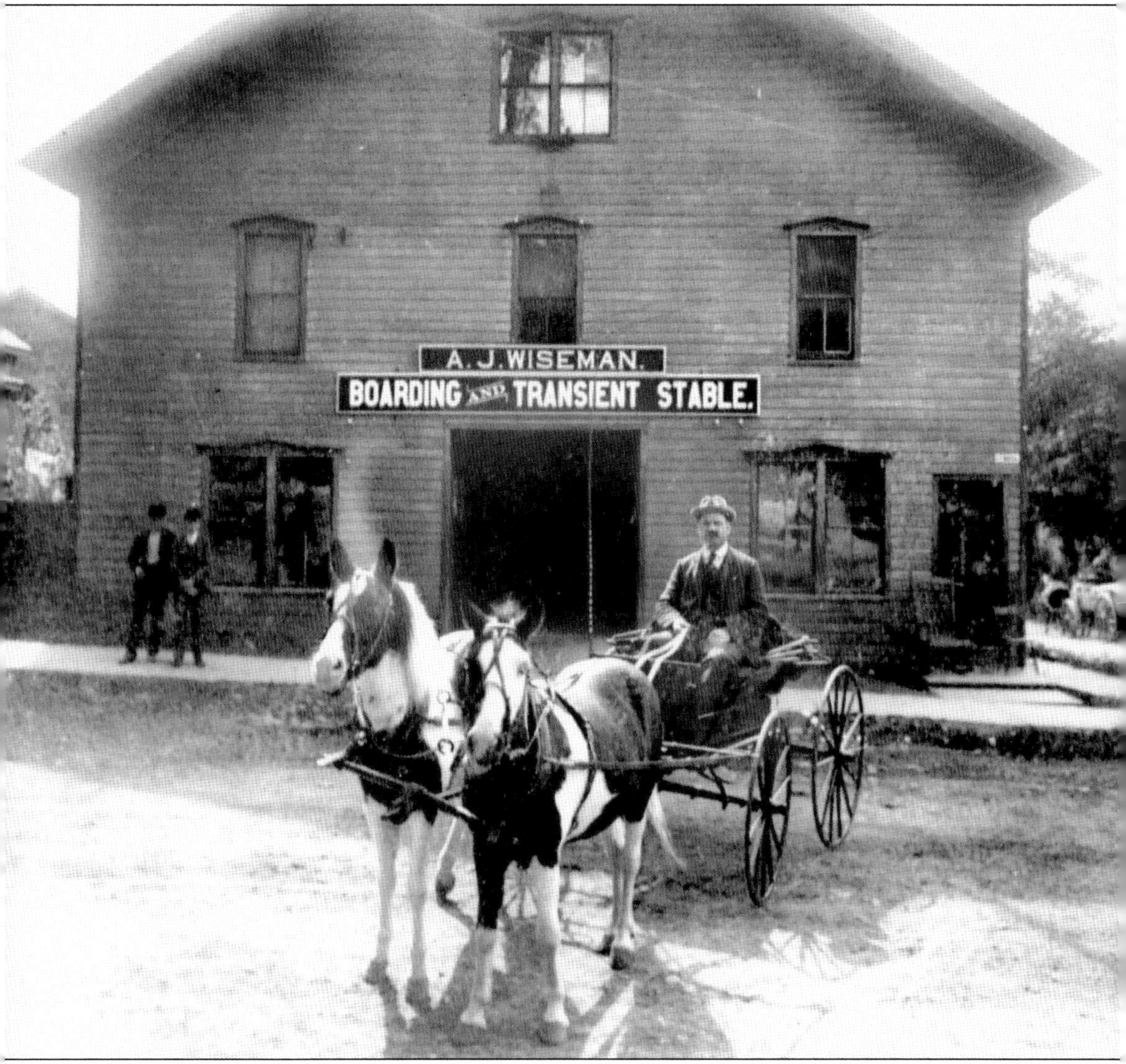

Anson J. Wiseman's Livery Stable stands on the northwest corner of the Hardscrabble Road and Old Route 29 in Fairfield. Anson Wiseman also ran "the stage" from Fairfield to Middleville, carrying passengers, packages, mail, and whatever had to travel up or down the hill. In 1827, this corner was the site of an early hotel, which, in 1891, was redone to serve as the armory for the Fairfield Military Academy. Since the Wiseman era, a gas station, variety store, country gift shop, and private home have been located on this site.

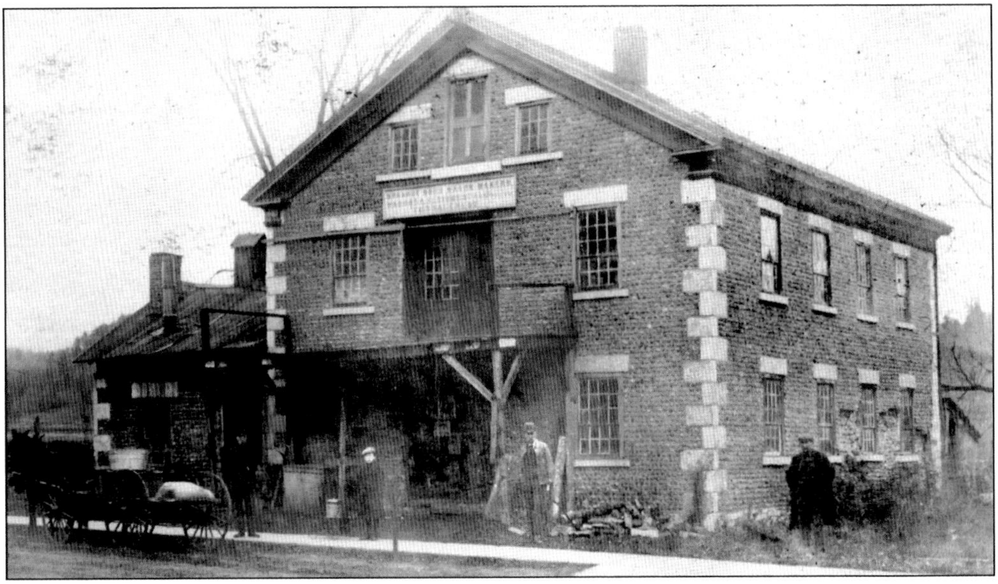

Daniel Sprague and his sons, Arnold and Charles Sprague, operated a carriage and sleigh business on Millington Avenue in Poland. In 1869, they moved their shop to the Old Cobblestone Shop (built *c.* 1800), on Cold Brook Street. They were widely known for their production of heavy wagons and sleighs used to haul lumber. They patented the Sprague wagon, which had a cross-reach that enabled the front and rear wheels to form the same arc when turning. The business flourished until the automobile made horse-drawn vehicles obsolete.

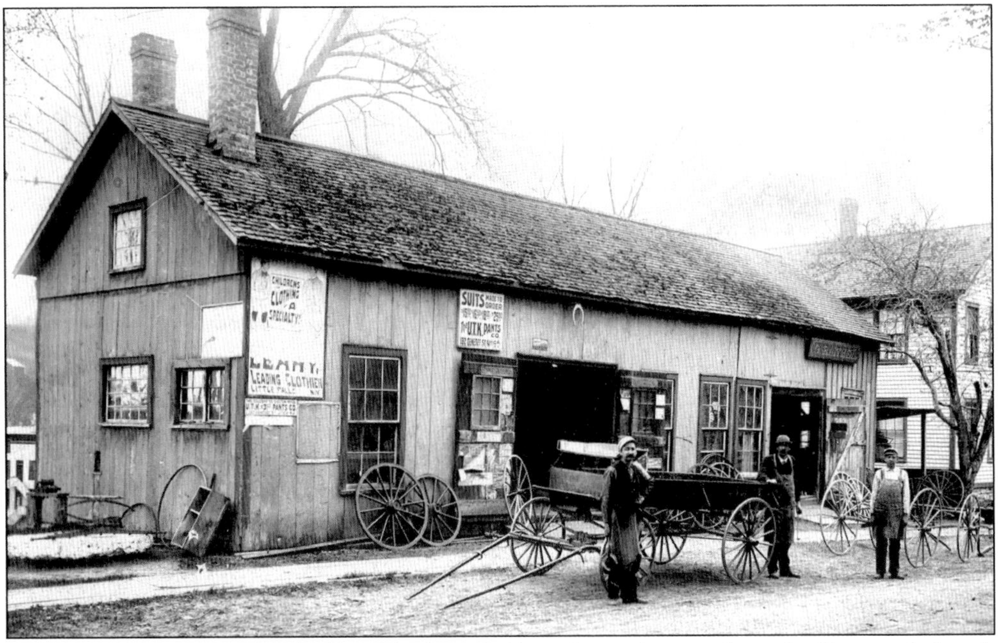

Shown *c.* 1895 outside the Sheldon Blacksmith Shop, located across from the Episcopal church in Middleville, from left to right are blacksmith William Sheldon and wagon makers George Raithel and son Fred Raithel. German immigrants, the Raithels used the right end of the building for their wagon shop when they first arrived in this area in 1885. Later, they built a wagon shop on Bridge Street.

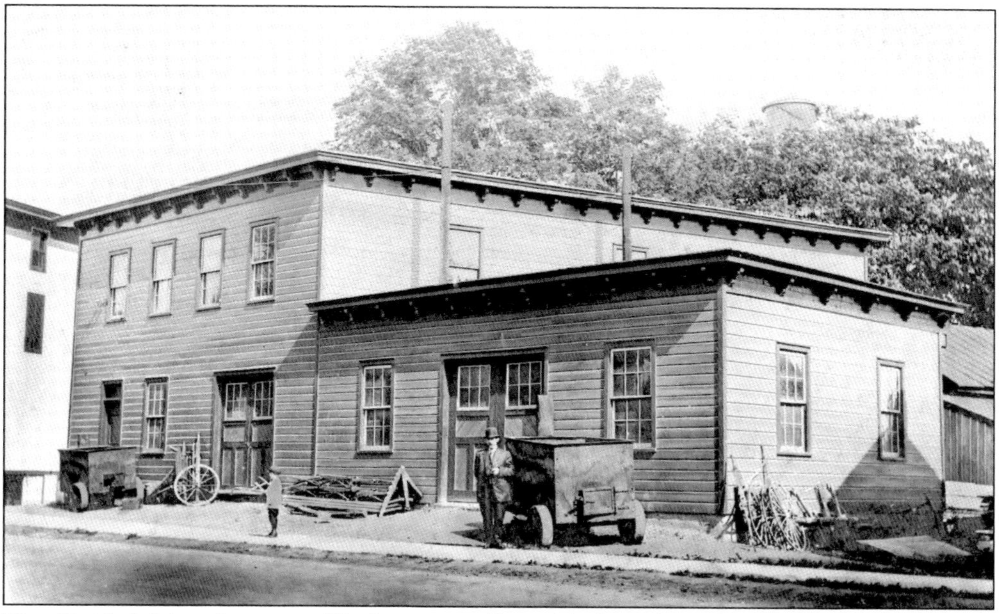

The Raithel Manufacturing Works, originally a blacksmith and wagon shop, did metal work, blacksmithing, and woodworking. The Raithels produced the famous convertible baby buggy-sleigh. It had runners for winter use and wheels for summer use. This shop, built in 1906, did work for the tannery and the felt mill in Middleville. It also made storm windows and doors, watering tubs, truck bodies, stone boats, and wagons. The Raithels were widely known for their craftsmanship.

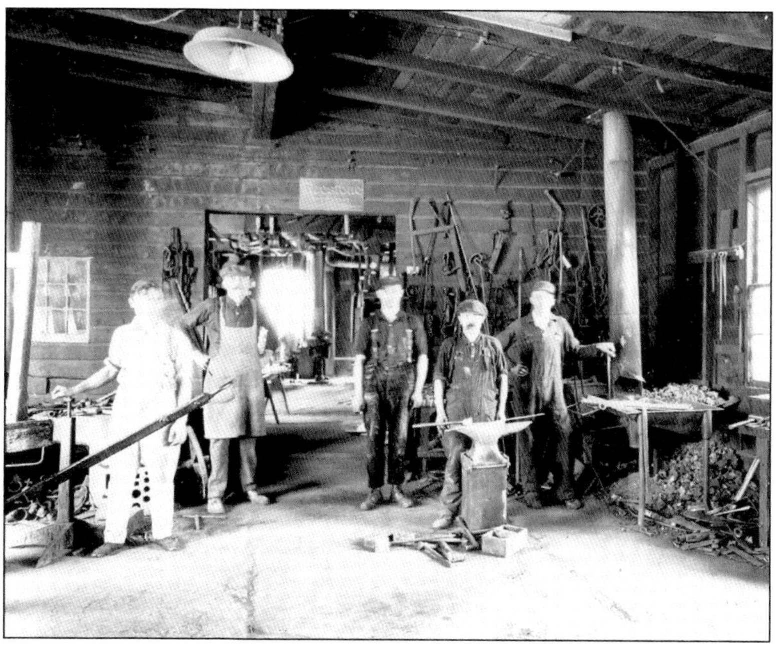

This 1907 photograph shows the blacksmith department of Raithel's shop on Bridge Street. From left to right are customer Tom Wagner, George Raithel, Charles Waller, William Brown, and Fred Raithel.

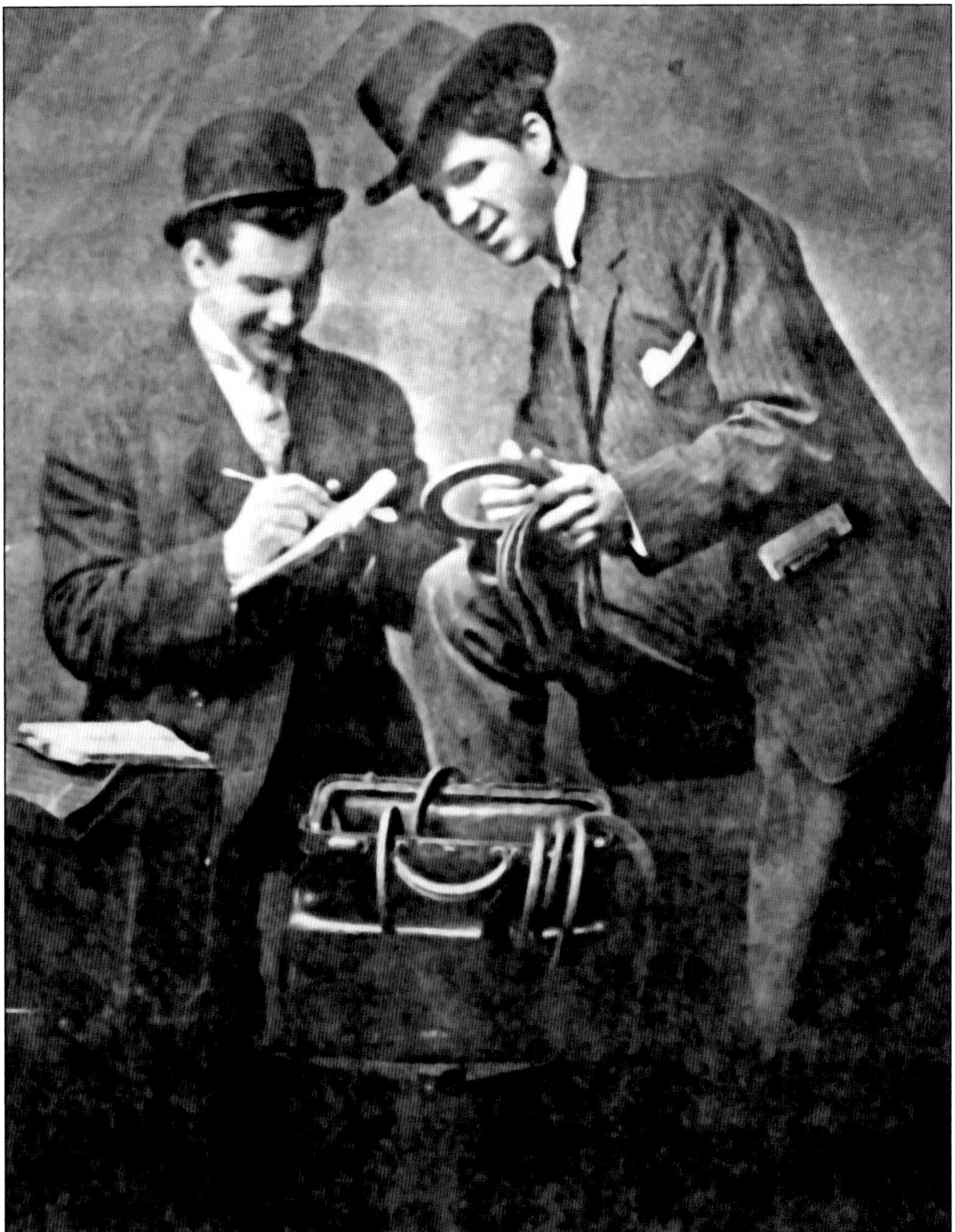

Charles Batchelder Spraker (right) was a horseshoe salesman in the early 1900s. Known as "C.B.," Spraker traveled up and down the Kuyahoora and Mohawk Valleys, supplying horseshoes to farmers and villagers.

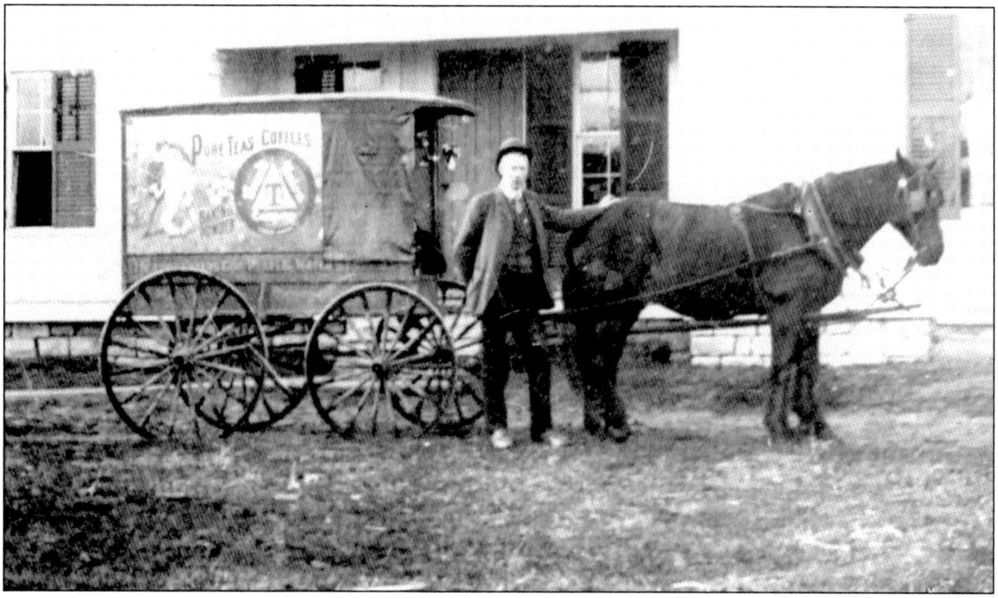

Peddlers with their horse-drawn wagons traveled the countryside, bringing their wares to farms and homes. Peddling teas and coffees from his Grand Union Tea Company wagon is Arch Blue of Grant.

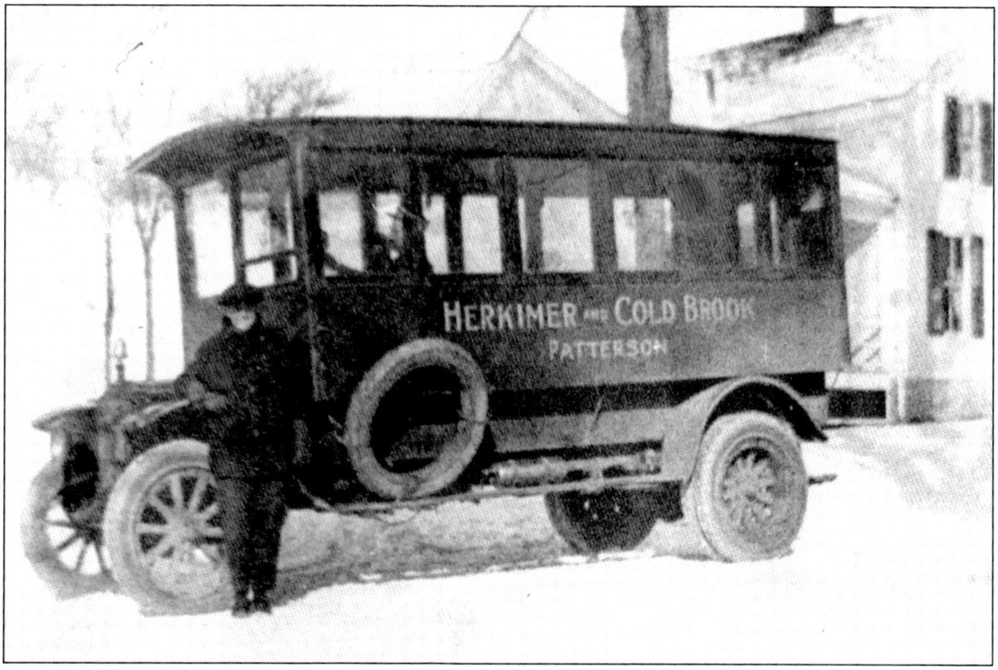

Beginning in 1912, the Patterson bus service provided three round trips daily to and from Herkimer and the villages of Middleville, Newport, Poland, and Cold Brook. William Patterson began the business and passed it on to his nephew Merrill George in 1921. The increasing number of privately owned automobiles caused patronage to decline, forcing the closure of the business in 1953.

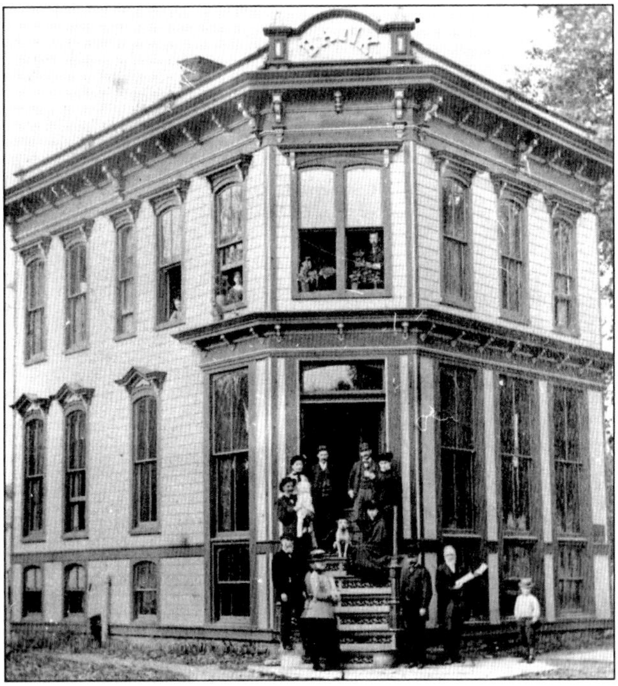

A group of businessmen organized the Bank of Poland in 1872 as a private bank. It operated out of Dr. Stephen Millington's old office until 1876, when it moved into a new wood frame, Italianate-style building in the Kellogg Block. The bank prospered, and in 1910, it became the Citizen's National Bank, which bought the building from the Kellogg heirs. Shown are the 19th-century cornice, brackets, second-floor window hoods, and two-over-two sashes. In 1927, the building was lowered three steps and the basement windows were eliminated. The bank escaped two major fires, survived the 1930s bank holiday without reorganization, and remained in continuous use for nearly 125 years.

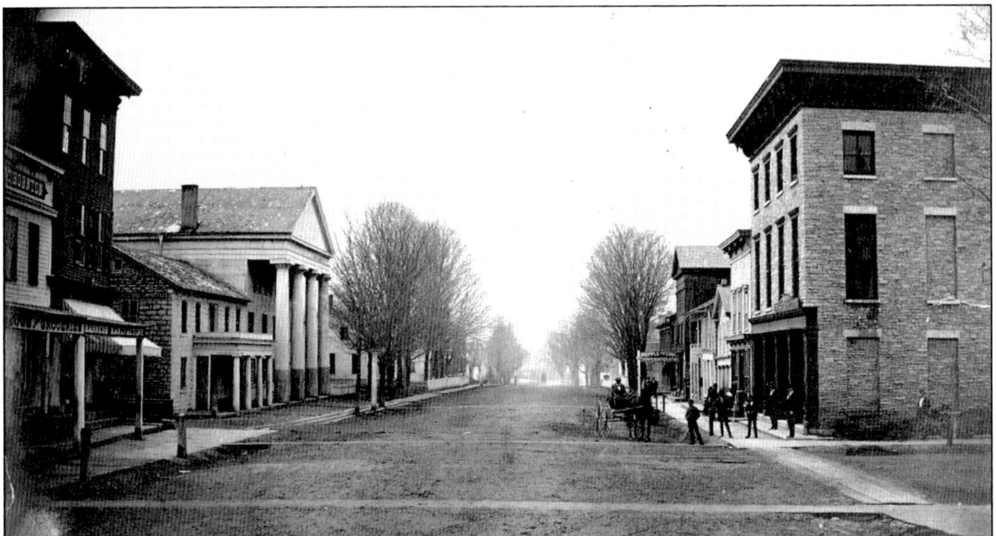

Shown at the corner of Main and Bridge Street is the Newport bank building (right), a three-story structure erected in 1854 by the firm of Swezey and Perry. The bank's native quarried limestone echoes other buildings and bridges in the Kuyahoora Valley. The building housed banks for 80 years: the Bank of Newport from 1858 to 1866 and the National Bank from 1866 until it closed in 1930s, a victim of the Depression. Across the street from the bank building is the Pioneer Inn.

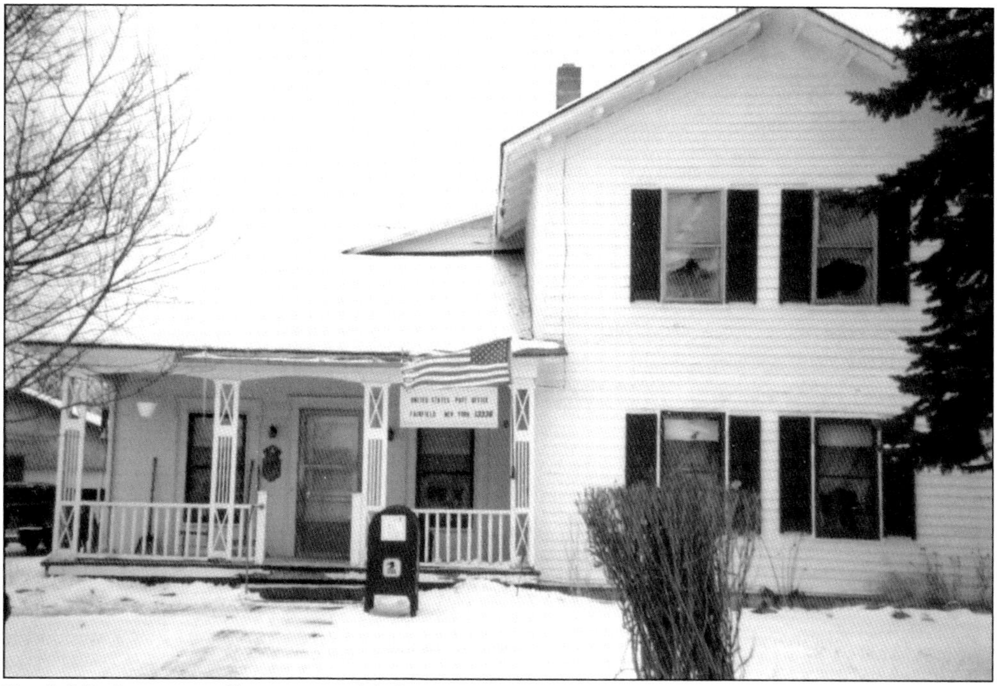

Fairfield's first post office was established in 1804, with William Smith as the first postmaster. Over the years, the post offices were operated from several different stores and a few private homes. Shown here is Fairfield's last post office, in the Bruce Windecker home on Old Route 29 (now known as Academy Walk). Barbara Windecker was postmaster from 1962 to 1990. The post office was officially closed on January 12, 1995, when it combined with Middleville.

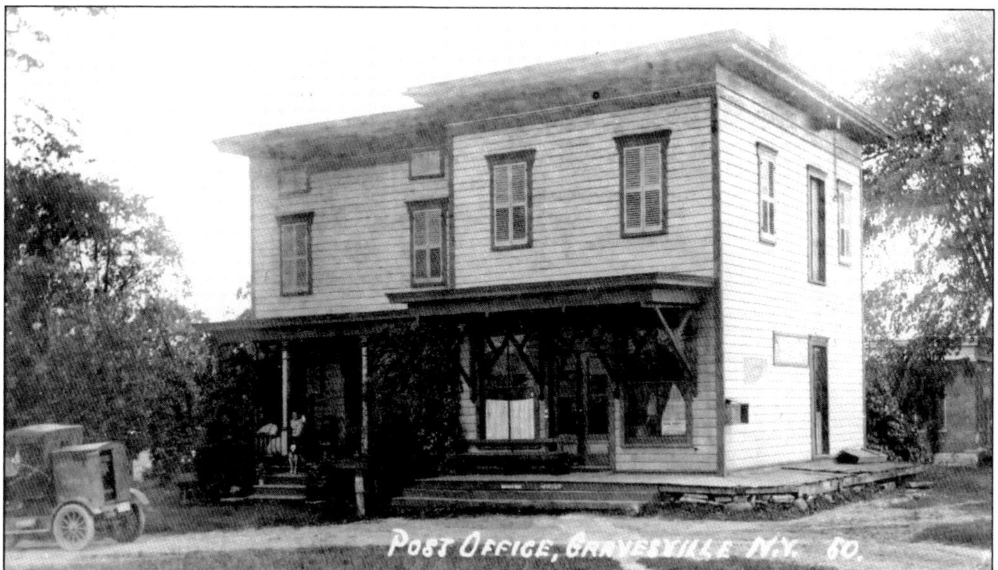

The first post office in Gravesville was established in 1845, with Elijah Seavy as the first postmaster. Like the one in Fairfield, this post office was in a general store for a few years and then operated out of the home of the postmaster.

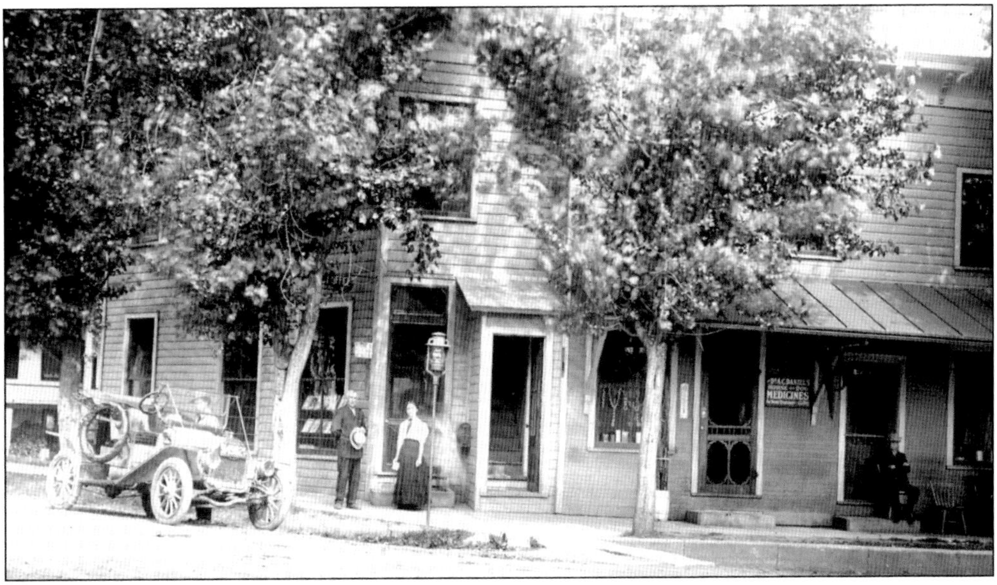

The first post office in Poland was established in 1838, with Joseph Benchley as postmaster. Over the years, it operated out of Benchley's hotel and several other sites, including the Poland Union, the basement of the bank, the Read Brothers Store, and the Wallace building (the wing of the bank that was moved down the street). In 1910, the post office was in the building shown here, at the corner of Cold Brook Street and Main Street. Standing in front of the office are John Read, postmaster, and Grace Read Lutz of Utica.

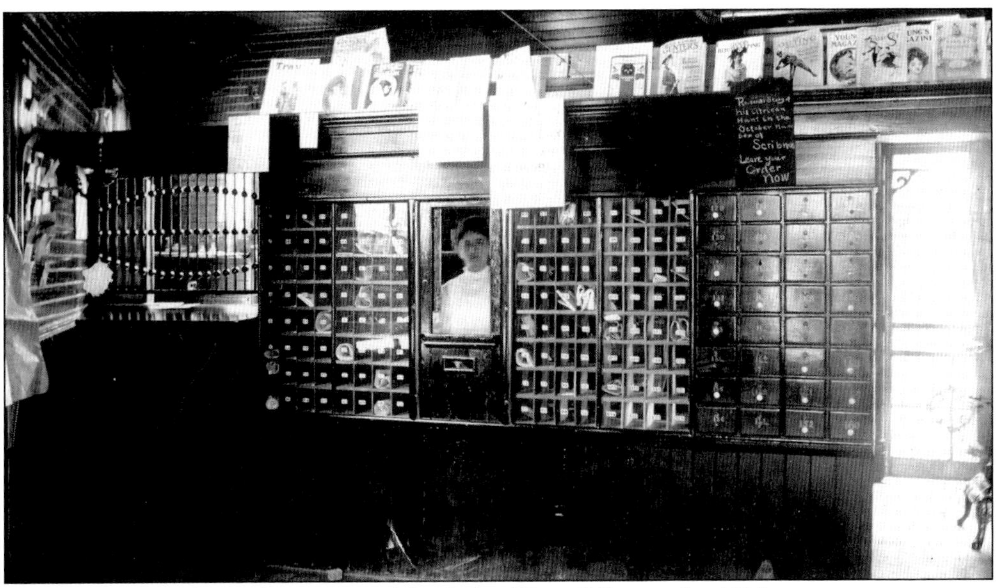

This photograph shows the interior of the Poland Post Office in the 1920s.

Seven

HIGHWAY AND BYWAYS

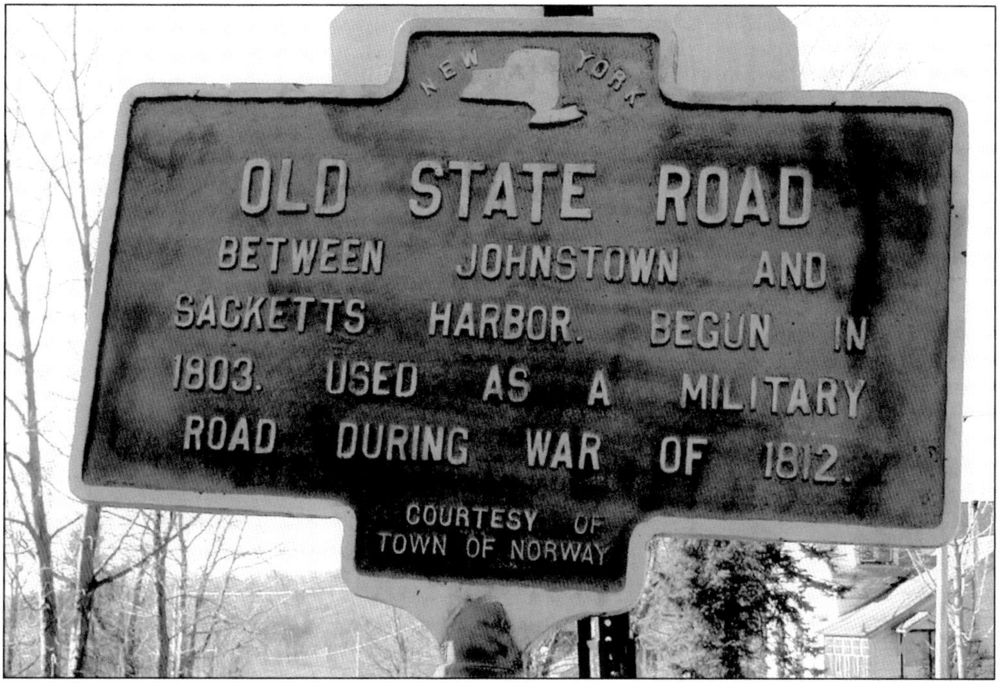

Travel in the Kuyahoora towns before 1800 was a hazardous adventure. Roads were rough trails, often full of mudholes and ruts, barely passable by horse or oxen teams. Without bridges, the pioneers were forced to ford streams in low-water areas. In 1803, the state legislature appropriated money to survey and construct a road from the Mohawk Valley north through the Black River Valley to Sackets Harbor, on Lake Ontario. The Old State Road was surveyed in 1806 and opened in 1808, passing through the towns of Fairfield, Norway, and Russia. The villages of Norway and Cold Brook grew rapidly and flourished. During this period traveling conditions were improved by the construction of plank roads and covered bridges that spanned the smaller streams and the West Canada Creek. Farmers expanded their markets for cheese and other products. Mail carriers on horseback brought news from throughout the northeast. Hotels, taverns, and stables were needed to accommodate the traffic on the roads. Blacksmith shops and wagon and harness shops were built along the highways to accommodate the travelers' needs. Threats of war with Britain loomed soon after the opening of the Old State Road. The War of 1812 was fought primarily on the northern frontier. Troops and munitions traveled from the Hudson and Mohawk Valleys north on the Old State Road. Thus, the road became known as the Military Road. This New York State historical marker stands at the four corners in the hamlet of Norway.

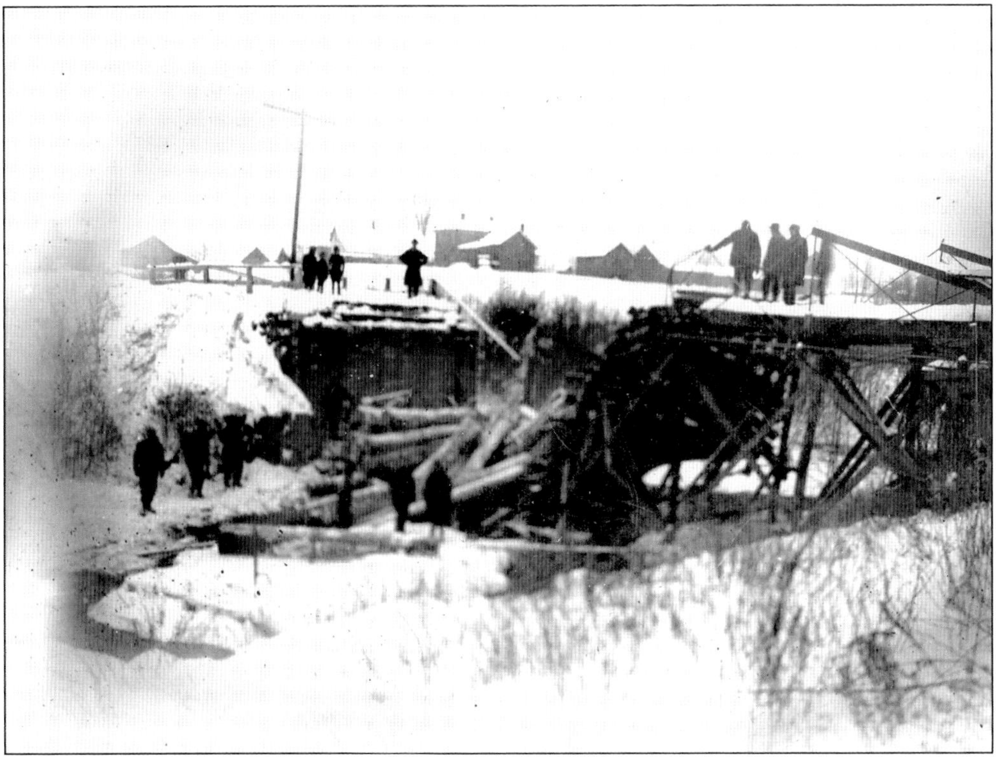

This wooden bridge over Black Creek in Gray collapsed when a Linn tractor pulling three loads of logs crossed it in December 1926. One of the workers, Archie Dutcher, was thrown into the creek, where he was pinned by the logs, which broke his leg. Unfortunately, it was not until the next day that his helpers could get him to a hospital in Utica.

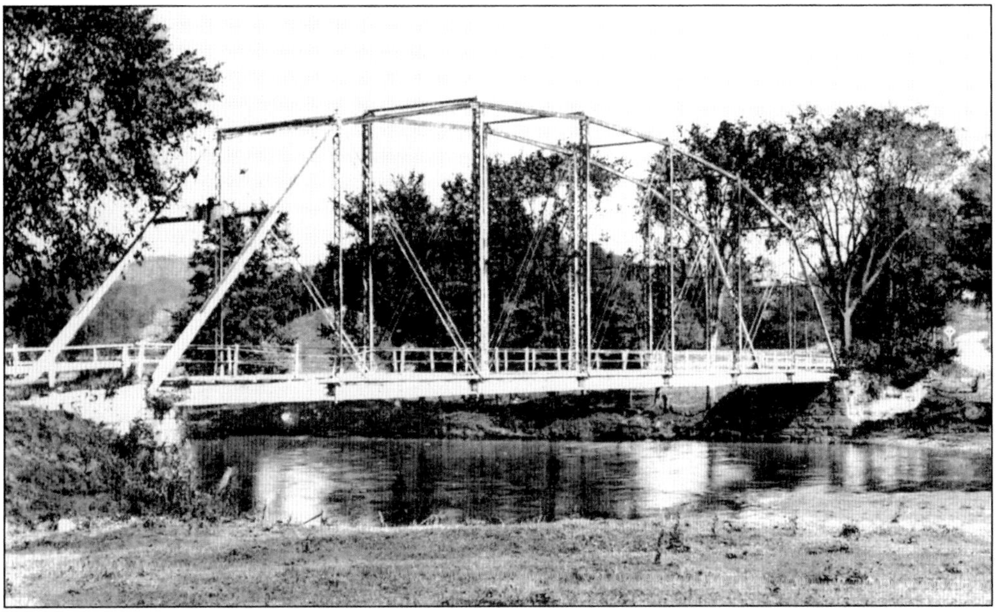

This iron bridge with limestone block abutments crossed the Kuyahoora south of Poland, providing access to the Brayton Corners area.

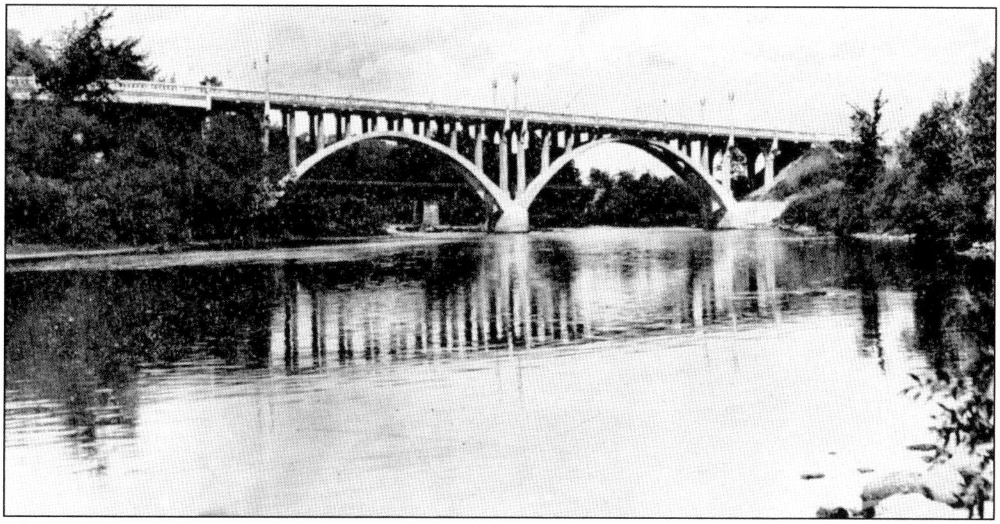

This concrete arch bridge, built in 1922, spanned the West Canada slightly upstream from the old iron bridge in Poland. The bridge was declared unsafe in 1996 and was replaced by a shorter (three-arch) steel beam and concrete bridge in 1997. In the background is the iron railroad bridge built in the late 1800s. It is still standing, but it has been blocked since the termination of the railroad.

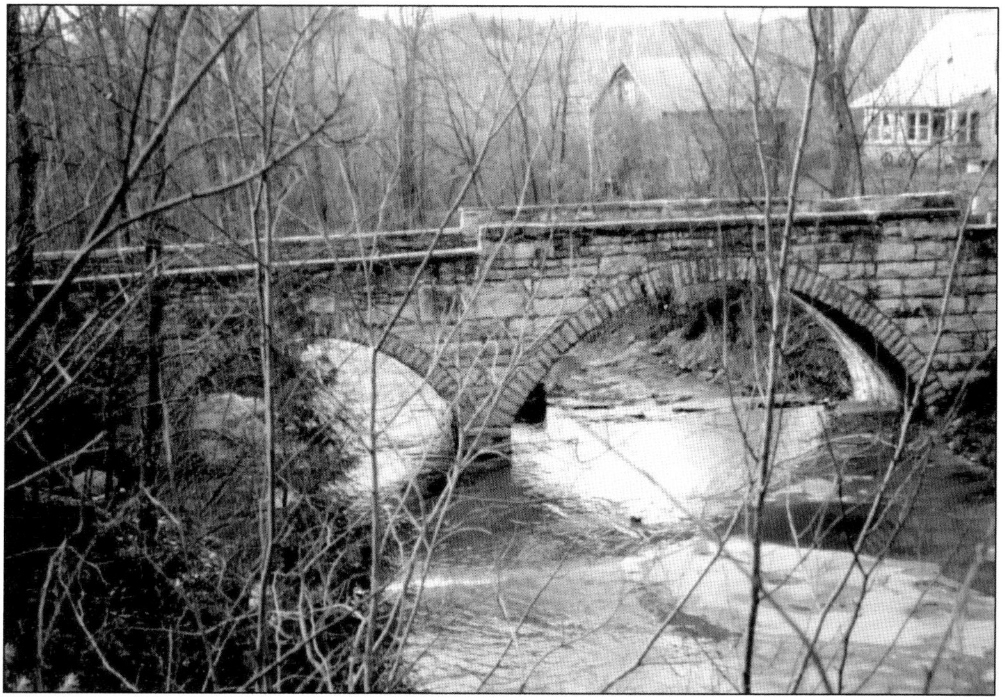

Using native limestone, local craftsmen constructed the Old City Road Bridge after the flood of 1898. Old City was an early industrial community that utilized the waterpower of City Brook, a series of falls with a vertical drop of more than 100 feet in a half-mile. Mills were present in this area of Fairfield in the 1790s. The house on the right was formerly an inn. One of the few remaining examples of this type of structure, Old City Road Bridge was listed on the National Register of Historic Places in 2001.

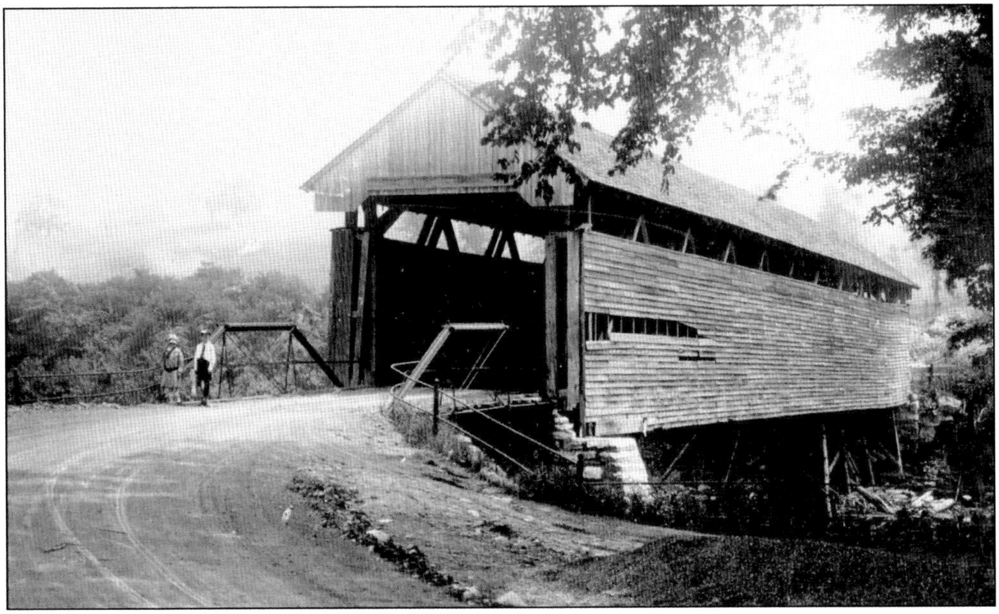

This old covered bridge outside of Poland was the original Schermerhorn Hill Bridge. One of the first bridges in the area, it was built in the early 1800s to cross the West Canada Creek upstream from Sunny Island. It was replaced with a steel through-truss bridge in 1929. In 1996, the steel bridge was replaced with a higher, longer, crescent-shaped, steel multi-beam and concrete bridge.

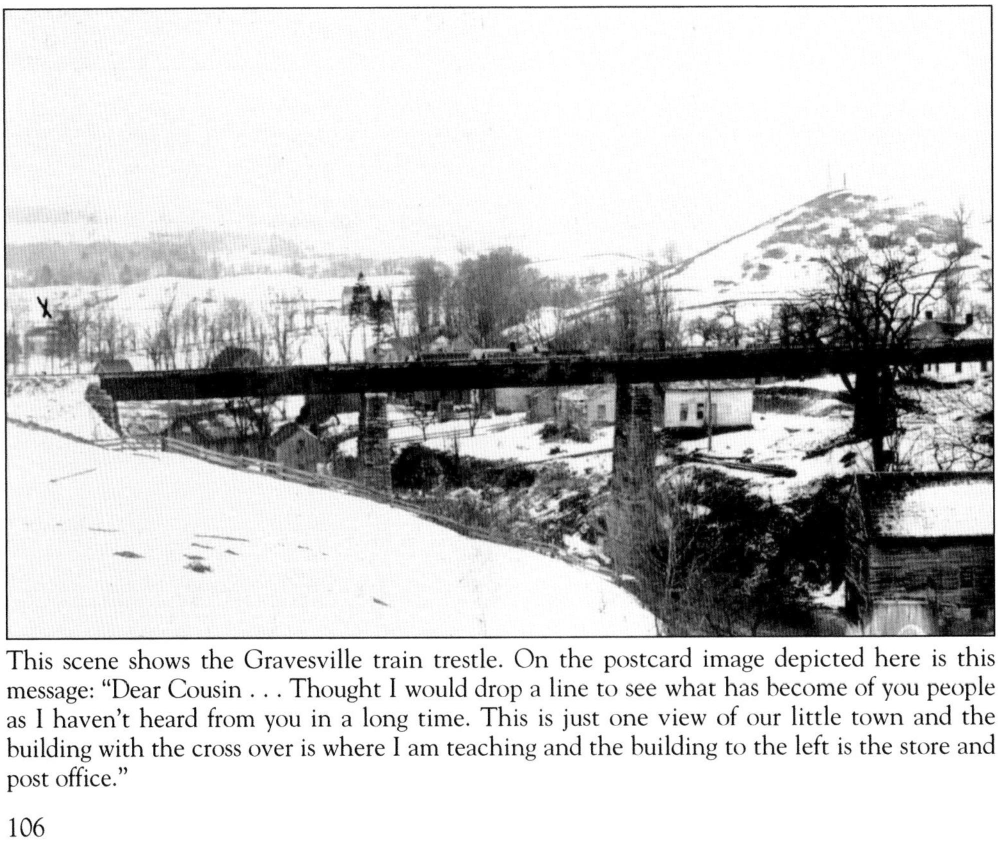

This scene shows the Gravesville train trestle. On the postcard image depicted here is this message: "Dear Cousin . . . Thought I would drop a line to see what has become of you people as I haven't heard from you in a long time. This is just one view of our little town and the building with the cross over is where I am teaching and the building to the left is the store and post office."

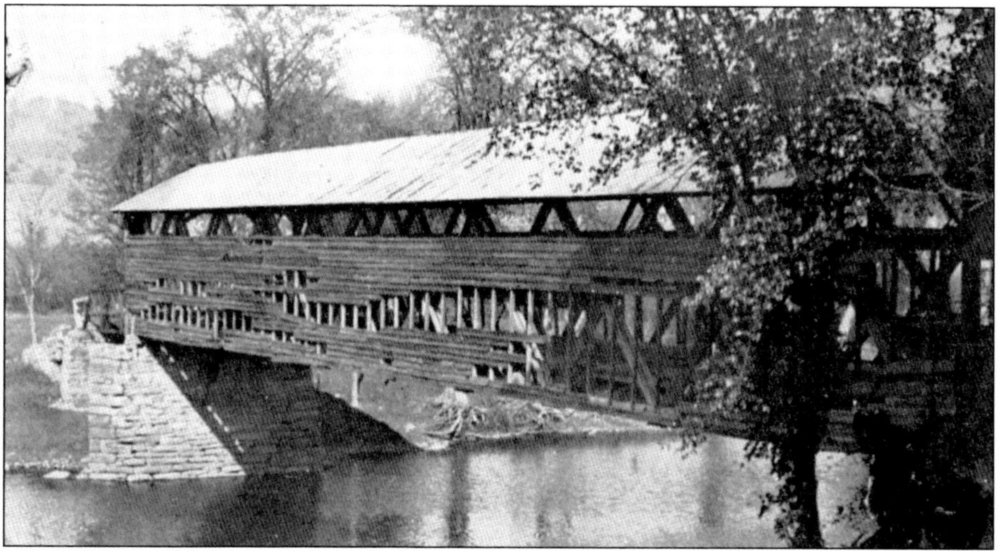

built in the early 1800s, the Cameron Bridge crossed the West Canada Creek between Poland and Gravesville and remained in use for more than 130 years. A covered bridge replaced the original bridge when a plank road was built in 1849. During the War of 1812, hundreds of troops marched across the original bridge on the road that connected the Utica area to the Albany–Sacketts Harbor Military Road.

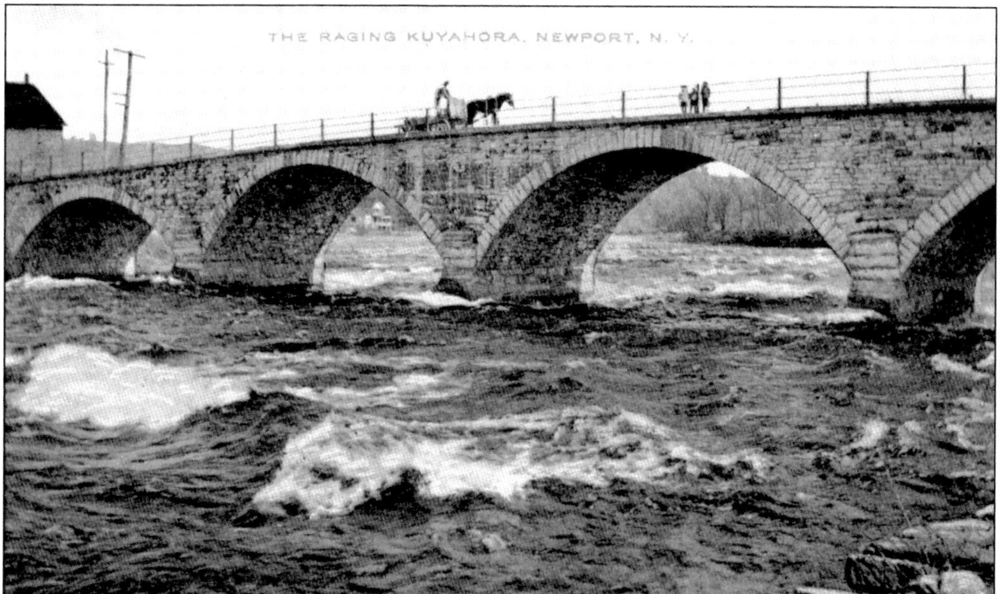

In 1853, the Four Arch Limestone Bridge was built over the West Canada Creek in the village of Newport at a cost of $4,000. This stone came from the nearby Fenner Farm. The four- by six-foot limestone blocks were lowered into the creek bed by a horse and pulley. The height of the two middle spans is 24 feet above the creek. The bridge is now on the National Register of Historic Places.

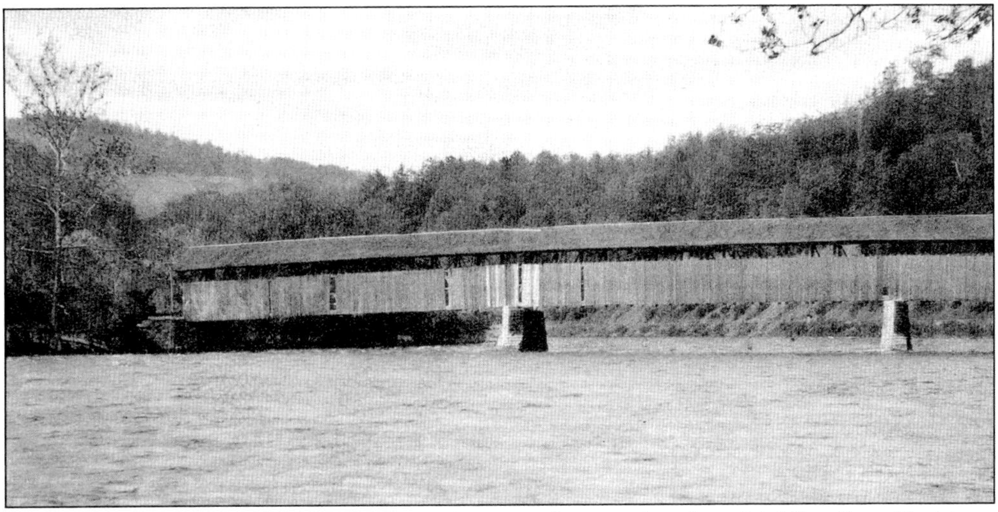

Dempster's Bridge was one of two bridges to be crossed in traveling from Middleville to Herkimer on what is today Route 28. This very long bridge had a problem. It was a car length from the railroad track at its northern exit. A severe accident in 1911 caused the removal of the side boards to increase visibility, but it remained very hazardous. Meetings to address the issue were begun in 1917, but it was not until 1921 that a new concrete Dempster's Bridge was completed. The two-lane concrete bridge was removed when the state highway department changed the channel of the West Canada Creek in 1965.

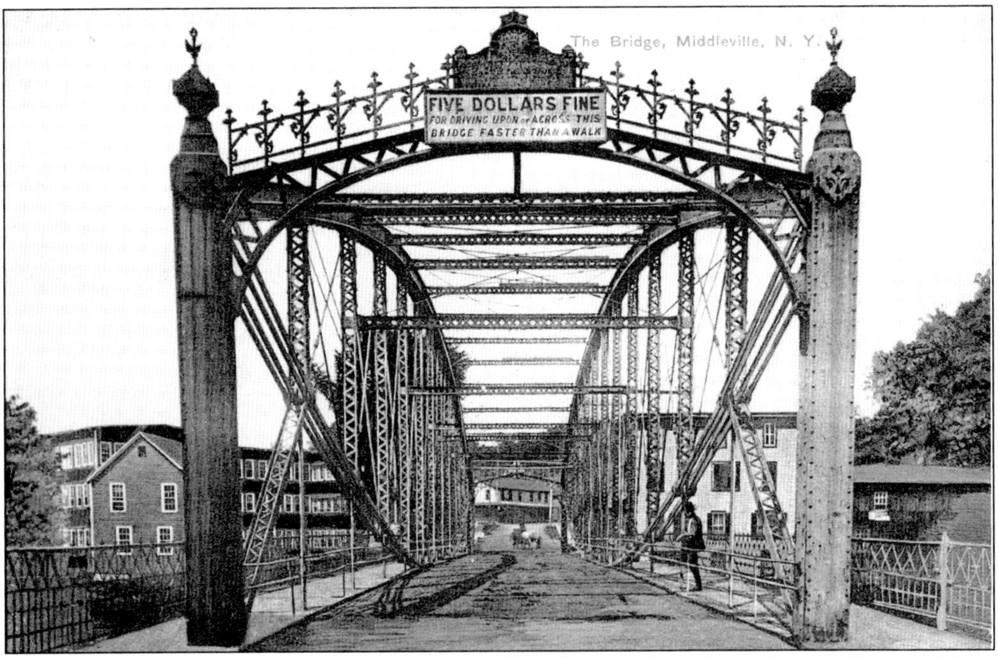

This iron bridge over the West Canada in Middleville served residents from 1888 to 1935. It was preceded by several wooden bridges, all of which were destroyed by floods. Maj. Edward Burns of Middleville watched the construction closely and declared that the bridge would not last 50 years. He was proved correct when it was discovered that the builders had not met the specifications. Residents recall that every time a vehicle passed over the bridge, the vibrations were loud enough to be heard all over the village. A steel bridge replaced the iron one in 1935.

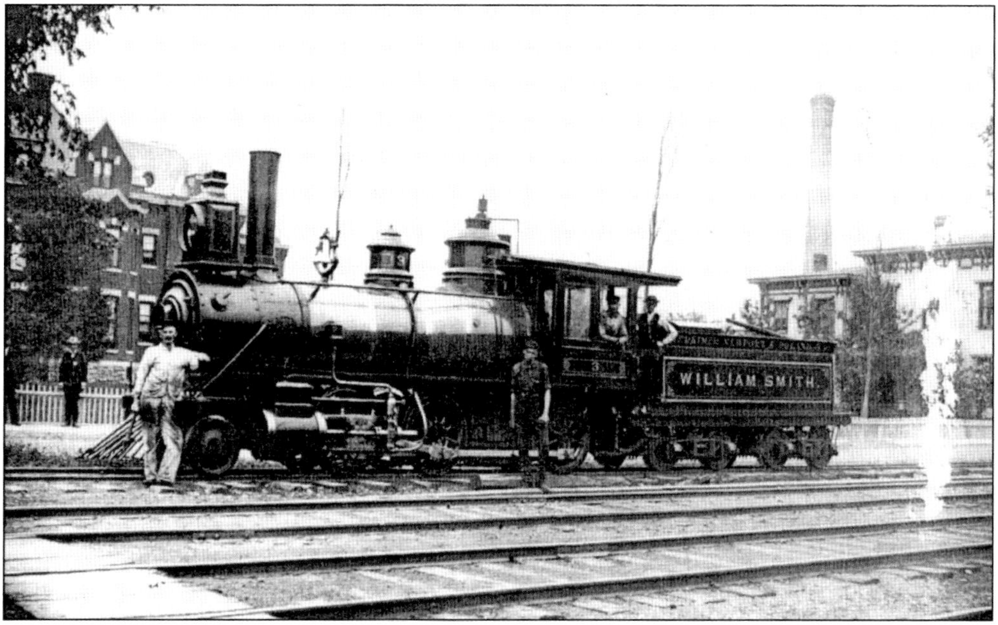

This train is shown on the tracks passing through the center of Herkimer. In 1880, train service connected Herkimer to the Kuyahoora towns of Middleville, Newport, and Poland with the narrow-gauge railway. The wide-gauge railroad replaced the narrow rails in 1891.

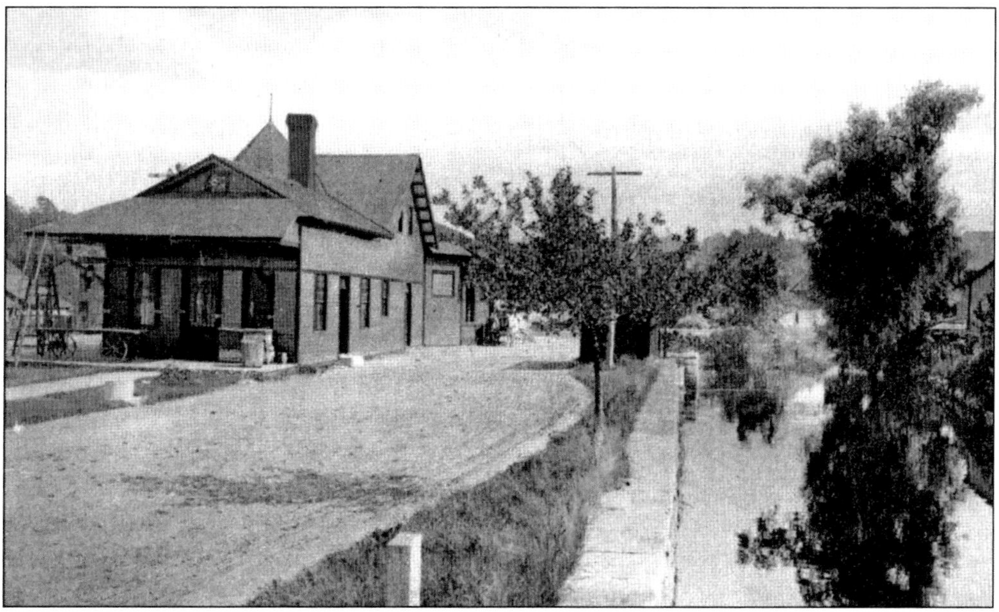

The Middleville Depot was located on the Herkimer-to-Poland line. A hydraulic canal ran alongside the tracks in this area, serving the industries of Middleville.

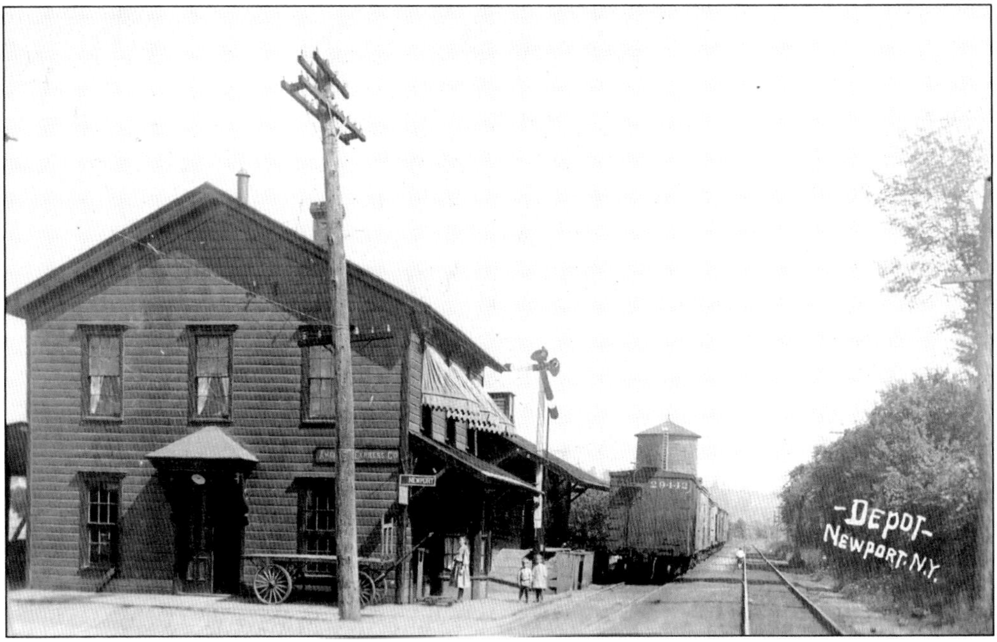

The Newport train depot was completed in December 1882. By the following February, receipts for freight totaled $130 and for passengers $150. In 1887, three or more carloads of cheese were shipped to New York weekly, with England being their final destination. Local quarries shipped stone on the railroad as well.

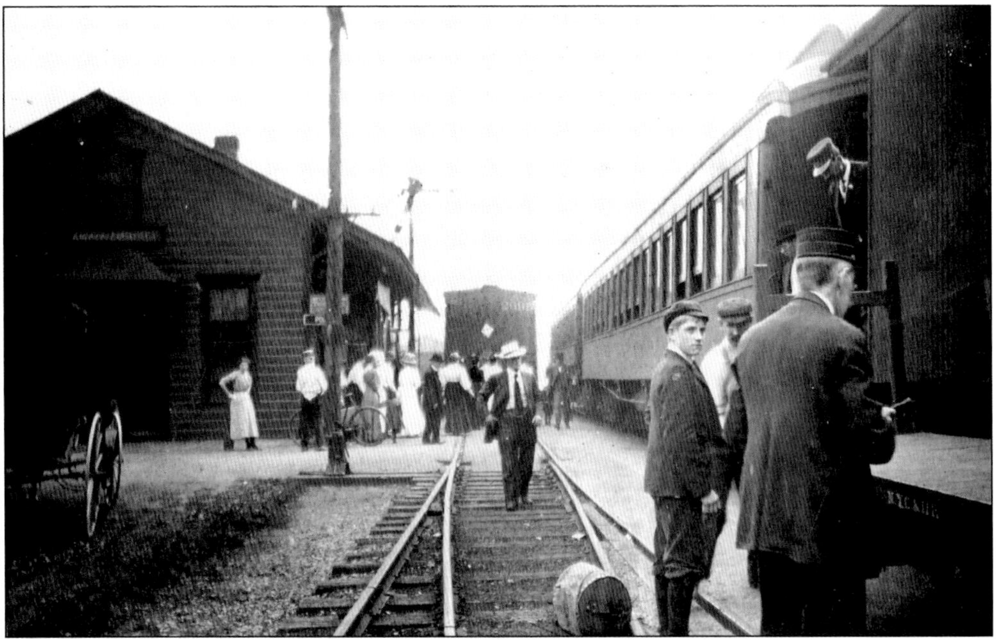

In 1909, three passenger trains and one freight train arrived daily in Poland. Three mails arrived daily on the passenger trains, which made stops at Kast Bridge, Countryman, County Home, Middleville, Newport, Poland, Gravesville, Trenton Chasm, Prospect Junction, and Remsen. A popular pastime was to watch the Sunday night excursion trains from the North Country pass through the station.

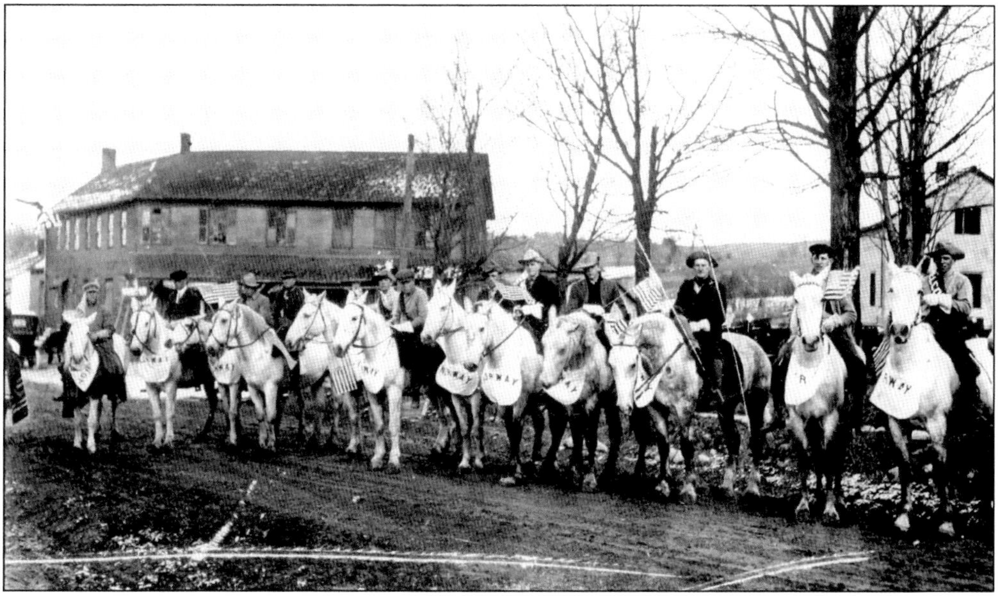

A new state road between Newport and Norway was opened in 1914. A parade of horses displaying "Norway" signs traveled over the new road to the celebration ceremonies held in the village of Norway. In front of the old Norway store from left to right are Millard Smith, Walter Rank, George Weakley, Ernest Willoughby, Irving Weakley, Adelbert Gould, Hollis Helmer, Adolph Hasler, unidentified, John Frank, Raymond Snyder, Will Ossont, and Fred Farber.

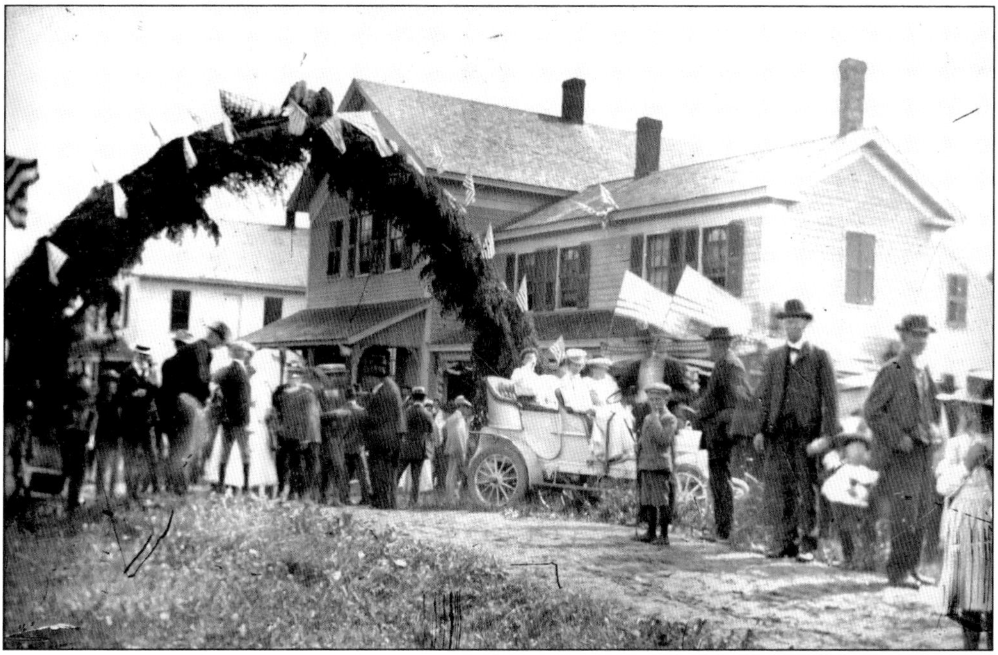

The crowds at this early-1900s Fourth of July celebration in Gray are looking at the automobile driven by Frank Coonradt from Cold Brook to Gray. Frank Coonradt had one of the first automobiles in the area, and it attracted much attention.

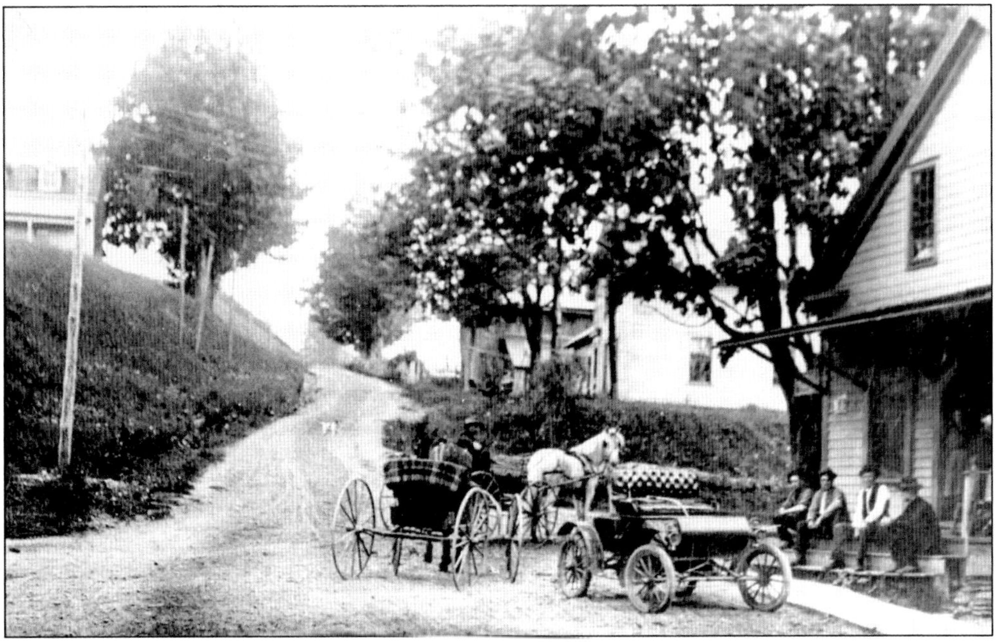

The junction of Grant, Pardeeville, Southside, and Stormy Hill Roads was known as the Busy Corner of Grant. As shown here, local residents stopped to talk at the store and pick up mail at the post office. Times were certainly changing: note the horse and carriage alongside the horseless carriage.

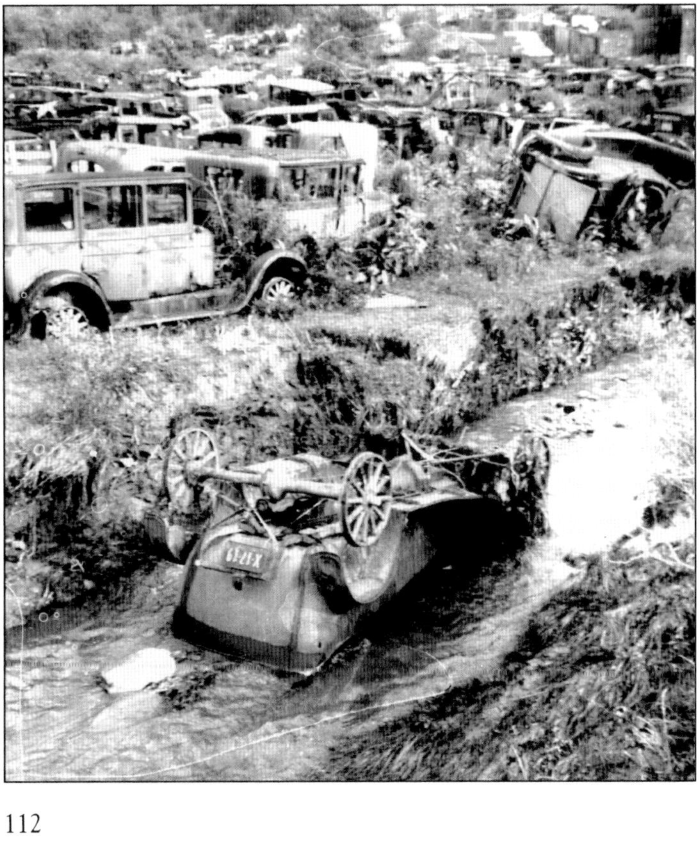

As newer model vehicles replaced early cars and trucks, junkyards became graveyards for the worn-out vehicles. Greiner's junkyard, along Cold Brook stream, was a popular spot to find used parts to repair one's ailing car or truck. Considered unsightly, junkyards were later required to be fenced from sight along highways.

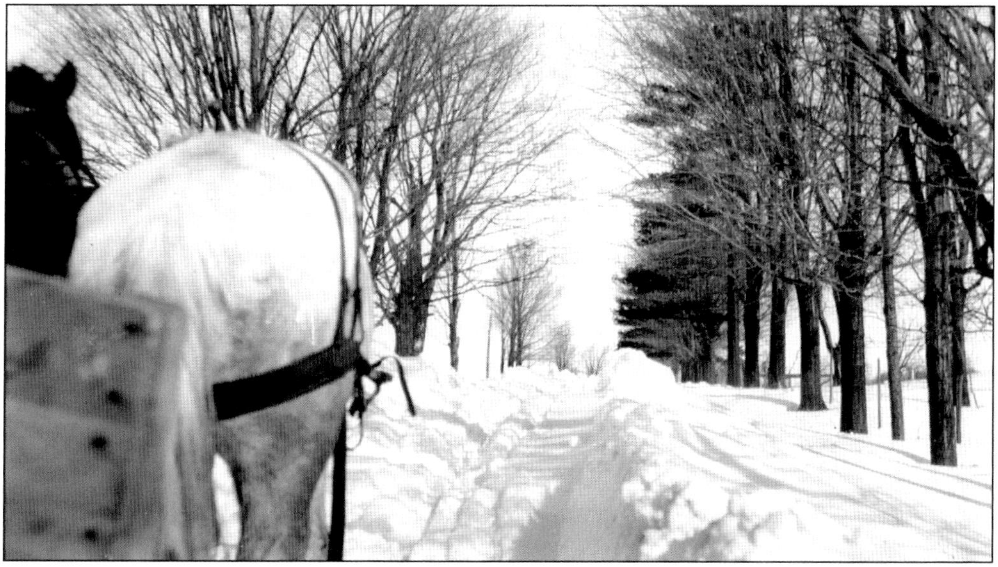

Winter travel around the countryside was difficult before the advent of heavy snowplowing equipment in the late 1930s. This scene shows a horse and sleigh on the Hurricane, in the town of Norway.

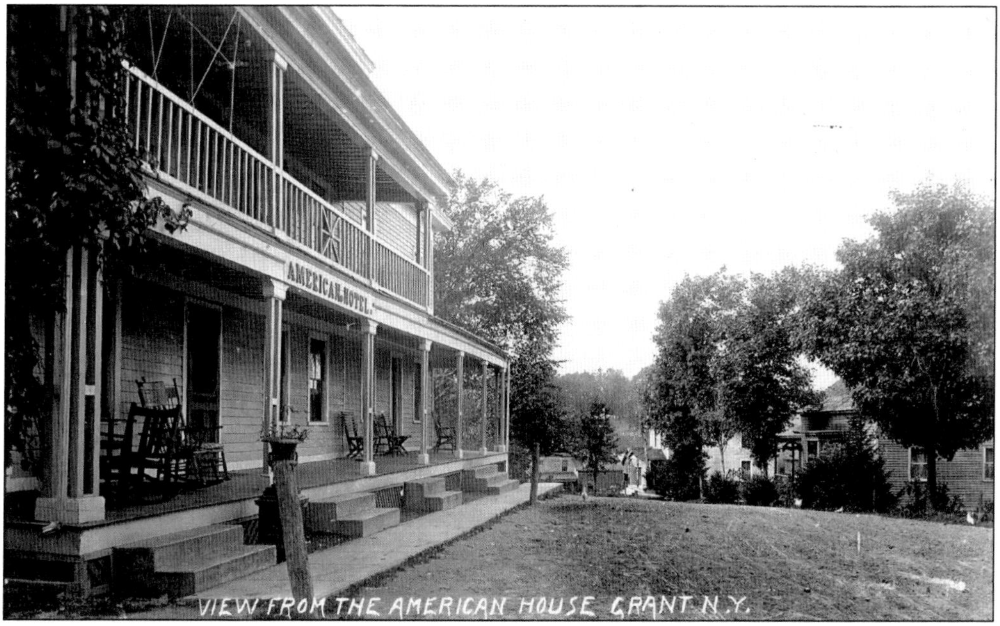

After operating for 30 years, the American House in Grant was destroyed by fire in 1915. Dewitt Nichols, a handyman, was rescued from the flaming structure when it burned, but he lived for only a few more days. The building was a three-story structure with a ballroom on the third floor. At one time, there was a livery and stable located here, providing service to Hinckley and Wilmurt.

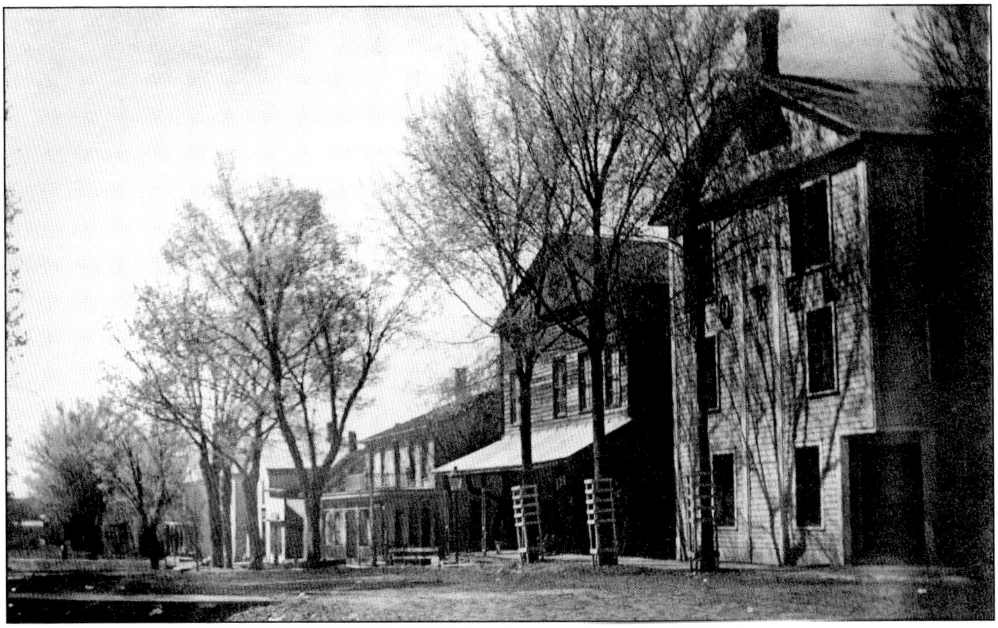

The old Fairfield Hotel (right) stood on the corner opposite the Fairfield Seminary. It was three stories high, with the top floor serving as a large ballroom. An extension on the west end served as a shelter for teams of horses and wagons, with the upper end used as a polling place. The building burned in 1932. It was replaced by a two-story hotel, popular in the 1950s and 1960s for delicious steak dinners. The hotel was destroyed by fire in 1975.

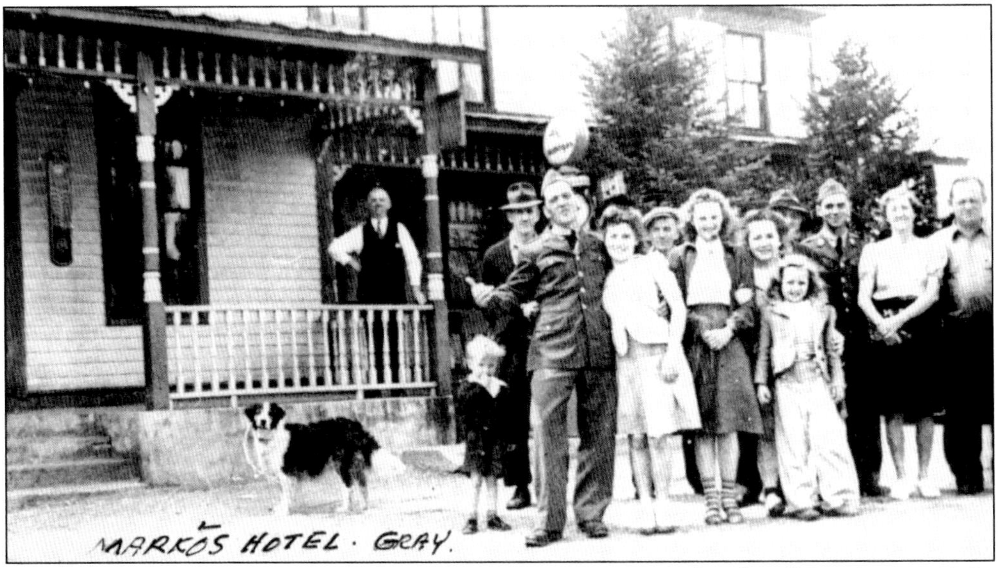

The Gray Hotel was built at the intersection of Gray-Wilmurt and Bull Hill Roads in 1852. In the early 1900s, Frank Turner operated it. In the 1920s, he sold it to John Marko, who operated it as a barroom and small grocery store. In 1940, a dance hall was added to the back part of the building. From left to right in this 1942 photograph are John Marko, Ronald Farber, John Becraft, Art Shafer, Nellie Davis, Louis Gibson, Dorothy Farber, Betty Davis, Shirley Farber, Albert Farber, Paul Farber, Ola Rachon, and Charles Stanley.

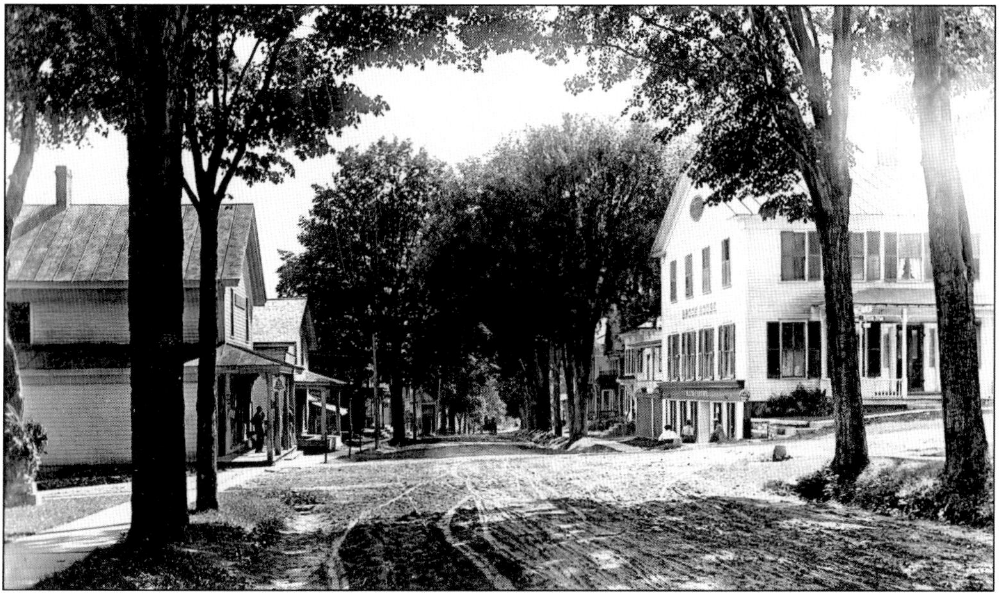

The three-and-a-half-story Brook House was erected in Cold Brook in 1832. In its early years, it was known as the Mansion House. Operators of the hotel included Edward Heyer, Daniel McCarthy, Charles Brondstatter, Jeff Moon, and H.V. Newberry. The hotel served as a community center and hosted traveling shows, dances, orchestras, singers, and magicians in its upstairs ballroom. The historic structure burned in August 1937.

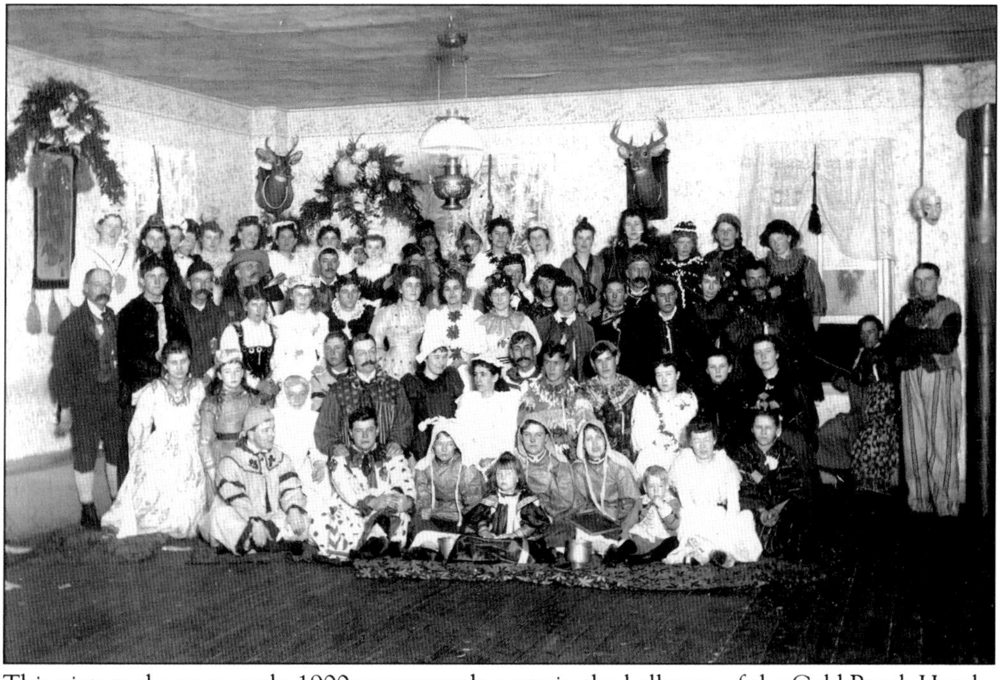

This picture shows an early-1900s masquerade party in the ballroom of the Cold Brook Hotel.

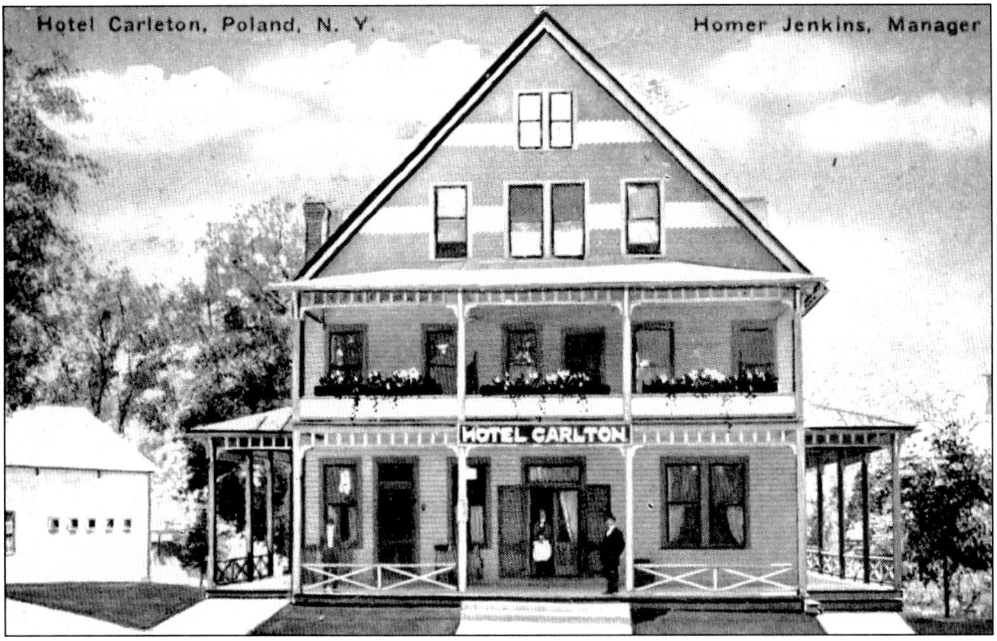

Poland's Hotel Carlton was built in 1898 and named after its first owner, Carlton Willoughby. In the early 1920s, Homer Jenkins purchased the hotel and changed its name to the Kuyahoora Inn. The inn, facing the park and fountain in the village, was a popular stopping place for tourists heading to or returning from the Adirondacks. The Kuyahoora was recently sold to Stewart's, which razed the building and replaced it with a gas station and convenience store.

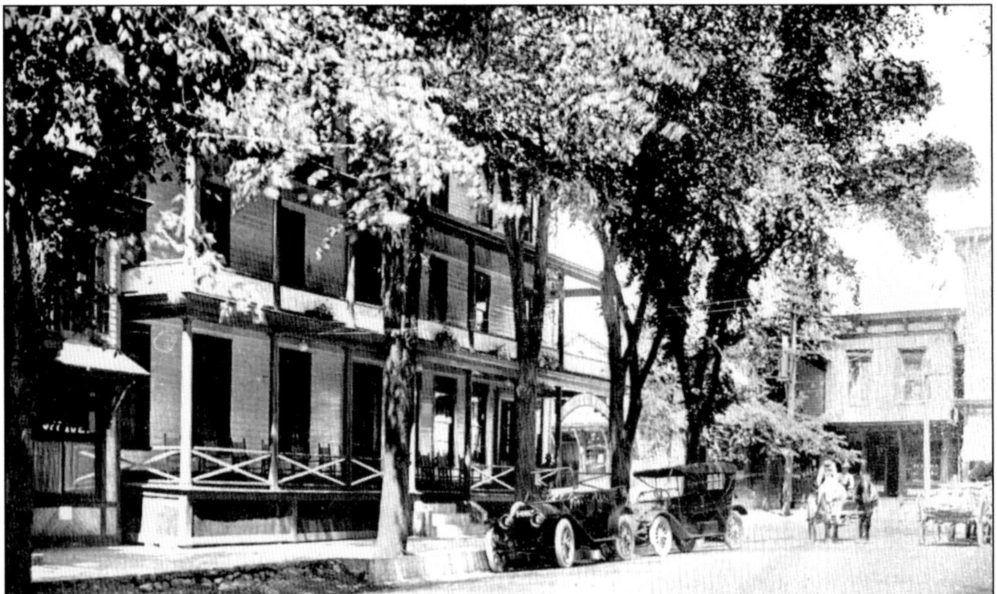

This historic three-story hotel was located on Bridge Street in Newport. Its first operator was William Benchley, who ran it from 1821 to 1836. At the beginning of the 20th century, it was owned by Dan Post and operated by Seymour Bowen as the Post Hotel. Mack Bateman operated the hotel from 1908 to 1926, when it was destroyed by fire.

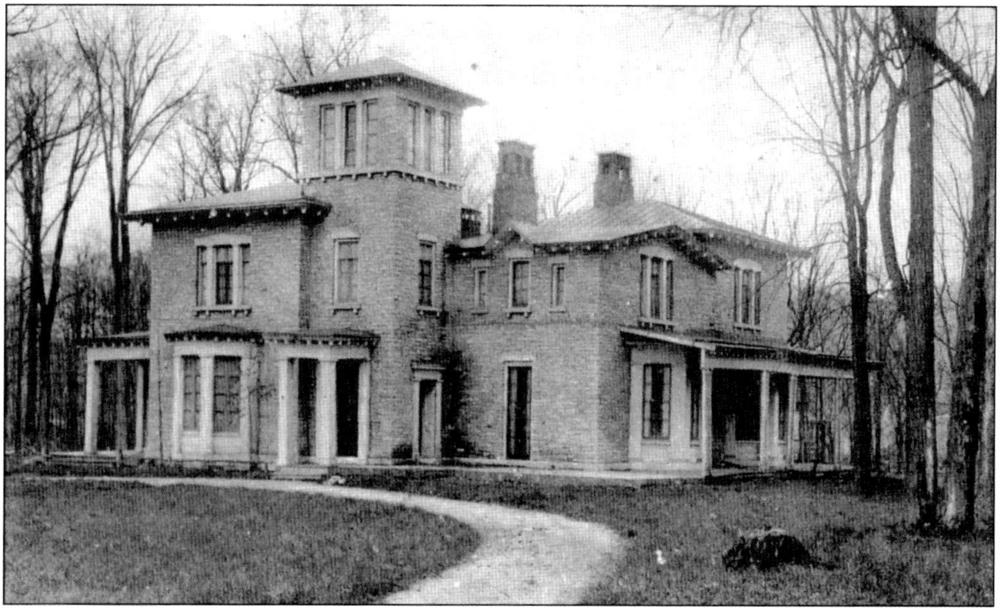

William Sweezy, partner of Stuart Perry and president of the National Bank of Newport, built a replica of the Perry home on the lot adjacent to Perry's. In the 1930s, Helen Lattimer of New York City opened the home during the summer season as the Green Tea Cup Inn. Lodging there cost $1 a night. A wooden structure behind the villa was used for wedding receptions, women's bridge club meetings, and other social functions. The Johannes Neckerman family from Frankfort, Germany, arrived in 1981, completely renovated the home, and renamed it Villa New Life.

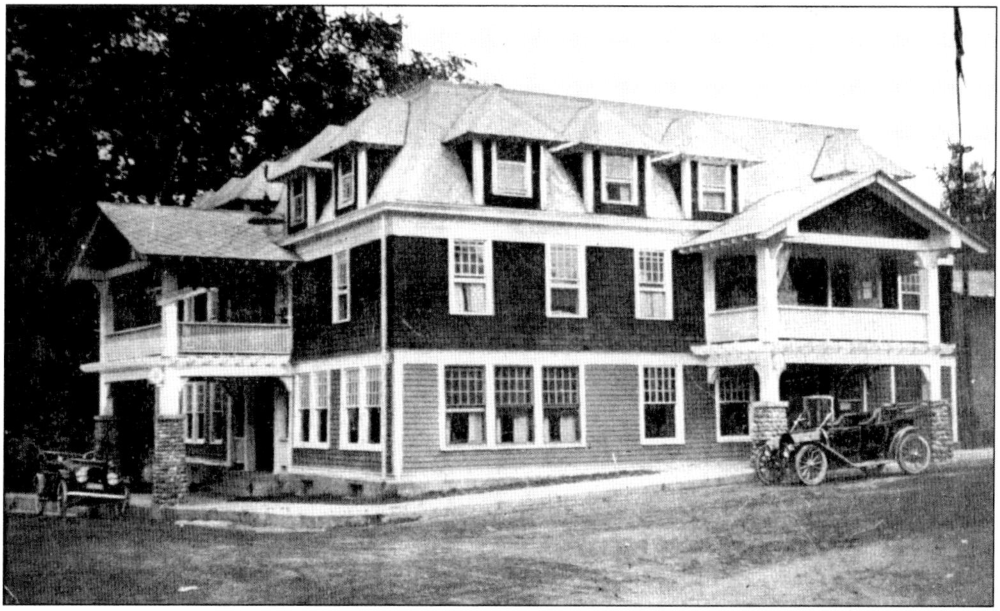

The first building in Middleville was built on this site as a public house in 1806. In its early years, it had a number of proprietors. Charles Lake, a former stagecoach driver, operated the business as the Lake House from 1899 until his death in 1935. After another series of operators, the hotel burned in 1994.

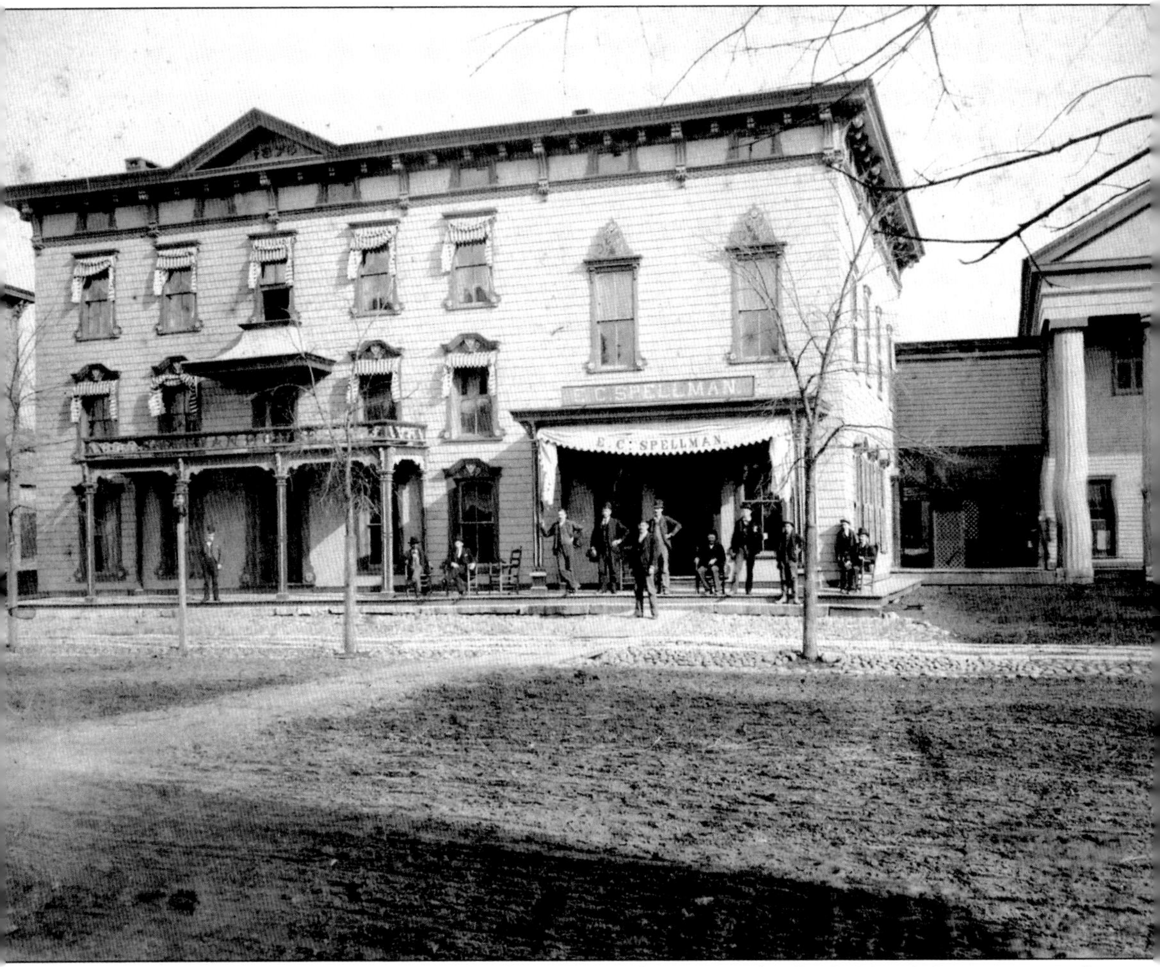

This Newport hotel, originally built of stone, was known as the Eagle Hotel. It was encased in wood in one of its several remodeling phases. Large pillars were added later. This scene shows the hotel when it was known as the Spellman House. In 1887, when he was 27 years old, Edward Spellman purchased the hotel, then known as the Hawkins House, made many improvements, and operated it until his death in 1899. The Spellman House was known as one of the best hostelries in Herkimer County. An enterprising man, Spellman was among the first to promote advancements that would benefit the entire village. The hotel was later known as the Pioneer Inn.

Eight

The Hills and Streams of Home

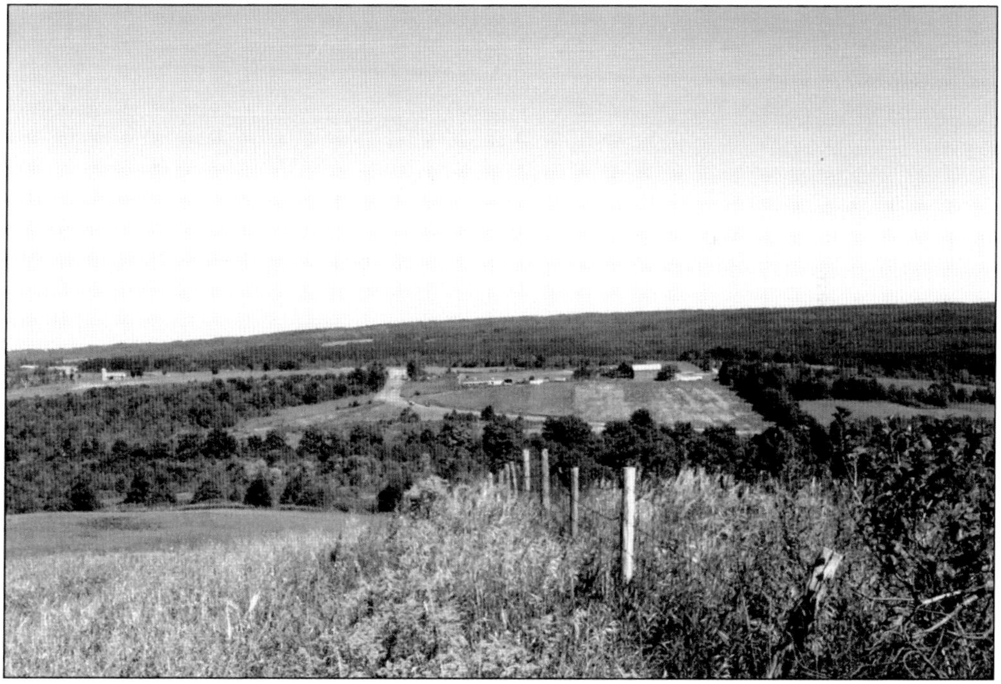

From the foothills of the Adirondacks in the towns of Fairfield and Norway to the West Canada Valley in the towns of Russia and Newport, beautiful vistas lie around every corner. Over the years, the streams have not only provided waterpower for local industries and businesses but also given the area a natural beauty. Both those who call the Kuyahoora area home and those who pass through and vacation here enjoy the scenic beauty and the recreational opportunities afforded by the streams and forests. Bartow Hill, on Route 29 east of the hamlet of Fairfield, provides spectacular scenery four seasons of the year. Overlooking the Kuyahoora Valley, the Adirondacks to the north, and the Mohawk Valley to the south, it provides breathtaking views for motorists and hikers. Named for Andrew A. Bartow, who lived on the hill from 1806 to 1820, the hill has an elevation of 1,653 feet. It provides a challenge for Fairfield highway crews in the winter, due to the winds that sweep across the hill.

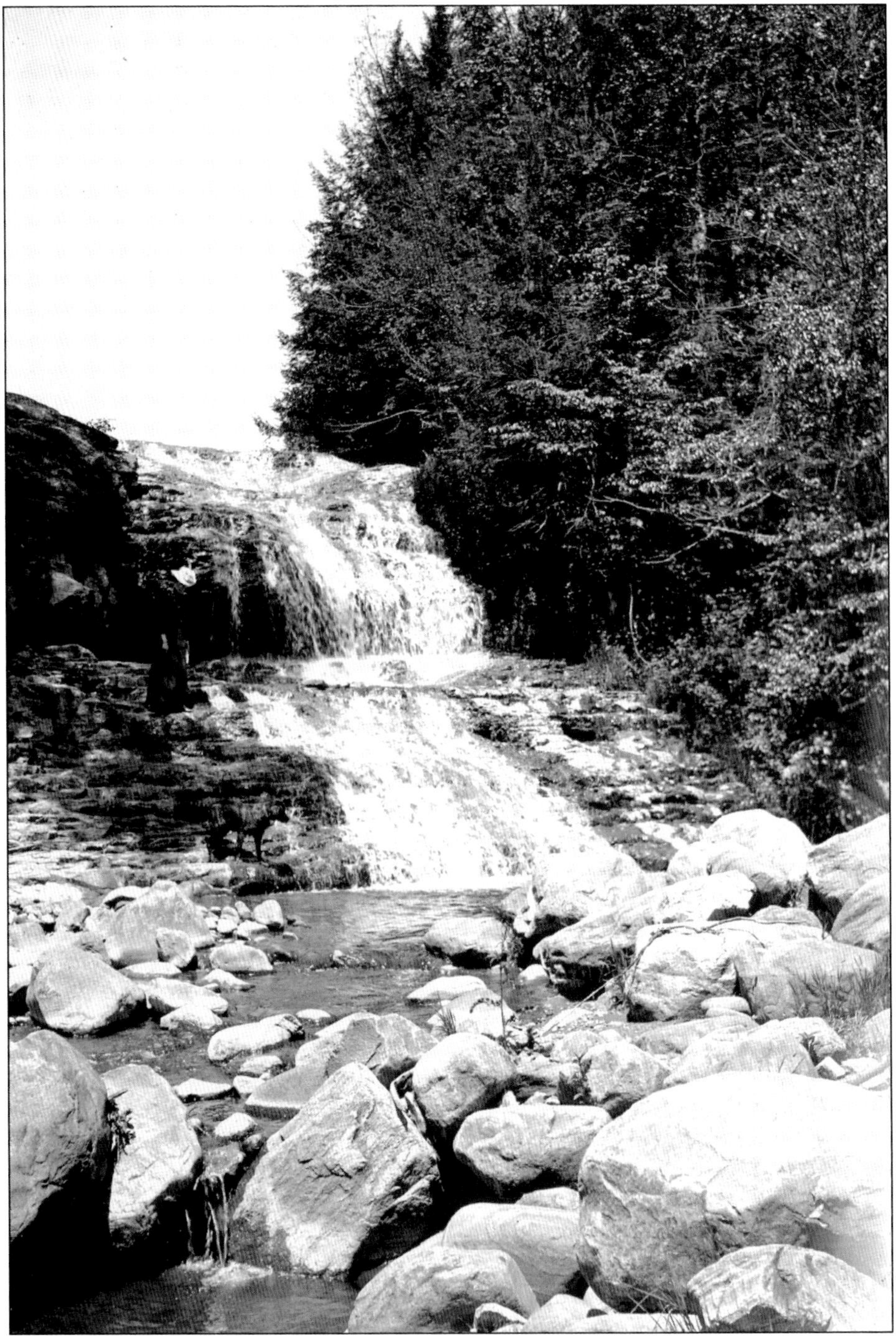

Cupid's Retreat is on Maltanner Creek as it descends down the hill to Middleville. This popular picnic area for Fairfield Academy students was once the location of early mills. Most of the cascades in the area were used for waterpower before the West Canada Creek was utilized. The spring snowmelt brings torrents of water over the falls, but by summer, the flow is considerably less. Today, the falls are located on private property, and cattle meander through the area during good weather.

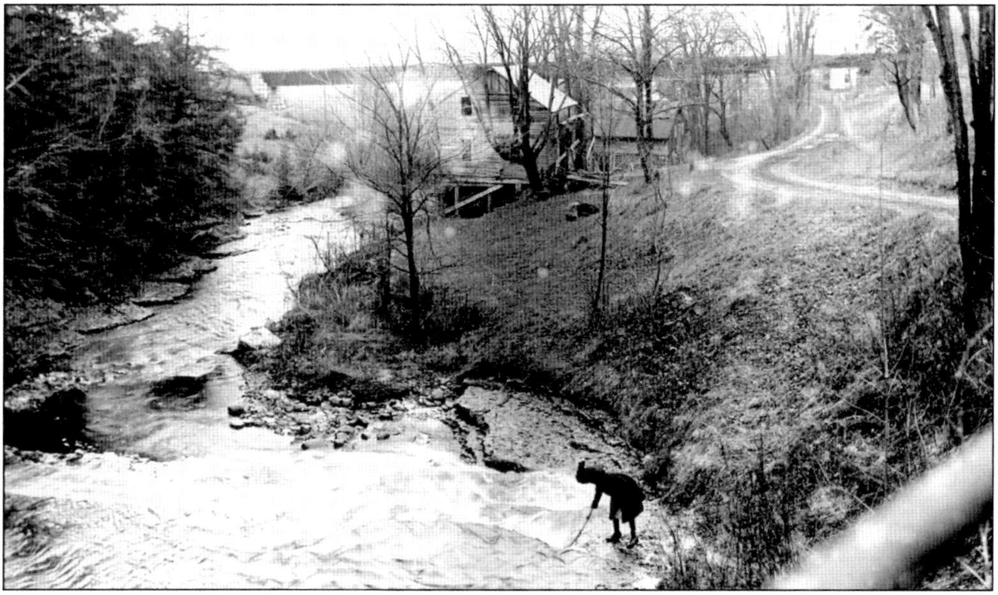

This photograph shows the view below the train trestle along Mill Brook in Gravesville. Just out of sight on the left is the site of the old milk station. In a half-mile radius along the brook, a number of enterprises were located: sawmill, gristmill, cooperage, blacksmith, furniture factory, and carriage wheel factory. Today, the stream meanders down the hill toward the West Canada Creek.

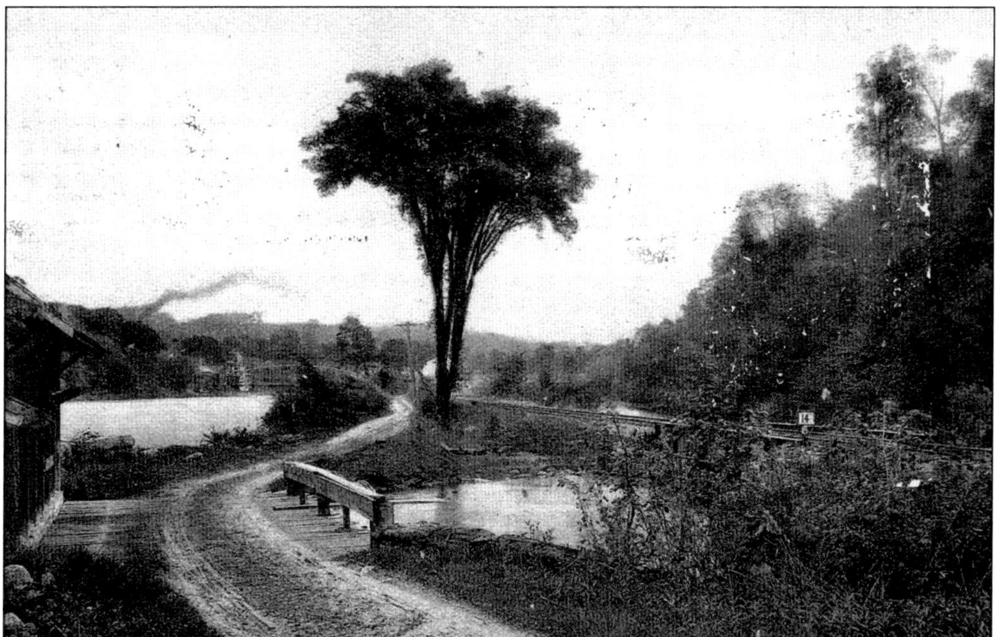

The Flume House Road followed the present-day Fishing Rock Road in Middleville. A hydraulic canal was constructed on the Newport side of the West Canada Creek to provide power for several mills and factories present in the village from the early 1800s. Visible on the right is the railroad, which was extended to Newport in 1881.

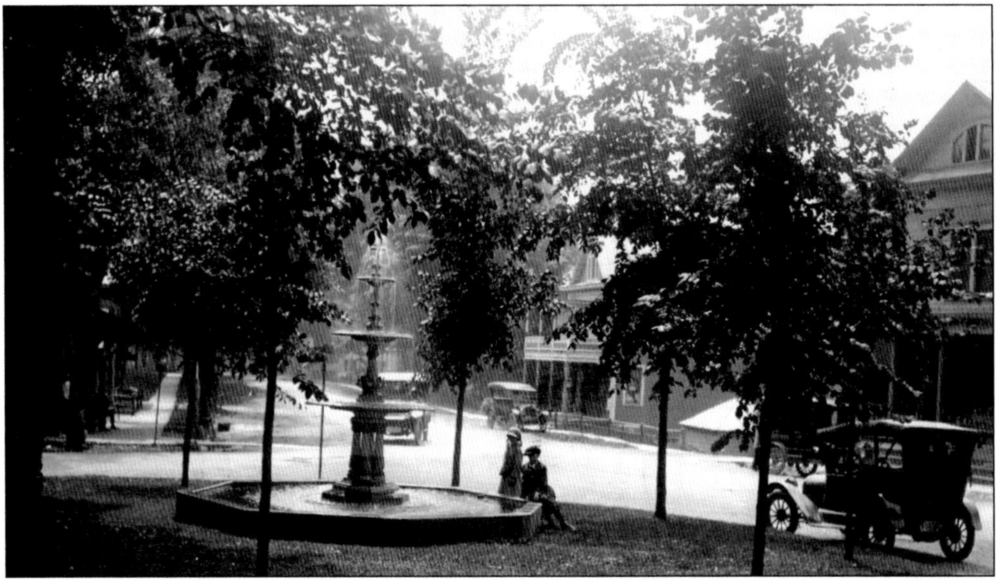

This cast-iron fountain, the centerpiece of the triangular park at the intersection of Main Street and Cold Brook Street, is a Poland landmark. A spring-fed horse watering trough was previously located in the same area. In 1904, after the Poland water system was constructed, a need was felt for a more decorative water feature. The fountain uses a recirculating pump to minimize the drain on the village water system. It is repainted every few years. In 2001, the concrete pool at the base was rebuilt.

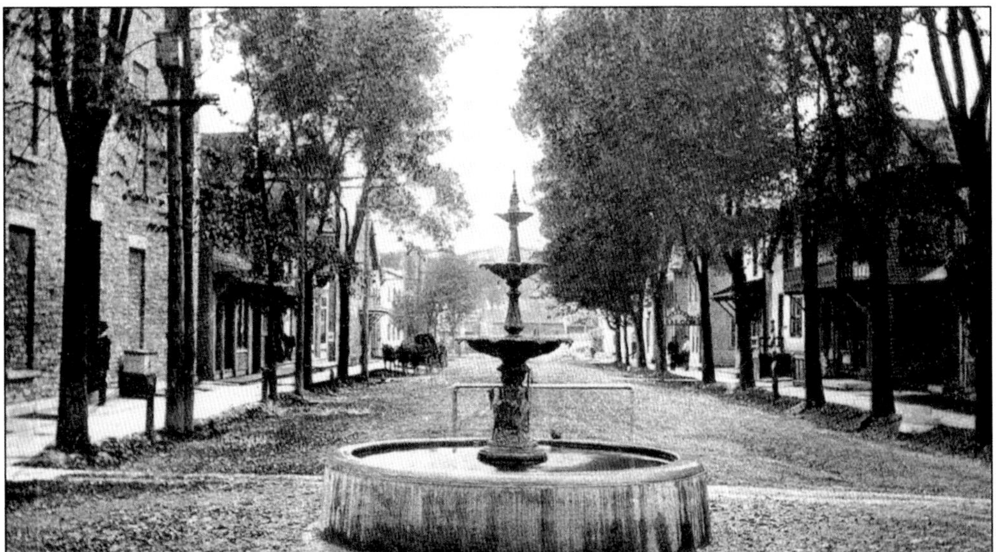

The first wooden watering tub was installed at the corner of Bridge and Main Street in Newport in 1876. H. Burlingame made a gift of a spring to feed the tubs and deeded the rights to the village. The tub was to be used to water passing horses and cattle, as well as to provide water for fire protection. In 1906, the Centennial Fountain replaced the wooden tub. Prof. Daniel Boynton, school commissioner, organized schoolchildren to contribute to the building of the fountain in honor of the first 100 years of Newport (1806–1906). The fountain was removed from the street in 1925.

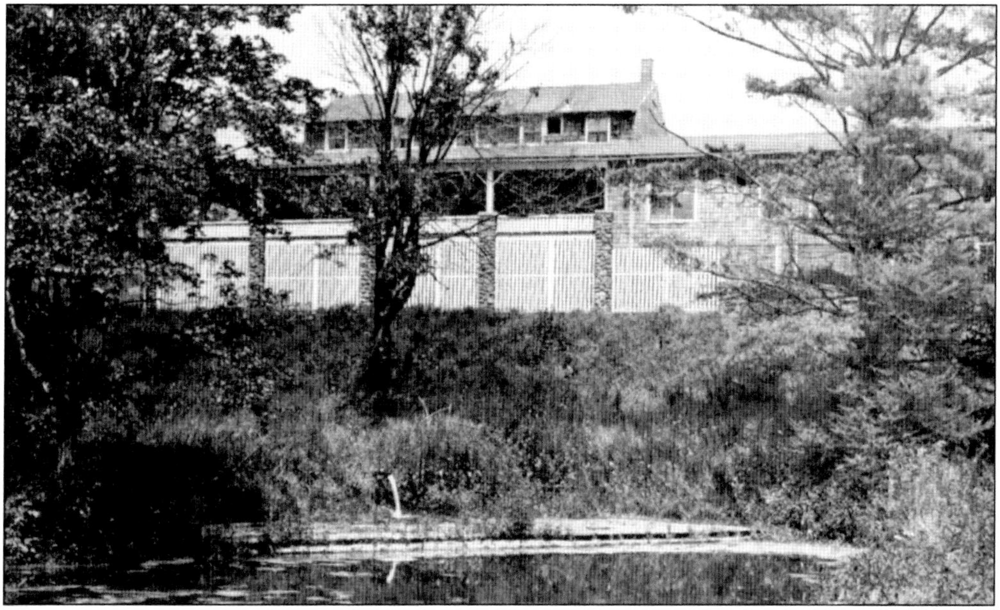

The Trout Brook Inn, in Gravesville, was famous for its trout, frog legs, and chicken dinners. On a direct route from New York to the Adirondacks and the Thousand Islands, the inn was a popular dining spot for tourists. Famous chefs from New York City worked here during the summer months, and an orchestra played for evening dancing.

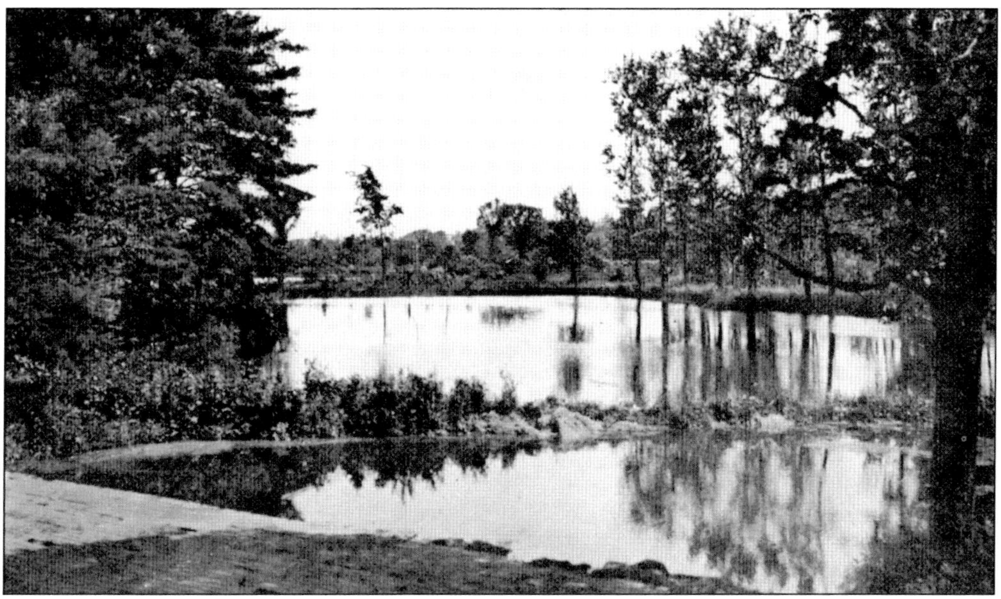

This is a view of one of the beautiful trout ponds, seen from the veranda of the Trout Brook Inn. Dining accommodations for 300 provided an ideal spot for banquets, weddings, and parties.

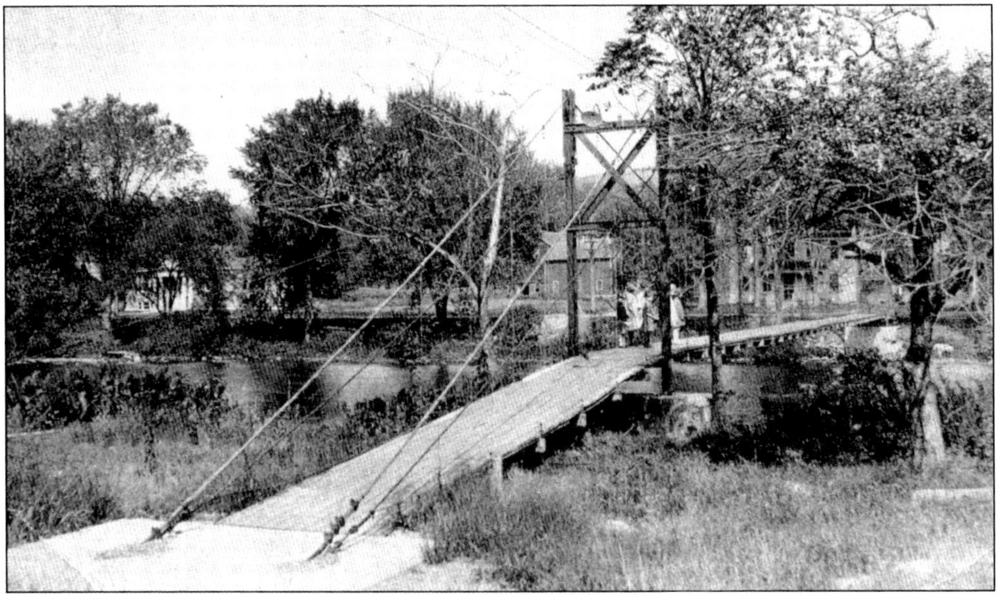

A suspension bridge was built across the West Canada Creek in 1921 to provide access to Brown's Island and Memorial Park. Group picnics, fireman's field days, ball games, and even dances were held in the park over the next 50 years. Heavy twisted wire cables held the bridge's wooden floor. Walking on the bridge gave one a special staggering sensation, especially when it was deliberately rocked. A tablet was placed near its entrance in 1925, dedicating the bridge to three local soldiers who lost their lives in World War I: Guy Bateman, Theodore Morey, and Daniel Toomey. In the 1970s, first the floor and later the cables were moved.

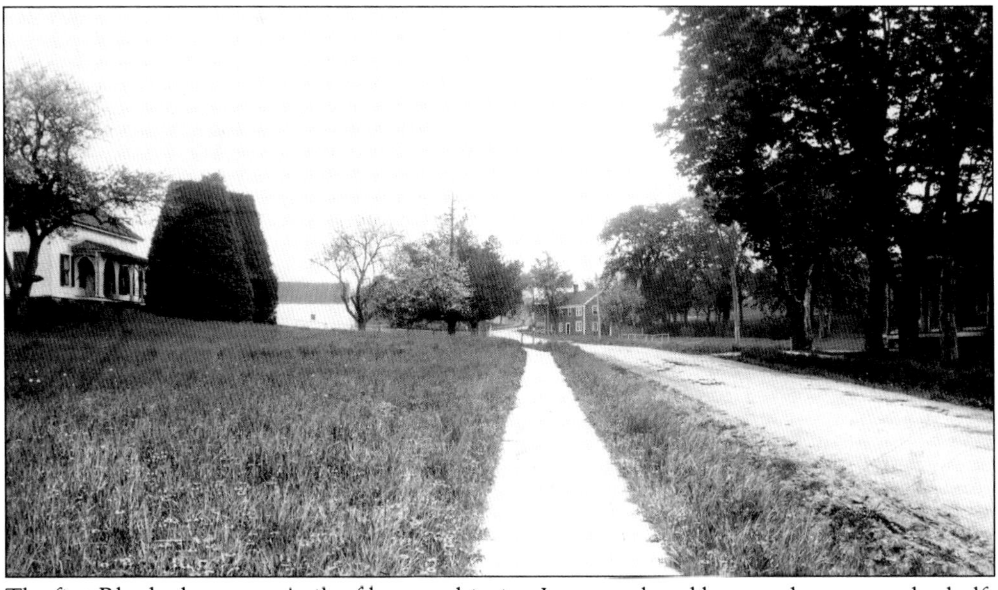

The first Rhodes home was built of logs on this site. It was replaced by a modest one-and-a-half-story home. In 1878, the roof was raised to its present height. Note the tall trimmed evergreens in front. This Cold Brook home was recognized for years for the unique archway carved between the branches of the pines.

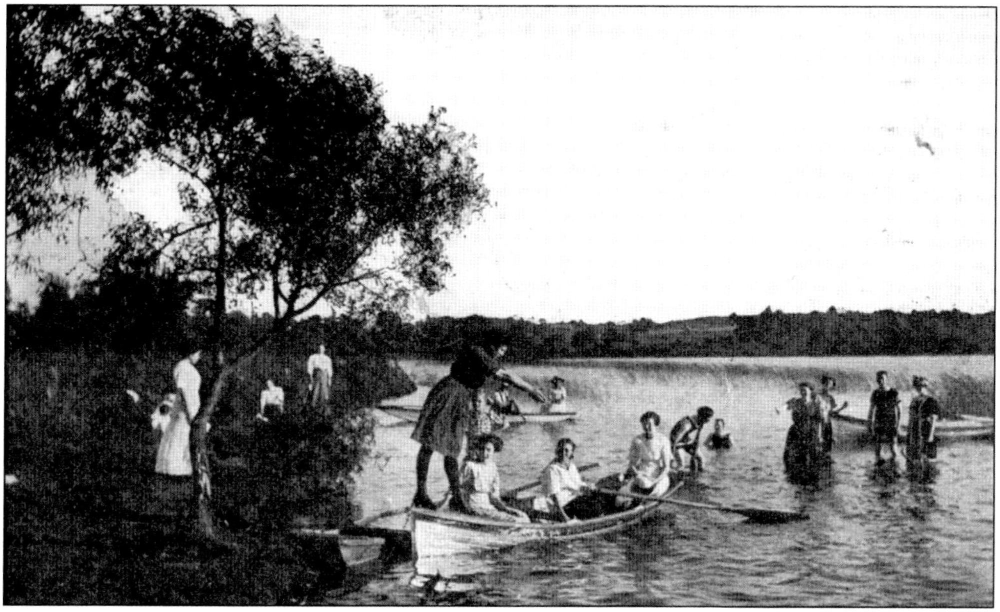

This scene shows the boating and swimming opportunities on the West Canada Creek near the dam in Grant.

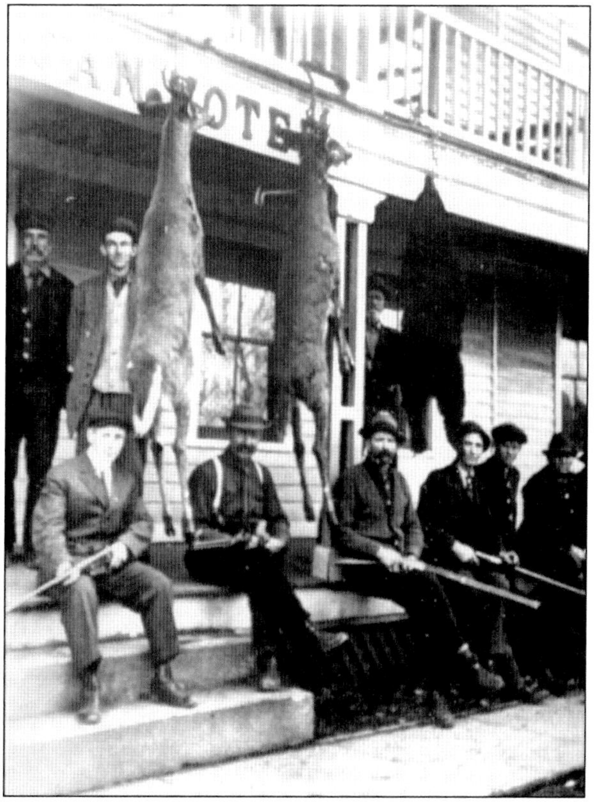

Hunting and fishing have always been popular in the uplands of the valley. Here, hunters sit in front of the American Hotel in Grant, with their deer and bear hanging from the porch.

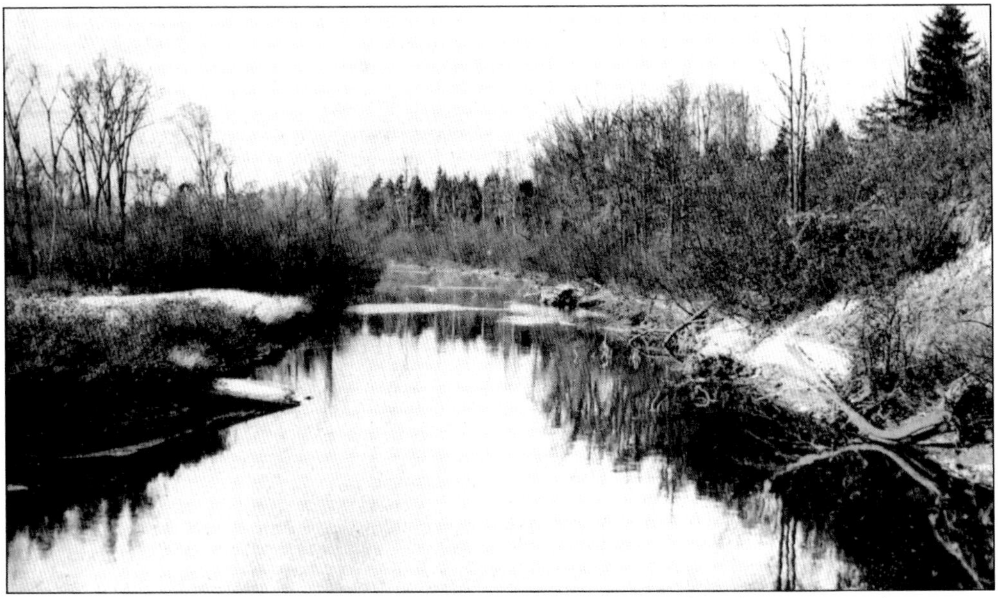

This tranquil scene shows the Shawngunk Bridge over Black Creek. Fishing is a popular pastime along the West Canada Creek and its tributaries.

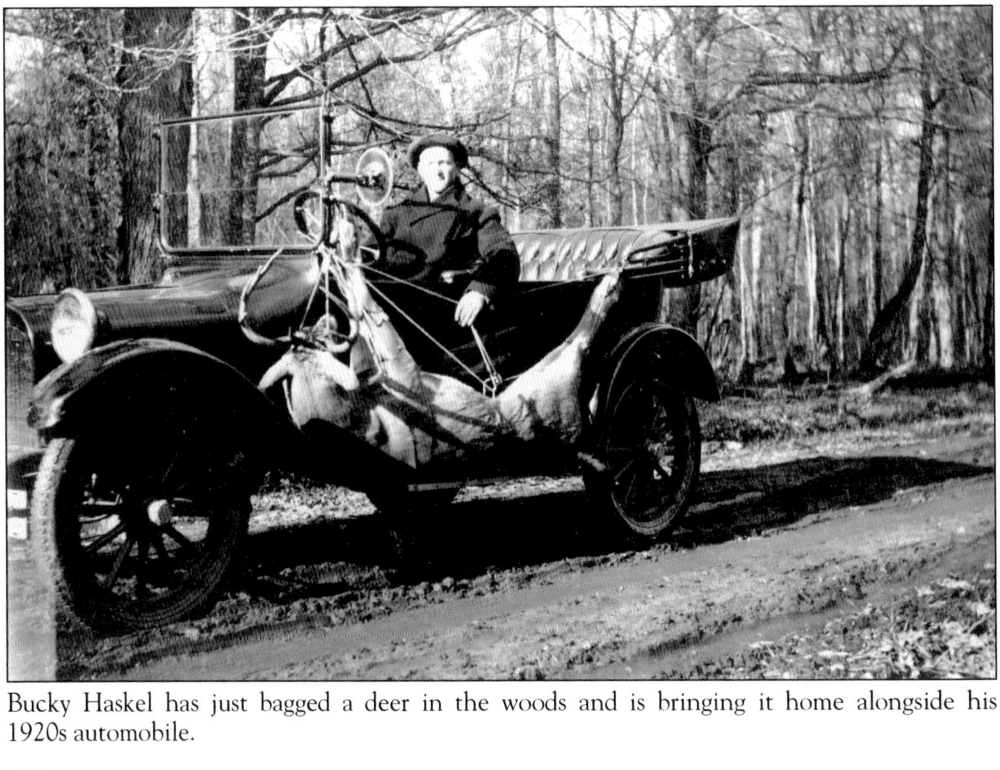

Bucky Haskel has just bagged a deer in the woods and is bringing it home alongside his 1920s automobile.

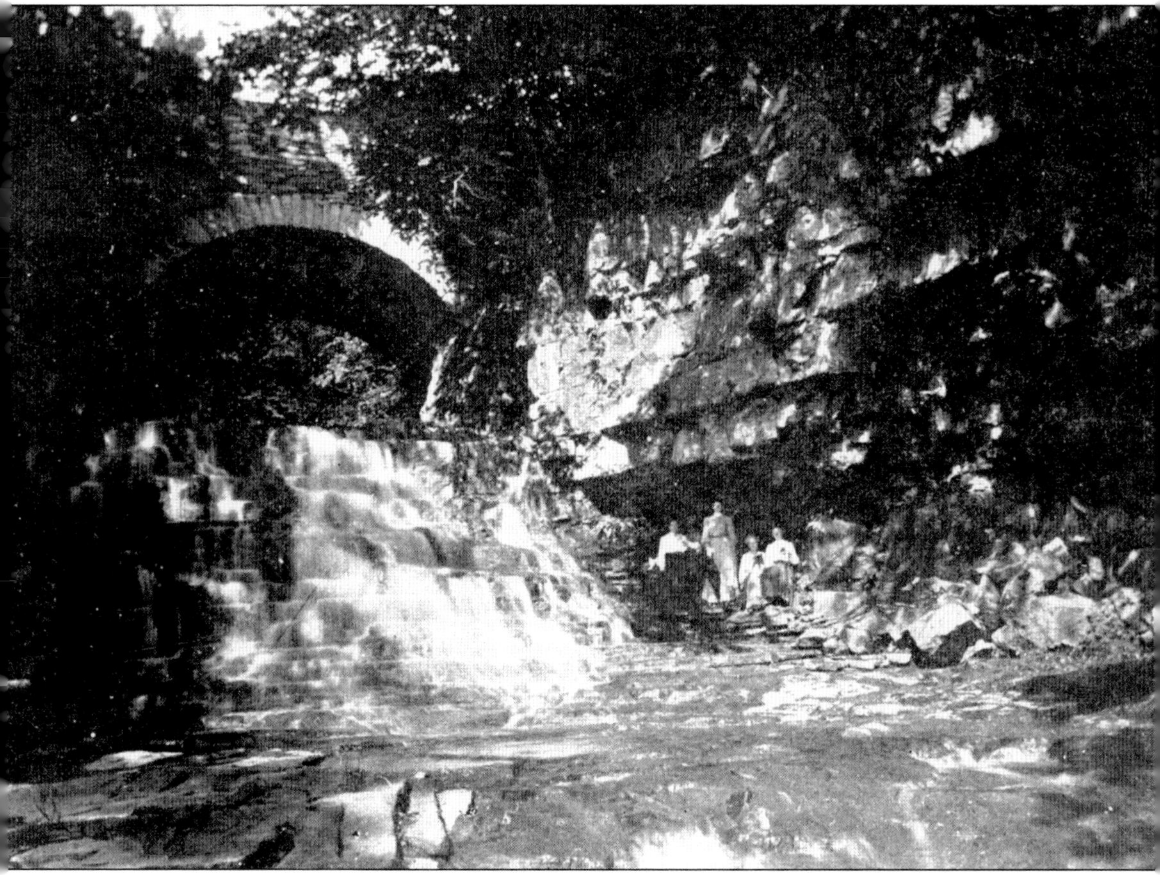

Before Route 29 connected Fairfield and Middleville, a road that crossed two stone arch bridges was used. This picture shows the arch, currently visible from Route 29, as it appeared in the past. The cascade, formed by an unnamed creek flowing south, is now under the present highway. It was a favored picnic spot of local people and Fairfield Seminary students. Members of the Todd family who were masons constructed most of the limestone arches in the town of Fairfield.

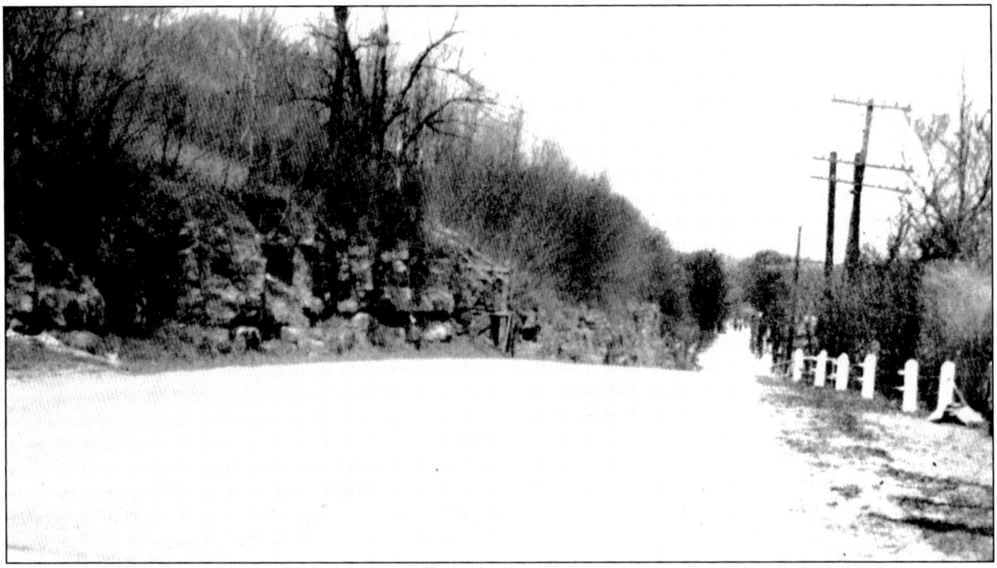

When this highway leading into Middleville was cut back to widen Route 28, thousands of crystals fell from cavities in the porous dolomite rock. Collectors have sought these Herkimer diamonds (so named in early 1900 because they were found in Herkimer County) for nearly 200 years. The brilliant quartz crystals are hard enough to cut glass.

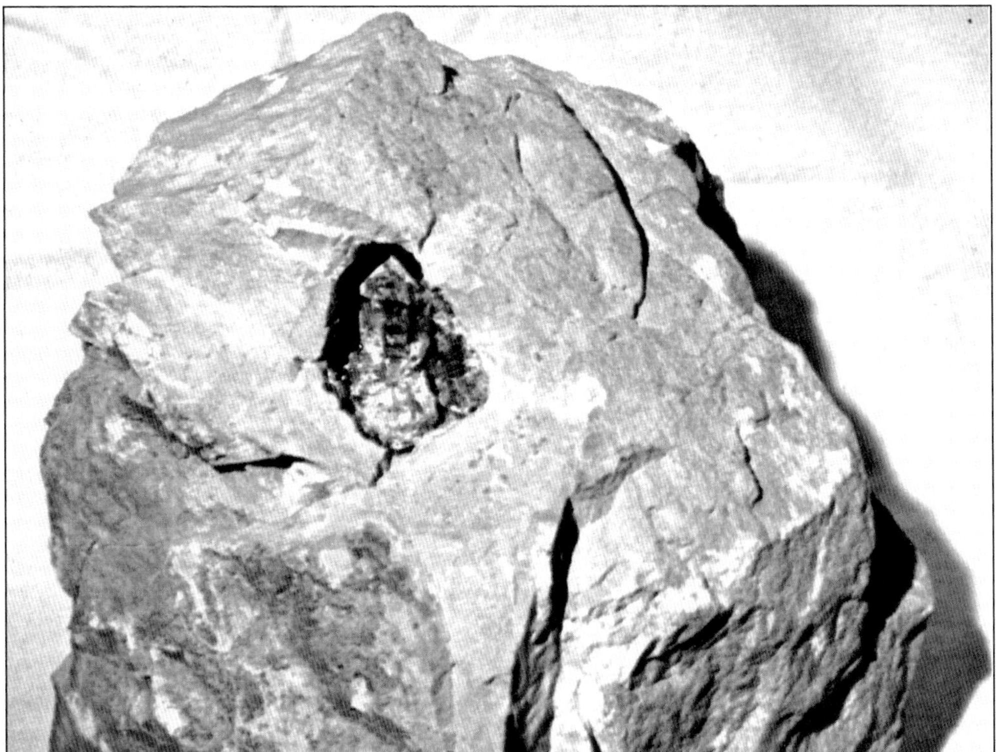

In 1842, New York State geologist Lardner Vanuxem said, "There is probably no locality in the world which produces more perfect or more beautiful quartz crystals than Middleville." This picture shows a large crystal formation within the limestone rock.